Bears' Guide to
Earning High School
Diplomas Nontraditionally

Bears' Guide to Earning High School Diplomas Nontraditionally

A Guide to More Than 500 Diploma Programs and Schools

Thomas Nixon, M.A.

TEN SPEED PRESS
Berkeley / Toronto

Other Degree.net books:
Bears' Guide to Earning Degrees by Distance Learning
Bears' Guide to College Degrees by Mail and Internet
Bears' Guide to the Best Computer Degrees by Distance Learning
Bears' Guide to the Best Education Degrees by Distance Learning
Bears' Guide to the Best MBAs by Distance Learning

Degree.net
A division of Ten Speed Press
PO Box 7123
Berkeley, California 94707
www.degree.net

Distributed in Australia by Simon and Schuster Australia, in Canada by Ten Speed Press
Canada, in New Zealand by Southern Publishers Group, in South Africa by Real Books, and
in the United Kingdom and Europe by Airlift Book Company.

Cover design by Catherine Jacobes
Text design by Jeff Brandenburg, ImageComp

Disclaimer:
While the author believes that the information in this book is correct as of the time of publication, it is possible that errors may have been made, which will be corrected at the first available opportunity. The publisher is not responsible for any problems that may arise in readers'
interactions with any schools or programs described in the book.

Library of Congress Cataloging-in-Publication Data
Nixon, Thomas.
     Bears' guide to earning high school diplomas nontraditionally : a guide to more than 500
  diploma programs and schools / Thomas Nixon.
       p.   cm.
     Includes bibliographical references and index.
       ISBN 1-58008-442-7 (pbk.)
       1. Alternative education—United States—Directories.   2. Education, Secondary—
  United States—Directories. I. Title.
  LC46.4.N59   2003
  371.04'02573—dc21   2003007040

First printing, 2003
Printed in the United States of America

1 2 3 4 5 6 7 8 9 10 — 07 06 05 04 03

To Billie and Gary Heisinger, high school educators both.
They have been and continue to be my second parents.

and

In memoriam, to William Heisinger (1969–1996) and Lewis Nixon II (1959–2000),
both of whom would have greatly appreciated alternative education.

Contents

Acknowledgments

No book is written in isolation. This is particularly true when you build upon the work of others. John and Mariah Bear have trusted me with their child. I hope that I do not disappoint. I must also acknowledge the behind-the-scenes pushing, shoving, and cajoling of Tom Head, my sometime writing partner. He, in no small part, made this happen.

I would like to particularly acknowledge Mike Lambert, Rich Douglas, Mariah Bear, Jesse Richman, and Leslie Bowman for agreeing to be interviewed for this book. Their expertise provided the foundation from which I built.

I also owe a debt of gratitude to the fine folks at Ten Speed Press for believing in this project. Justin Wells, the original editor, pushed hard to make this book a reality, and Holly Taines White, my project editor, brought the book to fruition. I am thankful to her for taking on this project midstream. It is certainly a better book due to her guidance. I am also grateful to Catherine Jacobes, for a visually stimulating cover; Jeff Brandenburg, for making the interior just as stimulating; Brady Kahn, for making sense of my grammatical structure; and Tom Southern, for approving the project and providing the link from original editor to ultimate editor.

Finally, much appreciation, admiration, and love to Elizabeth Nixon, mother to David, Maria, and Sarah, for how she is able to not only put up with me, but to support me in this grand adventure.

Introduction

"I have never let my schooling interfere with my education."

—Mark Twain

Once upon a time there was only one way to go to high school. You got up in the morning and were in your seat by eight o'clock. You then had six or so different classes and you went home.

Boy, have times changed! There are now high schools on university campuses, a high school for gay and lesbian teens (Harvey Milk High School in New York), high schools for different religious groups, and more performing arts high schools than you can shake a stick at.

Millions of American children don't go to public schools—nor are they required to. Many adults don't go to night school to earn a diploma anymore—nor should they, unless they want to.

You're reading this book because you don't have a high school diploma and you want one. Thousands of books out there will tell you why one particular method of earning a high school diploma is best. What you will find here, however, is a general introduction to the many ways to earn a high school diploma or its legal equivalent. Which is best for you depends on many factors, including your age, where you live, and your determination, motivation, and ability.

This book was written for:

- Adults who have never earned a high school diploma.

- Teens who wish to avoid the traditional high school experience.

- Families living abroad who wish their children to earn an American high school diploma.

You may want to complete your diploma as quickly as possible. You may be willing to take longer, but you don't want the traditional high school journey. This book covers both possibilities.

There are a number of options available for the teen or the adult returning student. While some programs require a great deal of work, others just require you to show that you already possess the knowledge that a high school student should have. The options profiled in this book fall into the following general categories.

Online High Schools

With the advent of the World Wide Web, the number of online programs has grown exponentially. There are numerous high schools on the Internet where students can complete a high school diploma. For additional information on these programs, see chapter 1.

Mike Lambert has been executive director of the Distance Education and Training Council (DETC) since 1992. He joined the DETC staff in 1972 and has served on more than 650 accreditation review teams, including service on teams from other accrediting associations. Besides developing dozens of distance-learning courses, he has published articles and edited handbooks on the method and lectured around the world on distance learning.

Bears' Guide: What do you see as the future of distance learning for high school education?

Mike Lambert: I see a continued surge in interest by three groups of people: newly arrived Americans, homeschooled children, and women who dropped out of high school and now wish to enter the workforce. There is no question that a high school diploma is the single most popular program in distance education for DETC, and the future looks brighter than it ever has before, as the public has come to believe that distance education is a legitimate way to earn a diploma.

We know from research that students who study at home are successful in college and that there is no significant difference in learning attainment. Distance graduates do as well as if not better than any class of high school students on standardized tests. The success of homeschooled students has been fairly well established by now.

I see more and more of our high schools adopting the Internet to conduct classes and that email will be largely supplanting snail mail for communications and exchange of lesson assignments.

Above all, the largest growth will be in the homeschool market, as knowledgeable parents demand sophisticated instruction from graduate-degreed faculty to ensure their child's opportunities to gain admission to prestigious colleges.

BG: How important is accreditation for high schools?

ML: Accreditation is vitally important. It helps institutions establish credibility with consumers. It assures that graduates will have their diplomas accepted by college admissions officers and employers and even ensures tuition reimbursement from employers and unions.

From the student's perspective, accreditation is the single best protection he or she has that the high school is reputable and offers sound instruction and prompt service. For an individual student, it would be nearly impossible to second-guess or duplicate the investigative work done by an accrediting body.

BG: Is there anything else that you would like to add?

ML: Just that everyone should earn his or her high school diploma! It means all the difference in the world in terms of self-esteem, job opportunities, and promotion possibilities. Over the course of your life, having a diploma can mean hundreds of thousands of dollars in lifetime income. There is no excuse not to earn a diploma today!

Independent Study Programs

These "correspondence" programs offer a great deal of flexibility and are often reasonably priced. The advantage for many is that they can be self-paced; you could finish much sooner than the traditional four years. This information is located in chapter 2.

Homeschooling

Homeschooling continues to be one of the more viable options for high school age students. Now legal in all fifty states, this can be a quite inexpensive alternative to traditional schooling. While many schools tend to have a religious focus, there are many that don't. Chapter 3 offers an introduction to this method.

Private Tutoring

Some states allow for homeschoolers and others to use a private tutor, such as a family member, to provide education through the high school level. Most states require that tutors be state-certified. Peruse chapter 4 for further information on this topic.

Alternative High Schools

One student's alternative high school is another's traditional venture. Alternative high schools tend to be guided by specific philosophies, most often political or religious. They tend to have fewer rules and hoops to jump through. In recent years, some of these private schools have converted to charter schools, sacrificing some of their freedom for financial stability. Chapter 5 is your destination for this information.

Charter Schools

Charter schools are publicly funded schools that don't have to comply with many of the rules regulating traditional schools. There are many different kinds of charter schools—from performing arts schools to auto mechanics schools, from computer technology programs to at-risk student programs. Read more on this in chapter 6.

University-Based High Schools

Universities across the country have long sponsored elementary and high schools located on their campuses. These schools tend to be more rigorous than much of what you could find off-campus. Find them in chapter 7.

GED Examination

The General Educational Development (GED) test is administered by the American Council on Education (ACE) and has been around since the end of World War II. More than 800,000 people a year now take the test (including some quite famous people). Check it out in chapter 8.

High School Proficiency Examinations

The GED is one route to receiving a diploma. A small number of states have produced their own proficiency examinations. In California, this can get you a diploma at age sixteen. For all of the rules and regulations, see chapter 9.

Skipping High School Altogether

While this option is certainly not for everyone, it works for some. Often people combine methods, such as passing the GED exam, then going off to college or finding volunteer opportunities. To find out more information, see chapter 10.

World War II Veterans

A program is now available in a number of states enabling World War II veterans to receive high school diplomas if they had to leave high school to fight in the war. Additional information can be found in chapter 11.

Which choice is the best for you will depend on your needs. Do you need a piece of paper attesting that you graduated from high school? Homeschooling may or may not be for you. Do you need to learn, or re-learn, high school knowledge? Quite possibly an online or correspondence course may be your best bet. Are you interested in getting the piece of paper as quickly as possible? Take the GED exam.

Some of these options are more suited for adult returning students and some are more suited for teenaged students. Some are good choices for either. The breakdown between high school age programs and adult student programs looks like this:

Teens

- Online high schools.
- Alternative high schools.
- Independent study.
- Homeschooling.
- Private tutoring.
- GED exam.
- High school proficiency exam.
- Charter schools.
- University-based high schools.
- Skipping high school.

Adults

- Online high schools.
- Alternative high schools (although very limited in number).
- Independent study.
- GED exam.
- High school proficiency exam.
- Charter schools (an extremely limited number for those aged eighteen to twenty-one).

For Teens

You may already know that you don't want to attend a traditional high school. Likewise, you may be attending one now and can't get away from it fast enough. There are many different possibilities. You can go somewhere else, you can accelerate your present program, or, depending on your age and your state, you can just drop out and go to college.

Why you want to escape the traditional high school experience is up to you, but make sure that leaving school is what you really want. Are you willing to miss the prom? How about football games? High school friendships? If you're willing to forgo these, this book is full of programs that may suit you.

For Adults

There are many reasons why you didn't get your high school diploma the first time around. Perhaps you had to go to work to support a family. Maybe it wasn't important to you at the time. Whatever the reason, you've decided that now is the time to finish up your high school education. Good for you! There are many opportunities described in this book that are geared toward the working adult.

Which program is best for you largely depends on your previous education. If you already have high school level knowledge, you may want to consider taking the GED. You can receive your diploma and be in college or in a better job in a matter of months (depending upon test dates). However, if you need to gain additional knowledge, then you should check out one of the online or correspondence programs that has a GED track.

Before proceeding further, you need to determine your goals. Is getting the diploma for self-satisfaction, or do you need it to fulfill a job or academic requirement? If the latter is the case, you need to do your research. For some programs, taking the GED test and passing it will be satisfactory. Others won't accept it.

Whatever your reasons, whatever your goals, if you want a high school diploma, this is the place to start.

Part I: Diplomas through Self-Paced Programs

CHAPTER 1

Online High Schools

"This is the first time in history that the teacher, student, and content do not have to be in the same place."

—*Willard Daggett, President, International Center for Leadership in Education*

If you've discovered that for whatever reason you need to actually go to high school, one way would be to do the entire diploma online. There are many programs available, and the number is growing quickly. While not for everyone, online school can work well for you. As opposed to other types of programs, online schools are available twenty-four hours a day, seven days a week.

There are two main kinds of accreditation that an online high school may possess. The first, regional accreditation, is similar to that of colleges and universities. This is the gold standard by which all other types of accredidation should be measured. Regional accreditation means that all fifty states will accept your diploma as being valid. The Distance Education and Training Council offers the second form of accreditation, national accreditation. DETC accreditation, although national, is perceived by some as lower in value than regional accreditation. Go figure.

Frequently Asked Questions

How can I tell if it is a good online program?

As with all education, it can be difficult to determine quality before you begin. However, there are some factors you can examine. How long has the school been in operation? Does it have a track record of college-admitted students? What kind of colleges do most of its students end up attending? As with all choices, but particularly with educational choices, it's up to you to do your own research.

How long has the school been providing online education?

While a school may be fifty years old, it certainly hasn't been providing high school diploma programs on the Internet for that long. The oldest online programs date from about 1994, with the explosion of the World Wide Web. You will probably want to look for a diploma program that has at least two to three years of online experience. This is not to say that brand-new programs are of low quality, but rather of unknown quality. Once a program has your money, it's a little late to realize that it is a waste of time.

A reference from a current or former student is always a plus. Never base your decision solely on a reference, but it's a good place to begin. If you do prefer personal recommendations, then get them from more than one source.

Should an online school be accredited?

Definitely check the accreditation. There are the six regional accreditation associations (also tasked with accrediting colleges; see appendix B) and the Distance Education and Training Council. For high school education, being accredited by either of these should be sufficient for colleges (and other high schools) to accept your diploma as valid.

What about other accreditors?

Blossoming all around are many other accreditors. While most seem quite serious, their accreditation is of more limited value. Other accreditors may be shams. Telling the difference can be quite difficult.

If a school has approval from its state department of education to provide education at the secondary level, then it is most likely an acceptable route for you. However, check it out with your college (or colleges) of choice. Also, feel free to ask the school where its graduates have gone to college. Reputable high school programs track this information and often put it up on their websites.

How much should I pay for an online high school diploma?

My preference is that you pay nothing at all. Failing that, pay what it's worth to you. The difference in cost can be extreme. Check out all the programs, and then decide what works best for your lifestyle. If your top choice costs too much, then consider your second choice.

Are online high schools only for high school age students?

Not at all. In fact, online high schools are a great choice for returning students. If you're a little embarrassed about not having received your diploma the first time around, why not try the facelessness of the Internet? Likewise, if it is difficult to find time to attend a brick and mortar school, the Internet can be a good choice. With almost all of these programs, you establish your own study schedule.

Will I be able to talk to other students? Will I need to do group projects with other students?

If you mean "talk" in the sense of "communicate," then certainly this will occur. Whether you actually talk face-to-face or on the telephone is primarily up to you. Whether you will need to do group projects depends on the program you have selected. If it is important to you to do collaborative projects, then make sure that you choose a school that offers that option. Ask your questions now!

What is the single most important skill that I should have in order to do well in an online program?

You need to be a good communicator, particularly in writing. With other forms of education, this might be less important, but, online, you will be judged by how well you are able to effectively communicate. Thankfully, this is something that you can work on. If communicating isn't a strength for you, you might want to make a writing or speech class a top priority.

Do homeschoolers use online programs?

Homeschoolers use many different types of programs or no program at all. Online programs can be a good option for homeschoolers who are not interested in developing their own curriculum. Some online programs are especially designed for inclusive (all viewpoints, including religious) and Christian homeschoolers.

Which program do you recommend?

I don't, with one exception. If you live in a state that has a charter school offering online diploma programs, it is probably your best choice, particularly if money is a concern. Most of these programs are free of charge to state residents (although sometimes only in certain regions). Free is usually the best price.

Having said that, you still need to do your research. Just because it's free doesn't make it a good program. Then again, you might be willing to compromise.

The Successful Online Student

There are certain qualities that most successful online students possess. While it is possible for most people to do well, having some of these qualities increases your likelihood of success.

1. Be self-motivated. If you are the type of person who can motivate yourself to get things done in a timely manner, then you will have a much easier time taking online courses. If you are not self-motivated, it certainly doesn't make success impossible, but recognize this challenge within you to work toward achieving your goal.

2. Commit the time. When online programs state that class preparation time is similar to site-based programs, they are serious. While you do save time in not having to go to a classroom, you really do need to spend time studying for your classes, logging into the course, and participating in discussions.

3. Be collaborative. While some of the work will be solo in nature, you will often be assigned group projects not unlike those in a traditional high school classroom. Being a reluctant group member is never a good idea. Being uninvolved in this environment will make it difficult for you to succeed. Conversely, good collaboration makes the online learning that much more effective.

4. Create relationships. Successful online learners establish relationships with their instructors and with their classmates. Not surprisingly, this is quite similar to site-based programs. See a particularly insightful post by someone? Send them an email and tell them so. Having a problem understanding the course? Let your instructor know.

5. Write. If you do not have adequate writing skills, working online can be quite challenging. In addition to papers and projects that must be written, you will need to write to communicate with your fellow classmates, your instructor, and possibly the online tech folks.

6. Be realistic. This course will be no more or less difficult than a site-based course. If you have difficulty in math, you may not want to take trigonometry online. Think about your learning style; in which courses might you need some face-to-face time? For those courses, it may make more sense to attend a class at your local community college.

Cost

Costs vary widely for online courses. Some programs have an annual fee that can range from around one thousand to several thousands of dollars. Other schools will charge a per course fee. Don't let the cost of a program dissuade you from participating. For some of the courses offered, it may be possible that your local high school will pay for them. This is particularly true if you attend the high school and are earning additional units or are taking Advanced Placement (AP) courses that are not offered locally.

However, even if you don't fall within these parameters, it may still be possible for your local school to pay. It never hurts to ask. The odds of a school paying for a course increase dramatically if you talk with a counselor and not with the principal.

Leslie Bowman is a designer and instructor of online courses. In addition to having taught for Michigan Virtual High School (www.mivhs.com), she has taught for California State University-Hayward, the Institute of Computer Technology, Walden University, and the University of Virginia. She trains teachers in online instructional methods. Her website, www.elearningprof.net, provides additional information about her ongoing activities.

Bears' Guide: Why is online learning a good choice for some high school students?

Leslie Bowman: There are many reasons for choosing online learning at the high school level. Reasons include everything from unavailability of courses due to lack of enrollment to a need to make up credits not earned during the previous year to negative socialization. Small schools may not have the enrollment or resources to offer a wide array of elective or advanced courses, and online courses can provide more opportunities for learning. Some high school students may take only a few courses online to supplement their traditional high school curriculum while others may choose to complete a high school diploma entirely online.

Online learning also provides different methods of learning beyond the traditional classroom lecture, including collaborative groups, independent and self-paced learning, and self-study. These different learning options address a variety of learning styles and, as a result, increase motivation and interest in courses. This can be a major advantage for students with special needs, whether those needs are for more time studying some subjects or a faster pace through classes.

BG: In what ways can online learning be better than the traditional classroom?

LB: Online learning can provide more opportunities for engaged and active learning, diverse courses, gaining up-to-date technical skills, earning college credit while still in high school, and interacting with teachers and students outside the local community as well as with experts around the world. Online learning encourages and supports a more personal interaction between student and teachers, as well as among students. In the online classroom, everyone starts on an even playing field. Absent are the common distractions that are a result of behavior, attitude, personality, or physical characteristics. The quiet student has as much opportunity to be heard as does the most outgoing student. With the classroom being available 24/7, students have access to information and communication with classmates and teachers on a more frequent basis than in traditional classes.

Students who learn together online often make friends with a more diverse population of classmates than can be found in the traditional class. This cultural diversity among classmates has the added advantage of teaching teenagers how to relate to and work with people of different ages, personalities, and cultural backgrounds. This type of positive socialization, albeit online, carries over into students' working and personal relationships with people in their daily lives.

BG: What should a high school student look for in a good online program?

LB: The first thing students should look for is accreditation. Will the credits count toward a high school diploma if a student is taking just a few classes to supplement a traditional high school curriculum? Another consideration is whether or not the online classes comply with state academic standards. Most states now have specific academic standards (and mandated standardized tests to assess those standards of learning), and online classes should address those state standards. Students should also ask if the state assessment tests would be a requirement of graduation.

Beyond that, students should ask direct questions about the classes, teachers, and instructional methods. If a student wants self-directed and independent learning classes, she or he should make sure that instruction method is available. If a student prefers collaborative learning and interaction with classmates, then she or he should make sure the instructional method promotes this type of learning.

Another major consideration is assessment. What kinds of tests and assignments are required? How are tests administered? Will the students take tests online and, if so, are these timed or open book tests? The other alternative is proctored tests. This means that the tests will be mailed to a proctor (usually a test center or a counselor at a high school) and the students will go to that location to take tests under the supervision of the proctor. Sometimes proctors can be arranged by the student, and in other cases proctors are located in national testing centers that can be found within driving distance of most places.

BG: What kind of student makes for a good online student?

LB: For students who are motivated, willing, and able to take responsibility for their learning, online education offers a richer variety of courses from which to choose than can be found in most high schools. Many students find online education to be an excellent alternative to traditional high school education because they can study and learn at their own pace within the parameters of the course schedule.

Students who want to take online classes need basic technical skills, good study skills, and time management skills. They need to be self-disciplined and able to work with minimal supervision. They need to have good written communication skills and be willing to commit to several hours per week of study and online time for each class. These students often have a clear purpose for taking online classes and in most cases also have clear educational goals.

The main concern that most students have is that they will be isolated and will learn all by themselves. This is not the case. Online students communicate regularly with classmates and teachers and through this interaction find that learning is more enjoyable, in many cases, than in the traditional classroom. This is another area of concern about which students should ask prospective online schools.

The Schools

I've divided the schools into categories based on accreditation. I have also included schools that are run by the state government but do not have accreditation. Many colleges and universities will accept diplomas from legally operating high schools regardless of accreditation.

Some of these programs will earn you a diploma outright while others will not. I've included non-diploma programs because some of them allow you to transfer the credits back to your local school. Many local schools do not limit the number of credits that they will accept in this manner, so you can easily do half or more of your required credits online. Doing so could accelerate your graduation or, at the very least, keep you off campus more of the time. Online schools all seem to have the same list to describe their students:

- Students who need to make up credit.

- Students who wish to take a class not offered at their school.

- Students who wish to take extra credit and graduate early.

- Students who are schooled at home.

Accredited Online High Schools

Alabama Online High School

PO Box 870372
Tuscaloosa, AL 35487-0372

PHONE: (205) 348-2647
FAX: (205) 348-2585
WEBSITE: www.onlinehighschool.org or aohs.state.al.us
EMAIL: aohs@pacers.org
YEAR FOUNDED: 2000
ACCREDITATION: None

Local schools typically pay for the cost of the courses. The school allows students to take courses that their local high school does not offer. Students in small rural schools with limited instructional resources can take all core courses and critical electives.

Arkansas Virtual High School

206 Pine Street
Dardanelle, AR 72834

PHONE: (479) 229-4349
FAX: (479) 229-2154
WEBSITE: arkansashigh.k12.ar.us/avhs_main.htm
EMAIL: sandyo@cox-Internet.com
YEAR FOUNDED: 1997
ACCREDITATION: None

Eventually the goal is to offer all of the courses available at a traditional high school. The school is very specific about who can take its courses, limiting enrollment to any public school student in grades nine through twelve who is a resident in an affiliated Arkansas school district. Part of this reasoning is that the school is not authorized to confer diplomas. You must be registered at your local school.

CCS Web Academy—North Carolina's Virtual High School

1624 Ireland Drive
Fayetteville, NC 28304

PHONE: (910) 484-3391
FAX: (910) 484-8231
WEBSITE: www.ccswebacademy.net
EMAIL: ajordan@ccswebacademy.net
YEAR FOUNDED: 1997
ACCREDITATION: State of North Carolina

Credits must be transferred to your home school. The school does not issue diplomas. Courses are free to students living in Cumberland County. If you live outside of the county, you will need to get the permission of your local education agency (LEA) and pay tuition.

Choice 2000 On-Line Charter School

155 East Fourth Street, Suite 100
Perris, CA 92570

PHONE: (909) 940-5700
FAX: (909) 940-5706
WEBSITE: www.choice2000.org

EMAIL: info@choice2000.org
YEAR FOUNDED: 1994
ACCREDITATION: Western Association of Schools and Colleges

Unlike many alternative schools, Choice 2000 has WASC accreditation and its curriculum is based on California state frameworks. As a charter school, tuition is free for students in Riverside, San Bernardino, San Diego, Imperial, and Orange Counties. All others must pay a fee of $175 per course. Compared to other programs, that seems a reasonable amount. Classes are offered synchronously (which means classes are scheduled where students must be present). A diploma is available.

Christa McAuliffe Academy

3601 West Washington Avenue
Yakima, WA 98903

PHONE: (509) 575-4989
FAX: (509) 575-4976
WEBSITE: www.cmacademy.org
EMAIL: CMA@cmacademy.org
YEAR FOUNDED: 1985
ACCREDITATION: Northwest Association of Schools and Colleges

Christa McAuliffe Academy is a regionally accredited school offering a diploma program. The focus is on the individual student.

Colorado Online Learning

259 South Broadway
Monte Vista, CO 81144

PHONE: (719) 852-4023
WEBSITE: www.cd.kiz.co.us
EMAIL: mpena@sargentk12.org
YEAR FOUNDED: 1998
ACCREDITATION: None

Colorado Online Learning (COSC) is for Colorado students only. School districts purchase "seats" for their students to take these online courses. Most of the school districts involved are quite small and are not able to provide a full range of courses for their students. Therefore, a diploma program is not available. COSC provides these districts with the additional courses online. Enrollment is arranged through your home district.

Delta Cyber School

PO Box 1672
Delta Junction, AK 99737

PHONE: (907) 895-1043 or (877) 895-1043

FAX: (907) 895-5198
WEBSITE: www.dcs.k12.ak.us:8001
EMAIL: mary_corcoran@dgsdmail.dgsd.k12.ak.us
YEAR FOUNDED: 1997
ACCREDITATION: None

This program, sponsored by the Delta/Greely School District, provides learning opportunities for the hinterlands of Alaska as well as elsewhere. As a charter school, it is free to residents of Alaska, but must charge a fee to others. The fee seems quite reasonable given the quality of education. A diploma is available.

ECO 2000 Cyberschool Project

PO Box 504
Washburn, ME 04786

PHONE: (207) 455-5972
FAX: (207) 455-5972
WEBSITE: www.eco2000.org/consortium/index.htm
EMAIL: eco2000@ainop.com
YEAR FOUNDED: 1995
ACCREDITATION: None

This project is a consortium of small school districts that are seeking to provide access to courses that they otherwise could not provide on their home campuses. In order to take the courses, you must be a student in one of the participating districts. The program does not offer enough courses to grant diplomas. Diplomas are issued by the homeschooling district. The member districts are: CSD #9 (Island Falls), Madawaska School Department (MSAD) #14 (Danforth), MSAD #24 (Van Buren), MSAD #25 (Sherman), MSAD #27 (Fort Kent), MSAD #29 (Houlton), MSAD #32 (Ashland), MSAD #33 (Frenchville), MSAD #45 (Washburn), MSAD #70 (Hodgdon), Union #122 (New Sweden, Woodland, Stockholm, and Westmanland), and Caswell.

Education Program for Gifted Youth

Stanford University
Ventura Hall
Stanford, CA 94305

PHONE: (650) 329-9920
FAX: (650) 329-9924
WEBSITE: www-epgy.stanford.edu
EMAIL: epgy-info@epgy.stanford.edu
YEAR FOUNDED: 1999
ACCREDITATION: None

This is an enrichment program, so no diploma is given. Students stay at their home schools and supplement their course work with these online classes. What it does give is the opportunity to learn at one of the world's most prestigious universities. Because this is a program for gifted children, proof of giftedness must be shown. Such proof may include a copy of your district's gifted student evaluation, sometimes called Gifted and Talented Education (G.A.T.E.) or Talented and Gifted (T.A.G.) or a copy of your SAT scores. In addition to the online course, some off-line work must be accomplished.

Educational Services Incorporated

PO Box 3363
Oshkosh, WI 54903

PHONE: (920) 688-3300
WEBSITE: www.educationalsi.com
EMAIL: jterzynski@educationalsi.com
YEAR FOUNDED: 1998
ACCREDITATION: None

Educational Services Incorporated (ESI) gets most of its students from referrals by school districts and with good reason. Students stay on the rolls of their local school district, so the home district gets the daily allotment of funds for that student. ESI charges the school district less than the allotment for the student, and the school district pockets the difference. Since ESI's student base is those students that often slip through the cracks, it's a win-win situation. The program also offers assistance to homeschooled children and their families. A diploma is available.

Electronic Classroom of Tomorrow

3700 South High Street, Suite 95
Columbus, OH 43207

PHONE: (614) 492-8884 or (888) 326-8395
FAX: (614) 492-8894
WEBSITE: www.ecotohio.org
EMAIL: Info@ecotoh.org
YEAR FOUNDED: 2000
ACCREDITATION: None

Sponsored by the Lucas County Educational Service Center, this is a statewide, nonprofit, computer-enhanced charter school. A diploma is available.

The Electronic High School

250 East 500 South
PO Box 144200
Salt Lake City, UT 84114

PHONE: (801) 538-7736
WEBSITE: www.ehs.uen.org
EMAIL: rsiddowa@usoe.k12.ut.us or blee@usoe.k12.ut.us
YEAR FOUNDED: 1994
ACCREDITATION: Northwest Association of Schools and Colleges and Universities

The Electronic High School (EHS) is free to students who live in Utah; those who live outside the state must pay a $100 per semester per course fee. The school's age makes it one of the older online high schools in existence. Students who complete courses from EHS will have a certificate of completion mailed to their local school of residence with the grade and credit earned. No diploma is offered.

E-School

Hawaii Department of Education
Advanced Technology Research Office
475 22nd Avenue
Building 302, Room 211
Honolulu, HI 96816

PHONE: (808) 733-4777
FAX: (808) 733-4730
WEBSITE: www.eschool.k12.hi.us
EMAIL: atr@k12.hi.us
YEAR FOUNDED: 1996
ACCREDITATION: None

This school is a project of the Hawaii Department of Education. It also has an E-magnet Academy to prepare students for electronic technology employment. Courses are free to students from Hawaii. No diploma is available.

Florida Virtual School

445 West Amelia Street, Suite 301
Orlando, FL 32801

PHONE: (407) 317-3326
FAX: (407) 317-3367
WEBSITE: www.flvs.net
EMAIL: info@flvs.net
YEAR FOUNDED: 1997
ACCREDITATION: Southern Association of Colleges and Schools

Florida Virtual School (FLVS) provides free online classes and instruction to all public, private, and home-schooled students in Florida. Classes are available for students outside the state on a tuition basis. Currently it has students in sixty-five out of sixty-seven Florida counties as well as students elsewhere. Students in FLVS consistently score higher than the Florida average on Advanced Placement tests. The mission of the Florida Virtual School is to provide students with high-quality technology-based educational opportunities to gain the knowledge and skills necessary to succeed in the twenty-first century. A diploma is available.

Futures International High School

2204 El Camino Real, Suite 312
Oceanside, CA 92054

PHONE: (760) 721-0121
FAX: (760) 721-6127
WEBSITE: www.internationalhigh.org
EMAIL: his@futures.edu
YEAR FOUNDED: 1985
ACCREDITATION: Distance Education and Training
Council

Futures International High School (FIHS) offers individualized one-to-one instruction via computer videoconferencing. Its diploma program is college preparatory.

Illinois Virtual High School

c/o Dr. Bradley Woodruff
Division Administrator, Secondary Education Division
Illinois State Board of Education (ISBE)
100 North First Street
Springfield, IL 62777

PHONE: (217) 782-2826
FAX: (217) 785-9210
WEBSITE: www.ivhs.k12.il.us
EMAIL: bwoodruf@isbe.net
YEAR FOUNDED: 2001
ACCREDITATION: None

This is one of the newer virtual schools, so it currently has few courses. This situation is expected to be temporary and the school should grow quickly. The Illinois State Board of Education administers it. It does not plan to offer a high school diploma program. A note of concern: the program's monthly updates web page has not been updated since February of 2001.

Indiana University High School

Owen Hall 001
790 East Kirkwood Avenue
Bloomington, IN 47405-7101

PHONE: (800) 334-1011
FAX: (812) 855-8680
WEBSITE: scs.indiana.edu
EMAIL: scs@indiana.edu
YEAR FOUNDED: 1999
ACCREDITATION: North Central Association Commission on Accreditation and School Improvement

Indiana University's School of Continuing Studies, provider of the university's distance-learning degrees, offers a high school diploma program. Courses, developed and taught by certified high school teachers, are mostly print based, though some employ the Internet, CD-ROMs, or other technologies. The program allows you to either complete an entire diploma program or finish a diploma program already in progress. The principal is a former linebacker for the Houston Oilers (and has his football card prominently displayed on the website).

Internet Home School

915 East Gurley Street, Suite 101
Prescott, AZ 86301

PHONE: (928) 708-9404
FAX: (928) 708-9384
WEBSITE: www.Internethomeschool.com
EMAIL: juliakf@earthlink.net
YEAR FOUNDED: 1997
ACCREDITATION: North Central Association of Colleges and Schools

This school works with homeschooling families to provide the best education possible for their children. The school was begun with the philosophy of working with children who have special needs. A diploma is available.

Juneau Cyber School

10014 Crazy Horse Drive
Juneau, AK 99801

PHONE: (907) 463-1700, ext. 318
FAX: (907) 463-1963
WEBSITE: http://jcs.jsd.k12.ak.us
EMAIL: hopkinsh@jsd.k12.ak.us
YEAR FOUNDED: 2000
ACCREDITATION: None

Juneau Cyber School (JCS) serves homeschoolers and others seeking a high school education. It provides access to the public services of the Juneau School District. It is up to parents and students to decide how much interaction they wish to have with the school district. Students are required to take the Alaska State Achievement Exam. If you desire a diploma, you must meet all of the requirements of the Juneau School District.

Kentucky Virtual High School

PHONE: (866) 432-0008 or (502) 564-4772
WEBSITE: www.kvhs.org
EMAIL: kvhspdreg@kde.state.ky.us
YEAR FOUNDED: 2000
ACCREDITATION: None

Kentucky Virtual High School (KVHS) provides supplemental courses for high school students and access to a challenging curriculum. To be admitted for course enrollment, students must be Kentucky residents. Interested homeschoolers should contact their local school to begin the application process. The state also offers Kentucky Virtual Adult Education and the Kentucky Virtual Advanced Placement Academy.

Keystone National High School

420 West Fifth Street
Bloomsburg, PA 17815

PHONE: (570) 784-5220
FAX: (570) 784-2129
WEBSITE: www.keystonehighschool.com
EMAIL: info@keystonehighschool.com
YEAR FOUNDED: 1995
ACCREDITATION: Distance Education and Training Council and Commission on Schools and Colleges of the Northwest Association of Schools and Colleges and Universities

Keystone offers its program in both correspondence and online formats. Its unique dual accreditation is a real bonus. A diploma is available.

Laurel Springs School

PO Box 1440
Ojai, CA 93024

PHONE: (800) 377-5890 or (805) 646-2473
WEBSITE: www.laurelsprings.com
EMAIL: info@laurelsprings.com
YEAR FOUNDED: 1991
ACCREDITATION: Western Association of Schools and Colleges

Students have online access to teacher-advisors, office staff, and other students. The school offers the option of either web-based or textbook-based courses. A diploma is available.

Louisiana Virtual High School

Louisiana Center for Educational Technology
Louisiana Department of Education
2758-D Brightside Drive
Baton Rouge, LA 70820

PHONE: (225) 763-5575
WEBSITE: lvhs.doe.apexvs.com
EMAIL: kbradford@lcet.state.la.us
YEAR FOUNDED: 2000
ACCREDITATION: None

Louisiana Virtual High School is run collaboratively by the Louisiana Department of Education and the Louisiana School for Math, Science, and the Arts. The program is free to all public and state-approved private high school students. A diploma is available.

Maryland Virtual High School of Science and Mathematics

51 University Boulevard East
Silver Spring, MD 20901

PHONE: (301) 649-2880
FAX: (301) 649-2830
WEBSITE: mvhs1.mbhs.edu
EMAIL: mverona@mvhs.mbhs.edu
YEAR FOUNDED: 1995
ACCREDITATION: None

Students conduct sophisticated scientific research. Although an incredibly unique program, it is really only a viable option for those already attending one of the partner schools. A diploma is available.

Michigan Virtual High School

University Corporate Research Park
3101 Technology Parkway, Suite G
Lansing, MI 48910-8356

PHONE: (517) 336-7733
FAX: (517) 336-7787
WEBSITE: www.mivhs.org
EMAIL: mivu@mivu.org
YEAR FOUNDED: 2000
ACCREDITATION: None

The goal of Michigan Virtual High School (MIVHS) is to provide a diverse set of courses for all students. The private, nonprofit Michigan Virtual University operates it. While the high school does not grant diplomas, a student could accelerate his or her graduation date by taking courses through both the local district and MIVHS.

Milwaukee Area Technical College

Adult High School Program
700 West State Street
Milwaukee, WI 53233

PHONE: (414) 297-6591
WEBSITE: www.milwaukee.tec.wi.us/featur/adult/index.htm
EMAIL: hopgooda@matc.edu
YEAR FOUNDED: 1997 for online courses
ACCREDITATION: North Central Association of Colleges and Schools

This program targets adults who have not earned a high school diploma. It is possible to study for either the GED or a traditional high school diploma.

Mindquest

Bloomington Public Schools, I.S.D. 271
2575 West 88th Street
Bloomington, MN 55431

PHONE: (952) 681-6123
FAX: (952) 681-6171
WEBSITE: www.mindquest.org
EMAIL: coordinator@mindquest.bloomington.k12.mn.us
YEAR FOUNDED: 1998
ACCREDITATION: None

Billed as "the world's first public high school diploma completely on the Internet," Mindquest is operated by the Bloomington Public Schools. The program is free to Minnesota residents, but citizens of other states must pay a fee. It offers a diploma program (for students at least seventeen or older and out of school) or a credit make-up program (for students aged seventeen to twenty-one). Minnesota residents must complete the Minnesota Basic Standards Test.

Monte Vista On-Line Academy

Monte Vista School District C-8
345 East Prospect Avenue
Monte Vista, CO 81144

PHONE: (719) 852-2212
WEBSITE: monte.k12.co.us/ola/index.htm
EMAIL: mrmac@monte.k12.co.us
YEAR FOUNDED: 1996
ACCREDITATION: None

Colorado residents pay no fees. The school does allow nonresidents to take classes, but they must pay tuition. A diploma is available.

New Mexico Virtual School

300 Don Gaspar
Santa Fe, NM 87501-2786

PHONE: (505) 827-6516
FAX: (505) 827-6696
WEBSITE: www.sde.state.nm.us
EMAIL: webmaster@sde.state.nm.us
YEAR FOUNDED: 2002
ACCREDITATION: None

The State of New Mexico has contracted with Intelligent Education Incorporated (IEI) to provide this virtual high school program. The school is still under construction.

North Dakota Division of Independent Study

PO Box 5036
1510 12th Avenue North
Fargo, ND 58105

PHONE: (701) 231-6007
FAX: (701) 231-6052
WEBSITE: www.ndisonline.org
EMAIL: jon.skaare@sendit.nodak.edu
YEAR FOUNDED: 1935
ACCREDITATION: North Central Association Commission on Accreditation and School Improvement; North Dakota Department of Public Instruction.

This school offers two diploma tracks: one for college-bound students and one for employment-bound students. It also offers a senior citizen discount.

Northstar Academy

690 North Meridian Road, Suite 204
Kalispell, MT 59901

PHONE: (406) 257-8680 or (888) 464-6280
FAX: (406) 257-8665
WEBSITE: www.northstar-academy.org
EMAIL: info@northstar-academy.org
YEAR FOUNDED: 1998
ACCREDITATION: Northwest Association of Schools and Colleges

This is a private Christian school that provides entire diploma programs and individual courses.

Oak Meadow School

PO Box 740
Putney, VT 05346

PHONE: (802) 387-2021
FAX: (802) 387-5108
WEBSITE: www.oakmeadow.com/school.htm
EMAIL: info@oakmeadow.com
YEAR FOUNDED: 1975
ACCREDITATION: None

The school asserts that it is pursuing national accreditation. It provides support for homeschooling families through the school and its publishing company. A diploma is available.

Plano ISD eSchool

Plano Independent School District
Student Services
2700 West 15th Street
Plano, TX 75075

PHONE: (469) 752-8017
FAX: (469) 752-8175
WEBSITE: www.planoisdeschool.net/home.htm
EMAIL: eSchool@pisd.edu
YEAR FOUNDED: 2001
ACCREDITATION: None

A project of the Plano Independent School District, eSchool charges tuition to all students. It plays up the possibility of taking courses at your local high school and at eSchool simultaneously. It allows students to take courses not offered on their home campuses and can accelerate graduation. You are only allowed to take two online courses per semester.

The Potter's School

c/o Janna Gilbert
8344 Carrleigh Parkway
Springfield, VA 22152

PHONE: (703) 912-7926
FAX: (703) 912-7926
WEBSITE: www.pottersschool.com
EMAIL: director@pottersschool.org
YEAR FOUNDED: 1994
ACCREDITATION: None

Classes meet online at least once each week using Internet video conferencing. The school does not provide a transcript; homeschooling students are encouraged to create a portfolio detailing their academic achievements. A portfolio is available.

Richard Milburn High School

Center for Distance Education
14416 Jefferson Davis Highway, Suite 8
Woodbridge, VA 22191

PHONE: (703) 494-0147 or (877) 888-9473
FAX: (703) 494-6093
WEBSITE: www.rmhs.org
EMAIL: inquiry@rmhs.org
YEAR FOUNDED: 1975
ACCREDITATION: Distance Education and Training Council

The curriculum is delivered online through video conferencing. The program also provides educational support to the military. A diploma is available.

seeUonline Program

Valley Pathways
690 Cope Industrial Way
Palmer, AK 99645

PHONE: (907) 745-1486
FAX: (907) 745-1496
WEBSITE: www.seeuonline.org
EMAIL: seeUonline@hotmail.com
YEAR FOUNDED: 2000
ACCREDITATION: None

Sponsored by the Matanuska-Susitna School District, this is an accelerated program for students who wish to complete high school in three years or less. Students who complete the full course are eligible for a Matanuska-Susitna diploma. The program is free to students in the participating boroughs; all others must pay a fee. Courses address Alaska academic standards.

University of California—Berkeley Extension Online

2000 Center Street, Suite 400
Berkeley, CA 94704

PHONE: (510) 642-4124
WEBSITE: http://explore.berkeley.edu/UCExt
EMAIL: askus@ucxonline.berkeley.edu
YEAR FOUNDED: 1996
ACCREDITATION: None

This program provides students with the opportunity to take courses at the prestigious University of California at Berkeley. While it does not offer a diploma, this program does have a myriad of courses from which to choose. Because of the traditional nature of the courses offered, students could use the courses to either accelerate their high school graduation or retake courses they did not pass.

University of Missouri—Columbia High School

Center for Distance and Independent Study
136 Clark Hall
Columbia, MO 65211-4200

PHONE: (573) 882-2491 or (800) 692-6877
FAX: (573) 882-6808
WEBSITE: http://cdis.missouri.edu/MUHighSchool/HShome.htm
EMAIL: cdis@missouri.edu
YEAR FOUNDED: 1999
ACCREDITATION: North Central Association Commission on Accreditation and School Improvement

This diploma program with more than 150 courses is open to adults and high school age students.

University of Nebraska—Lincoln Independent Study High School

Room 269, Second Floor
North Wing, Clifford Hardin Nebraska Center for Continuing Education
33rd and Holdrege Streets
Lincoln, NE 68583-9400

PHONE: (402) 472-4450
FAX: (402) 472-4422
WEBSITE: dcs.unl.edu/ishs and www.class.com
EMAIL: unlishs2@unl.edu
YEAR FOUNDED: 1929
ACCREDITATION: North Central Association Commission on Accreditation and School Improvement

University of Nebraska-Lincoln Independent Study High School (UNL) has a resident staff of certified teachers that provide instruction and support. It has recently increased the number of online courses offered. Graduates of the program receive a high school diploma.

Unaccredited or Unrecognized Accreditation

Some of the schools listed below have no accreditation whatsoever but quite likely offer a quality education. Some of the schools claim accreditation through various accreditors. While it is admirable that schools work on quality control issues (which is one of the important facets of accreditation), none of the accreditors below are recognized by the U.S. Department of Education. Is that important? It depends on your final goal. Graduates of the programs below will be able to get accepted into some colleges. Before you enroll, check to make sure that your dream college will accept your diploma. If you hope to transfer units to another high school, you may have more of a problem. Again, investigate your options before you sign up.

Also bear in mind that the state department of education or your local school district may recognize some good schools that do not have accreditation. If you attend one of these schools, most colleges will consider you for admission.

Abaetern Academy (formerly Montana Polytechnic Institute)

1627 West Main, #376
Bozeman, MT 59715

PHONE: (406) 920-1778
WEBSITE: www.abaetern.com
EMAIL: info@abaetern.com
YEAR FOUNDED: 1997
ACCREDITATION: Pursuing through Pacific Northwest Association of Independent Schools

This school provides a solid high school diploma program that is heavily focused on astronomy and other sciences. The staff has significant experience in science-related course work. There is an option to complete either an entire diploma program or to complete courses to transfer back to your home school. It is a mastery learning program; students must truly learn each course before moving on to the next.

ArabesQ Online Academy

PO Box 1031
Bronx, NY 10465

PHONE: (718) 518-1464
FAX: (253) 550-6223
WEBSITE: www.arabesq.com/Academy
EMAIL: Academy@ArabesQ.com
YEAR FOUNDED: 1999
ACCREDITATION: None

This is a program for homeschooling Muslim students and for adult women who may not have had the opportunity to get an education. The main office is in Saudi Arabia, but there are also offices in Washington, D.C., New York, and Egypt. A diploma is available.

Babbage Net School

PO Box 517
Port Jefferson, NY 11777

PHONE: (631) 642-2029
FAX: (631) 642-2029
WEBSITE: www.babbagenetschool.com
EMAIL: babbage@babbagenetschool.com
YEAR FOUNDED: 1996
ACCREDITATION: None

Courses are taught using interactive audio, synchronized web browsing, and a shared whiteboard. It has a relationship with the Board of Cooperative Educational Services of Suffolk County, so New York residents get a break on the price. In addition, all of the teachers are New York State certified and the classes conform to New York State academic standards. It does not offer its own diploma, but it supplements the educational offerings of other schools. Students are required to be online at specific times for classes.

Basehor-Linwood Virtual Charter School

PO Box 282
Basehor, KS 66007

PHONE: (913) 724-1727
FAX: (913) 724-4518
WEBSITE: http://vcs.usd458.k12.ks.us
EMAIL: Brenda_degroot@mail.usd458.k12.ks.us
YEAR FOUNDED: 1998
ACCREDITATION: None

Sponsored by the Basehor-Linwood Unified School District, this program provides an individualized curriculum to students through their home computers. The school's goal is to create and develop alternative approaches to education through the use of current and emerging technologies. A diploma is available.

Clonlara Compuhigh

1289 Jewett
Ann Arbor, MI 48104

PHONE: (734) 769-4511
FAX: (734) 769-9629
WEBSITE: www.clonlara.org/compuhigh.htm
EMAIL: info@clonlara.org
YEAR FOUNDED: 1994
ACCREDITATION: National Private Schools Accreditation Alliance

This popular program has been providing online courses since 1994, which is almost ancient for this format. It also offers an adult education program where students who are not high school age can earn a diploma. The accreditor is not recognized by the U.S. Department of Education.

Colorado State Academy of Arvada

7506 West 74th Place
Arvada, CO 80003

PHONE: (303) 425-1752
FAX: (303) 423-4461
WEBSITE: www.onlinehighschool.net
EMAIL: smedser@aol.com
YEAR FOUNDED: 1999
ACCREDITATION: None

This high school diploma program, in contrast to its name, is privately owned. The secretary of state of the State of Colorado accepts its diploma as valid.

Dennison Online Internet School

c/o Dennison Academy
PO Box 29781
Los Angeles, CA 90029

PHONE: (818) 371-2001
WEBSITE: www.dennisononline.com
EMAIL: principal@dennisononline.com
YEAR FOUNDED: 1981
ACCREDITATION: Accreditation Commission for International Internet Education

In addition to the traditional high school program for teens, the Dennison Online Internet School also offers an adult diploma program. The accreditor is not recognized by the U.S. Department of Education.

Eagle Christian High School

2526 Sunset Lane
Missoula, MT 59804

PHONE: (888) 324-5348
FAX: (406) 542-0632
WEBSITE: www.eaglechristian.org
EMAIL: eagle@eaglechristian.org
YEAR FOUNDED: 1996
ACCREDITATION: Montana Federation of Independent Schools

The school requires a statement of faith, and it is advisable to conform to the school's beliefs (or at least be in the ballpark). A diploma is available.

Eldorado Academy

PO Box 190
Nederland, CO 80466

PHONE: (303) 604-2822
FAX: (303) 258-3541
WEBSITE: www.eldoradoacademy.org
EMAIL: faculty@eldoradoacademy.org
YEAR FOUNDED: 1999
ACCREDITATION: National Private Schools Association

This is a private online high school, so all must pay. Eldorado Academy is a self-paced program; when the student completes all of the course requirements, the diploma is awarded. The focus is on integrating learning and technology.

Internet Academy

32020 First Avenue South, #109
Federal Way, WA 98003

PHONE: (253) 945-2230
FAX: (253) 945-2233
WEBSITE: www.iacademy.org
EMAIL: jbleek@iacademy.org
YEAR FOUNDED: 1996
ACCREDITATION: None

Provides online core courses that support the state of Washington standards and has Washington State–certified teachers. Internet Academy does not issue diplomas.

Regina Coeli Academy

9755 East McAndrew Court
Tucson, AZ 85748

PHONE: (520) 751-1942
FAX: (520) 751-2580
WEBSITE: www.reginacoeli.org
EMAIL: admin@reginacoeli.org
YEAR FOUNDED: 1995
ACCREDITATION: None

Regina Coeli Academy (RCA) was the first completely online school for Roman Catholics. It is operated under the authority of the Society for the Study of Magisterial Teaching. Its sister school is the Scholars' Online Academy. A diploma is available.

Scholars' Online Academy

9755 East McAndrew Court
Tucson, AZ 85748

PHONE: (520) 751-1942
FAX: (520) 751-2580

WEBSITE: www.islas.org/sola.html
EMAIL: admin@islas.org
YEAR FOUNDED: 1995
ACCREDITATION: None

Institute for Study of the Liberal Arts and Sciences, the parent of both Scholars' Online Academy and Regina Coeli Academy, offers three diploma tracks: math/science, languages, and vocation discernment (for potential priests and nuns). Graduates of the school have attended Ivy League schools.

The Southwest Secondary Learning Center

4122 Constance Place, NE
Albuquerque, NM 87109

PHONE: (505) 296-7677
FAX: (505) 296-0510
WEBSITE: www.sslc-nm.com
EMAIL: djuarez@sslc-nm.com
YEAR FOUNDED: 2001
ACCREDITATION: None

Sponsored by the Albuquerque Public School District, the school's goal is to improve, enhance, and change the educational delivery system through the integration of technology, service learning, and the development of personal and social responsibility. A diploma is available.

Sycamore Academy Online School

2179 Meyer Place
Costa Mesa, CA 92627

PHONE: (949) 650-4466
FAX: (800) 779-6750
WEBSITE: www.sycamoretree.com
EMAIL: sycamoretree@compuserve.com
YEAR FOUNDED: 1982
ACCREDITATION: None

According to information available on its website, the term "online" is a bit of a misnomer. Apparently the only time you're actually online is when you're sending completed assignments through email. The courses are actually on a CD-ROM. It does appear to have a solid curriculum and offers a high school diploma.

The Trent Schools

Admissions and Records
PO Box 7168
Bloomington, IN 47408

PHONE: It is of concern that the school does not provide a telephone number.
WEBSITE: www.theschools.com

EMAIL: TheTrentSchools@theschools.com
YEAR FOUNDED: 1996
ACCREDITATION: None

The Trent Schools focus on and believe they are successful with three types of students: exceptionally bright and motivated young men or women who demand challenges equal to their abilities; bright to normal students who, for lack of motivating instruction, have not been successful in public school programs; and able-minded students who have not yet discovered their full potential. This is a diploma program.

Virtual School for the Gifted

PO Box 549
Hurstbridge, Victoria 3099 Australia

PHONE: +61 3 9710 1558 or 03 9710 1558 (within Australia)
FAX: +61 3 9710 1592 or 03 9710 1592 (within Australia)
WEBSITE: www.vsg.edu.au
EMAIL: vsg-admin@vsg.edu.au
YEAR FOUNDED: 1997
ACCREDITATION: None

Don't let the Australian address scare you off. That's the advantage to online education; it's available anywhere at anytime. Virtual School for the Gifted (VSG) offers a unique approach to online learning for the truly gifted. A diploma is available.

Virtual School @ Liverpool

Liverpool Central School District
800 Fourth Street
Liverpool, NY 13088

PHONE: (315) 453-1512
FAX: (315) 453-0281
WEBSITE: www.liverpool.k12.ny.us/virtual.html
EMAIL: lblavine@liverpool.k12.ny.us
YEAR FOUNDED: 2000
ACCREDITATION: None

Although courses are available to all students, the school is particularly interested in offering courses for the medically challenged, homeschooled, and alternative education student. A diploma track is available.

Willoway School

PHONE: (866) 224-0464
FAX: (866) 224-0464
WEBSITE: www.willoway.com
EMAIL: information@willoway.com
YEAR FOUNDED: 1996

ACCREDITATION: Accreditation Commission for International Internet Education

An important goal of Willoway School is producing technologically literate adults. A diploma is available.

Virtual High Schools, Inc.

Virtual High Schools (VHS) (www.govhs.org) is a consortium of high schools that offer courses online through Virtual High Schools, Inc. In order to take courses from VHS, you must be a student in a member school. VHS offers courses in a number of academic disciplines. VHS is certainly not for those seeking a high school diploma entirely online, but if you do attend one of the member schools, this could be an opportunity to accelerate your learning.

The following schools are members of the consortium.

Alabama

JU Blacksher High School / Uriah
Monroe Senior High School / Monroeville

Arizona

Corona del Sol High School / Tempe
Desert Vista High School / Phoenix
Marcos de Niza High School / Tempe
McClintock High School / Tempe
Mountain Pointe High School / Phoenix
Tempe High School / Tempe

California

John F. Kennedy High School / Fremont
Mare Island Technology Academy / Vallejo

Colorado

Littleton High School / Littleton

Connecticut

East Windsor Junior/Senior High School /
    East Windsor
Metropolitan Learning Center / Bloomfield

Georgia

Carroll County Consortium / Carrollton
Central High School / Carrollton
Clarke Central High School / Athens
Crossroads Academy / Grovetown

Harris County High School / Hamilton
Lincoln County High School / Lincolnton
Mount Zion High School / Jonesboro
Newnan High School / Newnan
Portal High School / Portal
Temple High School / Temple
Villa Rica High School / Villa Rica
Ware County High School / Waycross

Idaho
Butte High School / Butte
Rigby High School / Rigby

Illinois
New Trier High School / Winnetka

Maryland
Maryland School for the Deaf / Frederick

Massachusetts
Abington High School / Abington
Algonquin Regional High School / Northborough
Archbishop Williams High School / Braintree
Avon Middle-High School / Avon
Beverly High School / Beverly
Bishop Fenwick High School / Peabody
Cathedral High School / Boston
Chatham High School / Chatham
Clinton High School / Clinton
Concord-Carlisle High School / Concord
Dennis-Yarmouth Regional High School / South Yarmouth
Douglas High School / Douglas
Dover-Sherborn High School / Dover
Fontbonne Academy / Milton
Franklin High School / Franklin
Harwich High School / Harwich
Holliston High School / Holliston
Hopedale Junior/Senior High School / Worcester
Hopkinton High School / Hopkinton
Hudson High School / Hudson
Ipswich High School / Ipswich
Leicester High School / Leicester
Leominster High School / Leominster
Lowell High School / Lowell
Marian High School / Framingham
Marlborough High School / Marlborough
Marshfield High School / Marshfield
Maynard High School / Maynard
Medfield High School / Medfield

Melrose High School / Melrose
Milford High School / Milford
Millis High School / Millis
Mt. St. Joseph Academy / Brighton
Nantucket High School / Nantucket
Natick High School / Natick
Newton South High School / Newton Centre
Nipmuc Regional Middle/High School / Upton
North Brookfield Jr./Sr. High School / North Brookfield
Northbridge High School / Whitinsville
Norton High School / Norton
Old Rochester Regional High School / Mattapoisett
Pope John XXIII High School / Everett
Quaboag Regional High School / Warren
Randolph High School / Randolph
Seekonk High School / Seekonk
Shrewsbury High School / Shrewsbury
Southeastern Regional Vocational Technical High School / South Easton
Southwick-Tolland Regional High School / Southwick
Sutton Junior/Senior High School / Sutton
Swampscott High School / Swampscott
Taunton High School / Taunton
Trinity Catholic High School / Newton
Tyngsboro High School / Tyngsboro
Ware Junior/Senior High School / Ware
Wareham High School / Wareham
West Boylston Middle/High School / West Boylston
Westborough High School / Westborough
Westwood High School / Westwood
Whitman-Hanson Regional High School / Whitman

Michigan
Bay City Central High School / Auburn
Bay City Western High School / Auburn
East Lansing High School / East Lansing
Everett High School / Lansing
Haslett High School / Haslett
Waverly High School / Lansing

Mississippi
Choctaw County Schools / Ackerman

New Hampshire
Newport Middle High School / Newport
Sunapee Middle High School / Sunapee
Winnacunnet High School / Hampton
Woodsville High School / Woodsville

New Jersey

Collingswood High School / Collingswood
New Egypt High School / Plumsted Township
Tenafly High School / Tenafly

New Mexico

New Mexico School for the Deaf / Santa Fe

New York

Silver Creek Central School / Silver Creek

North Carolina

Bandys High School / Catawba
Bunker Hill High School / Claremont
Charles B. Aycock High School / Pikeville
Eastern Wayne High School / Goldsboro
Fred T. Foard High School / Durham
Hillside High School / Durham
Maiden High School / Maiden
Myers Park High School / Charlotte
Orange High School / Hillsborough
Perquimans County High School / Hertford
Plymouth High School / Plymouth
Riverside High School / Durham
Rosewood High School / Rosewood
Southern Wayne High School / Dudley
Spring Creek High School / Seven Springs
Swansboro High School / Swansboro
Weldon High School / Weldon

Ohio

Anna High School / Anna
Fort Loramie High School / Fort Loramie
Groveport Madison High School / Groveport
Hamilton Township High School / Columbus
Hoover High School / North Canton
Jefferson Area High School / Jefferson
Mariemont High School / Cincinnati
North College Hill High School / Cincinnati
Tiffin Columbian High School / Tiffin
Whitehall-Yearling High School / Whitehall
Wickliffe High School / Wickliffe

Pennsylvania

Jenkintown High School / Jenkintown
Norristown Area High School / Norristown
North Penn High School / Lansdale
Perkiomen Valley High School / Collegeville
Ridley High School / Folsom
Springfield Township High School / Springfield

Texas

LaPorte High School / LaPorte
McKinney High School / McKinney
McKinney North High School / McKinney
McNeil High School / Austin
Round Rock High School / Round Rock
Stony Point High School / Round Rock

Vermont

Blue Mountain Union School / Wells River
Brattleboro Union High School / Brattleboro
Colchester School District / Colchester
Leland and Gray Union High School / Townshend
West Rutland School / West Rutland

Virginia

Chesterfield County Public Schools / Midlothian
Fluvanna County High School / Palmyra
Heritage High School / Newport

Washington

Clover Park Public Schools / Lakewood
Forks High School / Forks

Wisconsin

Madison Metro School District / Madison

International Schools

Asociacion Escuelas Lincoln and The American
   International / Buenos Aires, Argentina
Associacão Escola Gradauda de São Paulo / São Paulo,
   Brazil
Carol Morgan School / Santo Domingo, Dominican
   Republic
Colegio Franklin Delano Roosevelt / Lima, Peru
Colegio Internacional de Caracas / Caracas, Venezuela
Colegio Internacional de Puerto La Cruz / Barcelona,
   Spain
Dalat School / Penang, Malaysia
Escuela Campo Alegre / Venezuela
Escuela Las Morochas / Ciudad Ojeda, Venezuela
International School of Curitiba / Curitiba-PR, Brazil
International School of Port of Spain / Port of Spain,
   Trinidad
Taejon Christian International School / Daeduck,
   Taejon, South Korea
Uruguayan American School / Montevideo, Uruguay

CHAPTER 2

Independent Study High Schools

"That reality is 'independent' means that there is something in every experience that escapes our arbitrary control."

—*William James*

Independent study programs, formerly called "correspondence courses," are still a tried-and-true method for earning a high school diploma. This is particularly the case for people living outside the United States who do not have access, or at least reliable access, to the Internet. The only thing that you must rely on is the postal service.

In a former incarnation, correspondence courses were seen as entirely pencil-and-paper endeavours. Why the name change? The term *correspondence* brings to some people's minds the schools that used to advertise inside matchbook covers. In recent years, there has been a subtle shift to the term *independent study*, but, for the most part, independent study is still pencil and paper and the occasional software program.

An added benefit of pursing a diploma through an independent study program is that many independent study schools have a proven track record. In sharp contrast to online programs, it is possible to find independent study programs that are more than one hundred years old.

As with most distance-learning high schools, how much it will cost and how long it will take to complete course work depends solely on you and your academic history. If you left school as a junior, then you would likely not have to repeat course work from your freshman and sophomore years. This can mean a substantial savings.

Frequently Asked Questions

How "independent" will this independent study be? What if I need support for certain subjects?

Make sure you ask these questions before putting down any money. While some courses provide no support at all, others provide constant support and feedback. The following should be the minimum acceptable standards for student support:

- A toll-free number. Make sure that the toll-free number is not just for admissions but is also available for class questions. It is unreasonable (and impossible, in most cases) to expect a school to have a toll-free number that works outside the United States and Canada.

- An email address for questions. Same point: make sure that you can reach instructors and not just admissions folks.

- A quick turnaround time with mail. One good gauge is how long it took the program to send you the original information. Figure that it will probably take twice as long to return assignments and tests.

- Real teachers with real teaching experience. At minimum, teachers should have a bachelor's degree. Teacher certification would be an added plus.

- A fax number. This is more essential for international students than for States-based students. Faxing assignments improves the turnaround time significantly.

Which is the best program?

There is no one best program. This is particularly true with independent study programs, where the individual student's strengths and weaknesses come into play. Decide what you need and work from there. You may need (or want) a regionally accredited high school. If a program has regional accreditation, it will make that information well known. If you need a program without time constraints, make sure that the program you choose has none (or at least quite liberal ones).

Is there a maximum age for independent study students?

In almost all of these programs, there is no maximum age. This makes this method particularly good for the over-eighteen crowd coming back to school. Whether you're eighteen or eighty-one, independent study will work for you if you're a pencil-and-paper kind of student. If you prefer to do your work on the computer, you might want to look at the online high schools in chapter 1. If either method works for you, then look at both kinds of programs and decide from there.

For whom is this type of program best?

While anyone of high school age or over could do well with this type of program, self-motivated people are most likely to succeed. There won't be any teachers, parents, or administrators pushing you to complete your assignments. In many cases, the only external influence will be the time limit set by the program. Think about what kind of student you are. If this doesn't sound like you, it might be better to choose a format with more structure.

How long will the program take?

This is difficult to answer because it is dependent upon how much course work you have already completed. If you have never attended high school, it still should take you less than four years because you're not taking summers off or waiting for slower students to complete the work. If you have already finished two years of high school, then it will most certainly take you less than two years to finish the program. As most programs will tell you, much depends on you.

I prefer schools that set a maximum time for the program. The deadline helps most students finish more quickly.

Are scholarships available?

Almost without exception, there are no scholarships available. However, if you have a charter school in your state that offers independent study programs, you may be able to go to school for free. See chapter 6 for additional information on charter schools.

Is accreditation important?

Accreditation can be vitally important, depending on your goal. If higher education is in your future, it becomes even more important that you go to a school with regional accreditation or accreditation by the Distance Education and Training Council (see appendix B). At the very least, the school should be recognized by the state in which it resides.

Programs

When you begin contacting the schools below, you will notice that costs vary widely. Some have no cost, some have minimal cost, and some cost a significant amount. The free programs are all charter schools, and these are only free to state residents. Each state has its own charter school laws, and not all states allow charter schools.

One piece of advice to take to heart: do not choose a program solely on the cost. There are many factors to take into account besides money. What good is a free program if you don't complete it? What good is a free program if it is unacceptable to college admissions offices?

Programs with Regional and National Accreditation

American High School

2200 East 170th Street
Lansing, IL 60438

PHONE: (708) 418-2800 or (800) 531-9268
WEBSITE: www.americanschoolofcorr.com
YEAR FOUNDED: 1897
ACCREDITATION: Distance Education and Training Council; North Central Association of Schools and Colleges

It's hard to argue with a school that has this long a history. The curriculum is quite traditional, and the school offers both a general high school course and a college-preparatory course. Having dual accreditation is an added bonus. The diploma should be accepted anywhere on the planet.

Brigham Young University Independent Study

High School Transcript Program
206 Harman Continuing Education Building
PO Box 21514
Provo, UT 84602-1514

PHONE: (800) 914-8931
FAX: (801) 378-5817
WEBSITE: http://ce.byu.edu/is
EMAIL: indstudy@byu.edu
YEAR FOUNDED: 1982
ACCREDITATION: Northwest Association of Schools and Colleges

A complete diploma program is offered with three emphases—college preparation, vocational/technical preparation, or GED preparation—along with a tremendous amount of available resources. Definitely a top choice!

Christa McAuliffe Academy

3601 West Washington Avenue
Yakima, WA 98903

PHONE: (509) 575-4989
FAX: (509) 575-4976
WEBSITE: www.cmacademy.org
EMAIL: CMA@cmacademy.org
YEAR FOUNDED: 1985
ACCREDITATION: Northwest Association of Schools and Colleges

This academically rigorous program offers courses in both the online and off-line format. A diploma is available.

Chrysalis School

14241 NE Woodinville-Duvall Road, #243
Woodinville, WA 98072

PHONE: (425) 481-2228
FAX: (425) 486-8107
WEBSITE: www.chrysalis-school.com
EMAIL: info@chrysalis-school.com
YEAR FOUNDED: 1983
ACCREDITATION: Northwest Association of Schools and Colleges

The goal is creating confident and competent students. A diploma is available.

Citizens' High School

PO Box 66089
Orange Park, FL 32065-6089

PHONE: (904) 276-1700
FAX: (904) 272-6702
WEBSITE: www.citizenschool.com
EMAIL: inforequests@citizenschool.com
YEAR FOUNDED: 1981
ACCREDITATION: Distance Education and Training Council

Citizens' High School offers a diploma program at a reasonable price. Because it is independent study, no Internet connection is required. The curriculum is standard high school education material. The program has a time limit of three years.

The Hadley School for the Blind

700 Elm Street
Winnetka, IL 60093

PHONE: (847) 446-8111 or (800) 323-4238
FAX: (847) 446-9916
WEBSITE: www.hadley-school.org
EMAIL: info@hadley-school.org
YEAR FOUNDED: 1920
ACCREDITATION: Distance Education and Training Council

Offers almost a hundred courses for the blind, parents (and other family members) of blind children, and teachers that work with the blind. The courses are available in a number of formats including braille, audiocassette, and large print. A diploma is available.

Home Study International

12501 Old Columbia Pike
Silver Spring, MD 20904

PHONE: (301) 680-6570
FAX: (301) 680-6583
WEBSITE: www.hsi.edu
EMAIL: enrollmentservices@hsi.edu
YEAR FOUNDED: 1909
ACCREDITATION: Distance Education and Training Council

Offers courses at all levels of elementary and secondary education, including a State of Maryland approved high school diploma program. This is a Christian school.

Indiana University High School

Owen Hall
790 East Kirkwood Avenue
Bloomington, IN 47405

PHONE: (800) 334-1011
WEBSITE: http://scs.indiana.edu/hs/hsd.html
EMAIL: scs@indiana.edu
YEAR FOUNDED: 1999
ACCREDITATION: North Central Association Commission on Accreditation and School Improvement

What makes the high school diploma program particularly appealing is the service that surrounds the actual learning. Students have a highly qualified academic advisor who guides them through the process all the way to graduation. The school accepts transfer students and most courses from regionally accredited high schools.

James Madison High School/PCDI

430 Technology Parkway
Norcross, GA 30092

PHONE: (770) 729-8400 or (800) 223-4542
FAX: (770) 729-9296
WEBSITE: www.jmhs.com
EMAIL: info@jmhs.com
YEAR FOUNDED: 1987
ACCREDITATION: Distance Education and Training Council

Offers both a general diploma program and an academic diploma program. It is a division of Professional Career Development Institute.

Keystone National High School

420 West Fifth Street
Bloomsburg, PA 17815

PHONE: (570) 784-5220 or (800) 255-4937
FAX: (570) 784-2129
WEBSITE: www.keystonehighschool.com
EMAIL: info@keystonehighschool.com
YEAR FOUNDED: 1995
ACCREDITATION: Distance Education and Training Council; Commission on Schools and Colleges of the Northwest Association of Schools and Colleges and Universities

Offers programs in both correspondence and online formats. Its unique double accreditation is a real bonus and combined with its dual formats, this school should be a top choice for many. It is a division of KC Distance Learning. A diploma is available.

Laurel Springs School

PO Box 1440
Ojai, CA 93024

PHONE: (800) 377-5890 or (805) 646-2473
WEBSITE: www.laurelsprings.com
EMAIL: info@laurelsprings.com
YEAR FOUNDED: 1991
ACCREDITATION: Western Association of Schools and Colleges

Students have online access to teacher-advisors, office staff, and other students. The school offers both web-based and textbook-based courses. A diploma is offered.

Learning and Evaluation Center

420 West Fifth Street
Bloomsburg, PA 17815

PHONE: (570) 784-5220 or (800) 255-4937
FAX: (570) 784-2129
WEBSITE: www.creditmakeup.com
EMAIL: info@keystonehighschool.com
YEAR FOUNDED: 1972
ACCREDITATION: Distance Education and Training Council

Another division of KC Distance Learning, the Learning and Evaluation Center provides opportunities for high school students to make up courses they failed during the regular academic year. A diploma is available.

North Dakota Division of Independent Study

PHONE: (701) 231-6007
FAX: (701) 231-6052
WEBSITE: www.ndisonline.org
EMAIL: jon.skaare@sendit.nodak.edu
YEAR FOUNDED: 1935
ACCREDITATION: North Central Association Commission on Accreditation and School Improvement; North Dakota Department of Public Instruction

This program with both online and independent study courses offers two diploma tracks: one for college-bound students and one for employment-bound students. It also offers a senior citizen discount.

Seton Home Study School

1350 Progress Drive
Front Royal, Virginia 22630

PHONE: (540) 636-9990
FAX: (540) 636-1602
WEBSITE: www.setonhome.org
EMAIL: info@setonhome.org
YEAR FOUNDED: 1975
ACCREDITATION: Southern Association of Colleges and Schools

Ten thousand currently enrolled students can't be wrong. Seton Home Study School is a large, Catholic-centered private school that offers a rigorous, college-preparatory education. A diploma is available.

Texas Tech University High School

Box 42191
Lubbock, TX 79409

PHONE: (806) 742-2352 or (800) 692-6877, ext. 244
WEBSITE: www.dce.ttu.edu/ttuisd/ttuhs.cfm
EMAIL: distlearn@ttu.edu
YEAR FOUNDED: 1993
ACCREDITATION: Texas Education Agency

Open to all students. Bear in mind that you will be receiving a State of Texas accredited curriculum. There is an interesting twist to this program—regardless of age or location, you are required to take the Texas Assessment of Academic Skills before you can graduate. It is possible to arrange to do this in your home state, but it is unlikely that you could do this from overseas. A diploma is available.

Thomson High School

925 Oak Street
Scranton, PA 18515

PHONE: (800) 275-4410
FAX: (570) 343-3620
WEBSITE: www.EducationDirect.com
EMAIL: info@EducationDirect.com
YEAR FOUNDED: 1890
ACCREDITATION: Distance Education and Training Council

The program appears to take more time than most (nine months for each year of high school needed), but the curriculum seems well thought out. A diploma is available.

University of Missouri—Columbia High School

136 Clark Hall
Columbia, MO 65211

PHONE: (573) 882-2491
FAX: (573) 882-6808
WEBSITE: cdis.missouri.edu
EMAIL: cdis@missouri.edu
YEAR FOUNDED: 1999
ACCREDITATION: North Central Association Commission on Accreditation and School Improvement

This school offers individual courses as well as a diploma program. The diploma program is offered in both a correspondence and an online format.

University of Nebraska—Lincoln Independent Study High School

Room 269, Second Floor
North Wing, Clifford Hardin Nebraska Center for Continuing Education
33rd and Holdrege Streets
Lincoln, NE 68583-9400

PHONE: (402) 472-4450
FAX: (402) 472-4422
WEBSITE: http://dcs.unl.edu/ishs
EMAIL: unlishs2@unl.edu
YEAR FOUNDED: 1929
ACCREDITATION: North Central Association Commission on Accreditation and School Improvement

University of Nebraska-Lincoln Independent Study High School (UNL) has a resident staff of certified teachers that provides instruction and support. Some courses are also available online with more projected for the future. A diploma track is available.

University of Texas—Austin High School Diploma Program

Continuing and Extended Education
Independent and Distance Learning
PO Box 7700
Austin, TX 78713-7700

PHONE: (512) 232-7695
FAX: (512) 475-7933
WEBSITE: www.utexas.edu/cee/dec/uths/diploma.shtml
EMAIL: uts@dec.utexas.edu
YEAR FOUNDED: 1998
ACCREDITATION: Texas Education Agency

This relatively new program should grow quickly over the next several years. Courses are available in CD-ROM and print formats. A diploma is available.

Unaccredited or Unrecognized Accreditation

Below you will find schools that either have no accreditation or accreditation unrecognized by the United States Department of Education. Again, many good schools are not accredited, and accreditation may or may not be important, depending on your ultimate goals. If you are heading off to college, you should check with a couple of your top choices to see if they will accept a diploma and transcripts from any of these schools.

Academy of Home Education

1700 Wade Hampton Boulevard
Greenville, SC 29614

PHONE: (877) 252-4348
FAX: (864) 271-8187
WEBSITE: www.bjup.com/services/ahe
EMAIL: ahe@bju.edu
YEAR FOUNDED: 1990 for high school

The school is a ministry of Bob Jones University. The typical student identifies with the homeschooling movement. This program is for traditional high school age students only. A diploma is available.

Accelerated Christian Education/Lighthouse Christian Academy

8200 Bryan Dairy Road, Suite 200
Largo, FL 33777

PHONE: (727) 319-0700
FAX: (727) 319-0733
WEBSITE: www.schooloftomorrow.com
EMAIL: CustomerService@ACEministries.com
YEAR FOUNDED: 1970

If you desire a diploma from this program, you will need to enroll in Lighthouse Christian Academy.

Alger Learning Center: Independence High School

121 Alder Drive
Sedro-Woolley, WA 98284

PHONE: (800) 595-2630
FAX: (360) 595-1141
WEBSITE: www.independent-learning.com
EMAIL: orion@nas.com
YEAR FOUNDED: 1989
ACCREDITATION: National Association for Legal Support of Alternative Schools

Alger Learning Center: Independence High School (ALC) provides curriculum for homeschoolers. It offers both local and distance-learning programs. A diploma is available.

Alpha-Omega Academy

300 North McKemy Avenue
Chandler, AZ 85226

PHONE: (602) 438-2717 or (800) 682-7396
FAX: (480) 893-6112
WEBSITE: www.aop.com/default.asp?chan_id=24
EMAIL: online@aop.com
YEAR FOUNDED: 1992
ACCREDITATION: National Association of Private Schools

The academy is run by Alpha-Omega Publications; courses are available in either print or CD-ROM format. A diploma is available.

Branford Grove School

PO Box 341172
Arleta, CA 91334

PHONE: (818) 890-0350
FAX: (818) 890-6440
WEBSITE: www.branfordgrove.com
EMAIL: branfordgrove@aol.com
YEAR FOUNDED: 1984

Families have the option of purchasing a packaged curriculum or inventing their own. Two concerns are that the school does not mail enrollment forms and calls can only be returned collect. A diploma is available.

The Bridgeway Academy

334 Second Street
Catasauqua, PA 18032

PHONE: (610) 266-9016 or (800) 863-1474
FAX: (610) 266-7817
WEBSITE: www.homeschoolacademy.com/academy/index.html
EMAIL: office@homeschoolacademy.com
YEAR FOUNDED: 1988

Christian in nature, this school provides support for families going through the homeschooling process. It uses the School of Tomorrow curriculum that is used by many private schools and homeschoolers. This was formerly the Homeschool Academy and Northeast Christian Academy. A diploma is available.

Christian Liberty Academy Satellite Schools (CLASS)

502 West Euclid Avenue
Arlington Heights, IL 60004

PHONE: (847) 259-4444
FAX: (847) 259-1297
WEBSITE: www.class-homeschools.org
EMAIL: custserv@homeschools.org
YEAR FOUNDED: 1970

This Christian school provides curriculum for homeschooling families. A diploma is available.

Malibu Cove Private School

PO Box 1074
Thousand Oaks, CA 91358

PHONE: (805) 446-1917
WEBSITE: http://seascapecenter.com/indexmab.htm
EMAIL: seascapecenter@aol.com
YEAR FOUNDED: 1989

In addition to a regularly paced high school program, this school offers an accelerated course that allows students to complete their requirements much earlier. A diploma is available.

North Atlantic Regional School

25 Adams Avenue
Lewiston, ME 04240

PHONE: (207) 753-1522 or (800) 869-2051
FAX: (207) 777-1776
WEBSITE: www.narsonline.com/nars
EMAIL: narsinfo@narsonline.com
YEAR FOUNDED: 1989

For homeschooled children of all ages, this program grants official credit for homeschool work. It offers an accelerated schedule. A diploma is available.

Oak Meadow School

PO Box 740
Putney, VT 05346

PHONE: (802) 387-2021
FAX: (802) 387-5108
WEBSITE: www.oakmeadow.com/school.htm
EMAIL: info@oakmeadow.com
YEAR FOUNDED: 1975

The school asserts that it is pursuing national accreditation. It provides support for homeschooling families through the school and its publishing company. A diploma is available.

Saint Thomas Aquinas Academy

PO Box 630
Ripon, CA 95366

PHONE: (209) 599-0665
WEBSITE: www.staa-homeschool.com
EMAIL: info@staa-homeschool.com
YEAR FOUNDED: 1995

Provides a classical Catholic education. While non-Catholics are allowed and encouraged, they should be aware that the focus will be on preparing students to become Catholic adults. A diploma is available.

School for Educational Enrichment

PHONE: (915) 584-9499
FAX: (915) 585-8814
WEBSITE: www.diplomahighschool.com
EMAIL: info@diplomahighschool.com
YEAR FOUNDED: 1997
ACCREDITATION: Texas Alliance of Accredited High Schools; Texas Education Agency

While the school does not presently offer all of the courses for a Texas high school diploma, it is in the process of building the program. All of the courses come in CD format.

The Sycamore Tree

2179 Meyer Place
Costa Mesa, CA 92627

PHONE: (714) 668-1343
FAX: (714) 668-1344
WEBSITE: www.sycamoretree.com
EMAIL: sycamoretree@compuserve.com
YEAR FOUNDED: 1982

In addition to the program, the Sycamore Tree offers a catalog of Christian-based homeschooling materials. One benefit is a monthly tuition fee per family instead of per child. Depending on the size of your family, this could be a real savings. A diploma is available.

Westbridge Academy

1610 West Highland Avenue, #228
Chicago, IL 60660

PHONE: (773) 743-3312
WEBSITE: http://home.flash.net/~wx3o/westbridge
EMAIL: westbrga@aol.com
YEAR FOUNDED: 1985

This school is geared toward the academically advanced child. Be warned that this is likely to be not a good choice if your child is currently functioning below grade level. A diploma is available.

CHAPTER 3

Homeschooling

"Homeschooling is to education what anarchy is to government."

—*Tom Head, former homeschooler*

People homeschool for many different reasons. This chapter is not meant to represent the divergent philosophies associated with homeschooling. There are many wonderful books that do an excellent job of that. Instead, this chapter will introduce you to the myriad of resources available for homeschoolers. These include support organizations, information on legalities, and publications.

Why homeschool? Think about not being influenced by high school peer pressure. Think about getting a quality education in the comfort of your own home and the teacher is your mother (or father or grandmother). If you're like many students and you don't like the bully mentality at schools, homeschooling may be an option for you.

There are two basic types of homeschooling systems, Christian homeschooling and inclusive homeschooling. Christian homeschooling families often have concerns about what is taught in public schools, particularly evolution theory, which is part of the high school curriculum. The Christian homeschooling contingent is large and well organized. Inclusive homeschooling organizations are open to anyone regardless of religion (or lack of it) or any other set of beliefs.

Something that you will need to decide from the beginning is whether you are a homeschooler or an "unschooler." Ask a hundred homeschoolers what the difference is between homeschooling and unschooling and you will get one hundred different answers. The simplest answer is that homeschooling tends to mirror in some fashion the public school experience (at least in terms of using established curriculum) and unschooling seeks to create individualized educational experiences. It's important to understand that there is a lot of crossover between the two. It's more of a continuum than two distinct approaches.

How do you choose between homeschooling and unschooling? There is no easy answer. Many people feel more comfortable using traditional materials (math books, science books, and so on) while others prefer to explore and find education wherever it might be. Both are acceptable; decide what you are like and start from there. Homeschooling tends to be more structured (although typically much less structured than public school).

Frequently Asked Questions

My parents are not college graduates. Can they still teach me at home?
There are two issues to consider. The first is whether they have the ability to teach children. While a college degree is certainly not essential, they could well benefit from taking some college courses (and couldn't we all?). The second issue is a legal one. Does your state require parents to have a college degree in order to homeschool your children? The broad answer is that most do not, but you will want to check with your state for the specific rules.

What about socialization? I have heard concerns about homeschooled children not getting exposure to other children.

Homeschoolers take art classes with public school children, Tae Kwon Do with other children, and are often involved in local homeschooling organizations that put on many events. Being homeschooled in no way means that you don't ever leave your house. Yes, if you are homeschooled, you might have to work a tiny bit harder to make sure that you learn to relate to people and the world around you, but certainly not much harder.

Is homeschooling preferable? My local high school is considered an excellent school.

If your local high school is that good, perhaps you shouldn't choose homeschooling. Or, conversely, it may be possible for you to do part of the day at the local high school and be homeschooled for the rest of the day. This might be particularly wise if you want to learn subjects, such as higher mathematics, that your parents may not be able to teach.

You should know that many parents choose homeschooling because

- They want to be in charge of their child's education.

- They don't believe the local schools will provide a quality education.

- They have religious differences with what is taught as part of the core curriculum in public high schools.

- They want to develop a better or different relationship with their child.

- They want to relieve their child of the burden of peer pressure in schools.

- All of the above.

All of these are certainly valid reasons for homeschooling as are many, many other possible reasons.

What are the arguments against homeschooling?

The number one worst reason to homeschool is that someone told you or your parents how bad your local schools are. This someone might be a homeschooler, a politician, or a religious leader. While you should trust your friends, you should also do your own investigations. In the United States, school quality is on a continuum, from schools that are clearly the best in the world to schools that are among the worst. You may discover that your district has both kinds of schools. If you could transfer to another school in your district, would you still want to homeschool? If getting your school of choice would change your mind, then for you there probably is no reason to homeschool. For most homeschoolers, school choice is not the only issue.

How do I get started homeschooling?

1. The first step you must take is to discover the specific homeschooling laws for your state. These vary widely from state to state. Some states give almost no oversight at all and others border on the intrusive. The single best source for such information is the Home School Legal Defense Association (HSLDA) at www.hslda.org. In addition to providing information on the legalities of homeschooling in your state, the HSLDA provides legal assistance to homeschoolers who are having difficulty with the implementation of a particular state's homeschooling laws.

2. Something else that you should do early on is talk to your state or local homeschooling organizations. A good source for contact information is the *Homeschooling Almanac* by Mary and Michael Lepper (as well as being a tremendous source on homeschooling in general). This book will describe what the scene is like in your area. Homeschooling has been around long enough that most organizations can tell you whom and, perhaps more importantly, whom not to contact locally to begin the process.

3. After getting this information, then it is time to talk with your parents about the possibility of homeschooling. If homeschooling will be a new adventure for you, it's probably better to gather the information from the above sources first. If you've been homeschooling through elementary school, then you likely will expect to continue doing so. You still should have a conversation with your parents about what the high school years might be like. One word of advice is that your parents are unlikely to throw a prom for you. Best to make sure that you really don't want one.

4. Who is going to do the teaching? It may seem obvious to you that one of your parents will be the one who does most of the teaching, but it is a good idea to discuss it. Although the learning day for a homeschooling family is almost always shorter than the regular school day, it still requires a specific time commitment. This is particularly true in states that require a certain number of school days or hours per year. Make sure that you have your parents onboard.

5. Finally, you must decide which curriculum you are going to use. If your parents are going to do the teaching, it is important that they feel comfortable with whatever final choice you make together. You could use a prepackaged curriculum similar to correspondence courses, you could sign up for an online program, or, depending on the case and the state, you may be able get materials from your county office of education or local school district. Conversely, you could just make it all up as you go along and design the curriculum from the ground up. In most places, this is perfectly acceptable, but make sure that you cover all of the required courses for your state.

If I homeschool, will I be able to get a high school diploma?
While some homeschooling parents issue their own diplomas, these are not seen as legally valid in any of the fifty states (unless that state has the "home school as a private school" option). Pennsylvania is the only state that recognizes diplomas from homeschooling organizations, but the number of states offering this service is expected to increase in the near future. There are other options. In some states, a homeschooled child can take a high school proficiency (or equivalency) exam. Another possibility is always the GED.

I am interested in homeschooling, but I am not a Christian. Aren't most homeschooling groups for Christians only?
There are homeschooling groups for non-Christians as well as Christians. Inclusive homeschooling is just what it sounds like—for all people, regardless of religious or any other orientation. Some Christian homeschoolers actually participate in inclusive organizations. Within the ranks of Christian organizations, some require a specific statement of faith, while others require nothing. And to make this even more confusing, some Christian groups gladly welcome non-Christians as well.

My family is living abroad and we are homeschooled. Which state's rules should we follow?

It probably doesn't matter, but check with the rules for your home state. Also, it is important to figure out how you are going to prove knowledge to college admissions people. Although most colleges are now aware of homeschoolers and some actively recruit from this group, it's still a good idea to determine if you will need to make up transcripts. If so, start keeping track of what you've studied and what grades you've received.

National Homeschool Organizations

American Homeschool Association

PO Box 3142
Palmer, AK 99645

PHONE: (800) 236-3278
WEBSITE: www.americanhomeschoolassociation.org
EMAIL: aha@americanhomeschoolassociation.org

One of the main sponsors for the American Homeschool Association is *Home Education Magazine.* One of the association's main functions is to be a network for homeschoolers around the country. It has many resources available to homeschoolers, media people, and educators.

Home School Legal Defense Association

PO Box 3000
Purcellville, VA 20134-9000

PHONE: (540) 338-5600
FAX: (540) 338-2733
WEBSITE: www.hslda.org
EMAIL: info@hslda.org

Yes, homeschooling is legal in all fifty states. However, just because it is legal does not mean that everyone agrees with homeschooling. The Home School Legal Defense Association can be the homeschooler's best friend, particularly if you live in a state that is not very open to homeschooling. HSLDA has gone to bat, time and again, to ensure that anyone who chooses homeschooling is allowed to do so. Some homeschoolers have expressed concern about the conservative bent to the organization, but for those who are either conservative or apolitical, it can provide much in the way of resources.

National Home Education Research Institute

PO Box 13939
Salem, OR 97309

PHONE: (503) 364-1490
WEBSITE: www.nheri.org
EMAIL: mail@nheri.org

National Home Education Research Institute (NHERI) conducts research on homeschooling issues. In addition, it functions as a clearinghouse for all things homeschooling. It publishes the periodical *Home School Researcher.*

Legal Information

The following information about the legalities of homeschooling is based on information from the Home School Legal Defense Association. As a general rule, most homeschoolers have a preference for little governmental intervention with their children's education. The good news here is that twenty of the states, plus the District of Columbia, require little or no notification to the state government of the intent to homeschool. You may begin your homeschooling without going through any type of bureaucracy.

While some states make it more difficult to homeschool than others, it's important to emphasize that homeschooling is legal in all fifty states. It is only the requirements that differ from state to state. Should you have trouble with your local school district in your quest to homeschool, immediately contact your local homeschooling organization. It has likely come across this problem before. Often the problem is isolated to particular individuals in the district and not with the school district as a whole.

When I caught up with Jesse Richman, he was doing a summer seminar at Harvard University. He is a Ph.D. student in Carnegie Mellon University's Department of Social and Decision Sciences, where he is studying political economy. He is married to Patricia, a fellow homeschooler. They live with their one-year-old daughter, Sarah, near Pittsburgh, Pennsylvania. Jesse was homeschooled from 1977 to 1995.

Bears' Guide: Describe what it was like to be homeschooled.

Jesse Richman: This is a broad question. Homeschooling gave me lots of freedom to explore and to do things for myself. For instance, I studied carpentry by building a fourteen by sixteen-foot cabin. But there was also structure. At the beginning of the year, my mother (with my input) would plan the courses I would take. For science and math courses, there was usually a textbook to work through. We met at least once a week with groups of homeschoolers for activities like writing club, square dances, math contests, French language nights, and so on.

BG: What role did you have in the decision to become a homeschooling family?

JR: I was homeschooled from birth through age eighteen. I was rather young when homeschooling started, but I was in accord with the decision. When I was four years old, I told my mother that I never wanted to go to school.

BG: Do you think you missed out on anything in high school because you were homeschooled?

JR: It is a bit harder to do laboratory science courses at home. Schools have the equipment that one has to make at home. But we did the making. Another of the things one misses would be foreign language classes. We used a video series by Annenburg/CPB publishing company. As it turned out, my accent was substantially better for that experience. In a traditional school language course, one is exposed to a teacher with (hopefully) a good accent and many students with American accents.

Sometimes people worry about socialization among homeschoolers. Socialization does tend to be a bit different. You wind up interacting with a wider range of age groups, for example. Overall I felt well prepared socially as well as academically, though my knowledge of popular TV shows and music was fairly restricted by the fact that I watched almost no TV.

BG: Describe how you earned your high school diploma.

JR: Act 169 of 1988 for Pennsylvania contains graduation requirements for homeschoolers, unlike nearly all other home education laws in the country. To implement these requirements, the state has chosen to recognize six or seven nonprofit organizations to award diplomas to (and keep transcripts on) homeschooled students. I graduated from the largest of these organizations, the Pennsylvania Homeschoolers Accreditation Agency (PHAA), which was founded by my parents. My graduating class had about a hundred students. Today PHAA graduates about five hundred students per year. Because graduation requirements are in the Pennsylvania home education law, homeschoolers' diplomas are recognized by the state for state education grants, by public colleges for admissions, and for various other purposes as well (for example, for homeschooling one's children, which requires a high school diploma in Pennsylvania).

Requirements vary somewhat from organization to organization, but all lay out basic guidelines for what counts as a substantive course of study. For instance, to earn an English credit I had to read twenty-five books of my choosing, three of which had to be classics, write a ten-page paper, as well as some shorter essays, and deliver a public speech. For a math course, I had to complete at least two-thirds of a textbook.

At the end of each school year, an evaluator affiliated with PHAA reviewed a portfolio of my work. Deborah Bell, my evaluator, continued to play an active role in my academic life as I moved on to college; she wrote an excellent recommendation letter for my college entrance, and she later wrote a letter for a scholarship competition I was entering. I continue to correspond with her occasionally.

BG: Describe growing up in your family with its rather active involvement in homeschooling.

JR: My family was very active in the homeschooling movement. My mother started a newsletter for homeschoolers when I was five or six and later wrote a book about homeschooling. Because we traveled around the state a lot when I was in high school, I had friends scattered all over. My family's intense involvement with passing a home education law during the 1980s helped shape later career choices. At ten I was a relatively old homeschooler for those days. I got to give a speech to legislators, and participated in lots of lobbying, rallies, and negotiations. Later I found that politics particularly fascinated me, and I became a political scientist.

BG: Describe what your academic life has been like since finishing high school.

JR: After finishing high school, I attended the University of Pittsburgh on a four-year academic scholarship. I studied history and political science there and then went on to Carnegie Mellon.

States Requiring No Notice

The following nine states do not require any notification of the intent to homeschool. You are free to homeschool in whatever manner you feel is best.

Alaska	Indiana	New Jersey
Idaho	Michigan	Oklahoma
Illinois	Missouri	Texas

States with Low Regulation

Almost as good, these eleven states plus the District of Columbia only require that you notify them that you will be homeschooling. No other contact is required.

Alabama	District of Columbia	Montana
Arizona	Kansas	Nebraska
California	Kentucky	New Mexico
Delaware	Mississippi	Wyoming

States with Moderate Regulation

These nineteen states make it more difficult to homeschool. They require state notification and test scores or professional evaluation in order to assure student progress.

Arkansas	Louisiana	South Carolina
Colorado	Maryland	South Dakota
Connecticut	Nevada	Tennessee
Florida	New Hampshire	Virginia
Georgia	North Carolina	Wisconsin
Hawaii	Ohio	
Iowa	Oregon	

States with High Regulation

These eleven states have chosen to make homeschooling more difficult, but many homeschooling families have been able to be quite successful in winding their way through the rules and regulations. These states require notification by parents, achievement test scores, and/or professional evaluation before allowing a child to homeschool. Some of these states also have other requirements.

Maine	North Dakota	Vermont
Massachusetts	Pennsylvania	Washington
Minnesota	Rhode Island	West Virginia
New York	Utah	

State Listings

Under each state listed below, I have included statewide homeschool contact information, a department of education contact, and information on homeschooling conventions. In addition, the following information is provided:

COMPULSORY ATTENDANCE: The number of days required of "school" attendance by the state.

TEACHING QUALIFICATIONS: The qualifications of the parents or other individuals to teach the children.

SCHOOL SETUP OPTIONS: The possible ways to homeschool legally in that state. Some states require parents to set up a private school or offer home correspondence courses.

SUBJECTS REQUIRED: Actual minimum course work required by the state. Where none is stated, this means that it is up to the discretion of the parents to choose suitable subjects for their children.

Alabama

Organization

Home Educators of Alabama Roundtable (HEART)

PHONE: (256) 974-3017
WEBSITE: www.heartofalabama.org
EMAIL: wdkmg@pipeline.com
FOCUS: Inclusive homeschooling

Convention

Alabama State Homeschooling Convention

c/o Christian Home Education Fellowship of Alabama
PO Box 20208
Montgomery, AL 36120

PHONE: (334) 288-7229
WEBSITE: www.alhome.org
EMAIL: pres@alhome.com
DATE: Held in May
FOCUS: Christian homeschooling

State Contact

Alabama State Department of Education

Director, Prevention and Support Services
PO Box 302101
Montgomery, AL 36104

PHONE: (334) 242-9700
WEBSITE: www.alsde.edu
EMAIL: sadams@alsde.edu
COMPULSORY ATTENDANCE: Ages seven to sixteen; no required number of days if a qualified church school and 140 days (times three hours per day) for private tutor.
TEACHING QUALIFICATIONS: None for church school. Private tutor must have teacher certification.
SCHOOL SETUP OPTIONS: Establish and/or enroll in church school; private tutor.
SUBJECTS REQUIRED: None for church school. Private tutor must teach reading, spelling, writing, arithmetic, English, geography, U.S. history, Alabama history, science, health, and physical education.

Alaska

Organization

Alaska Private and Home Educators Association

PO Box 141764
Anchorage, AK 99514

WEBSITE: www.aphea.org
EMAIL: membership@aphea.org
FOCUS: Christian homeschooling

Convention

Alaska Private and Home Educators Association

PO Box 141764
Anchorage, AK 99514

WEBSITE: www.aphea.org
EMAIL: board@aphea.org
DATE: Held in September
FOCUS: Christian homeschooling

State Contact

Alaska Department of Education and Early Development

801 West Tenth Street
Juneau, AK 99801

PHONE: (907) 465-2800
WEBSITE: www.educ.state.ak.us
EMAIL: webmaster@eed.state.ak.us
COMPULSORY ATTENDANCE: Ages seven to sixteen; 180 school days per year.
TEACHING QUALIFICATIONS: None (except teacher certification required for private tutor).
SCHOOL SETUP OPTIONS: Establish/operate a homeschool; use a private tutor; enroll in full-time state department of education approved correspondence program; school board approval for alternate educational experience; qualify as a private school (religious/other).
SUBJECTS REQUIRED: None (but private schools must use standardized testing and this must cover reading, spelling, math, and grammar).

Arizona

Organization

Arizona Families for Home Education

PO Box 2035
Chandler, AZ 85244

WEBSITE: www.afhe.org
EMAIL: afhe@primenet.com
FOCUS: Inclusive homeschooling

Conventions

Arizona Families for Home Education

PO Box 2035
Chandler, AZ 85244

WEBSITE: www.afhe.org
EMAIL: afhe@primenet.com
DATE: Held in July
FOCUS: Inclusive homeschooling

The Salt Seller's Arizona State Used Curriculum and Book Fair

Glendale Civic Center
5750 West Glenn Drive
Glendale, AZ 85301

PHONE: (602) 235-2678
FAX: (602) 249-6151
WEBSITE: www.thesaltseller.org
EMAIL: bookfairinfo@thesaltseller.org
DATE: Held in June
FOCUS: Inclusive homeschooling

State Contact

Director of Homeschooling Services

Maricopa County School Superintendent
301 West Jefferson, Suite 660
Phoenix, AZ 85003

PHONE: (602) 506-3144
WEBSITE: www.maricopa.gov/schools/home_school.asp
EMAIL: dmunoz@schools.maricopa.gov
COMPULSORY ATTENDANCE: Ages six to sixteen; no days-per-year requirement.
TEACHING QUALIFICATIONS: None.
SCHOOL SETUP OPTIONS: Establish/operate a homeschool.
SUBJECTS REQUIRED: Science, social studies, math, grammar, and reading.

Arkansas

Organization

Home Educators of Arkansas

PO Box 192455
Little Rock, AR 72219

PHONE: (501) 847-4942
WEBSITE: www.geocities.com/heartland/garden/4555
EMAIL: hearreport@juno.com
FOCUS: Inclusive homeschooling

Convention

The Arkansas Home School Convention

c/o Family Council
414 South Pulaski, Suite 2
Little Rock, AR 72201

PHONE: (501) 375-7000
FAX: (501) 375-7040
WEBSITE: www.familycouncil.org/eahms.htm
EMAIL: edu@familycouncil.org
DATE: Held in May
FOCUS: Christian homeschooling

State Contact

Arkansas Department of Education

4 State Capitol Mall
Little Rock, AR 72201

PHONE: (501) 682-1874
WEBSITE: http://arkedu.state.ar.us
EMAIL: gmorris@arkedu.k12.ar.us
COMPULSORY ATTENDANCE: Ages five to seventeen; no days-per-year requirement.
TEACHING QUALIFICATIONS: None.
SCHOOL SETUP OPTIONS: Establish/operate a homeschool.
SUBJECTS REQUIRED: None.

California

Organization

Homeschool Association of California

PO Box 2442
Atascadero, CA 93423

PHONE: (888) 472-4440
WEBSITE: www.hsc.org
EMAIL: info@hsc.org
FOCUS: Inclusive homeschooling

Convention

The Link Kid Comfortable Homeschool Conference

587 North Ventu Park Road, Suite F-911
Newbury Park, CA 91320

PHONE: (805) 492-1373 or (888) 470-4513
FAX: (805) 493-9216
WEBSITE: www.homeschoolnewslink.com
EMAIL: the.link@verizon.net
DATE: Held in June
FOCUS: Inclusive homeschooling

State Contact

California Department of Education

721 Capitol Mall, Room 552
Sacramento, CA 95814

PHONE: (916) 657-2453
WEBSITE: www.cde.ca.gov
EMAIL: Available at www.cde.ca.gov/writeform.htm
COMPULSORY ATTENDANCE: Ages six to seventeen; some options require 175 days per year.
TEACHING QUALIFICATIONS: Vague law requires capability of teaching. Teacher certification required for tutor.
SCHOOL SETUP OPTIONS: Private school; private tutor; independent study program through public school; private school satellite (for example, independent study) program.
SUBJECTS REQUIRED: Same as in the public schools. Must be in English.

Colorado

Organization

Christian Home Educators of Colorado

10431 South Parker Road
Parker, CO 80134

PHONE: (720) 842-4852
FAX: (720) 842-4854
WEBSITE: www.chec.org
EMAIL: office@chec.org
FOCUS: Christian homeschooling

Convention

Christian Home Educators of Colorado

10431 South Parker Road
Parker, CO 80134

PHONE: (720) 842-4852
FAX: (720) 842-4854
WEBSITE: www.chec.org
EMAIL: office@chec.org
DATE: Held in June
FOCUS: Christian homeschooling

State Contact

Department of Education

201 East Colfax Avenue
Denver, CO 80203

PHONE: (303) 866-6600
FAX: (303) 830-0793
WEBSITE: www.cde.state.co.us/cdeedserv/homeschool.htm
EMAIL: dam_a@cde.state.co.us
COMPULSORY ATTENDANCE: Ages seven to fifteen; 172 days per year.
TEACHING QUALIFICATIONS: None. Teacher certification required for tutor.
SCHOOL SETUP OPTIONS: Establish/operate a homeschool; private school with home instruction; private tutor.
SUBJECTS REQUIRED: U.S. Constitution, reading, writing, speaking, math, history, civics, science, and literature.

Connecticut

Organizations

Connecticut Home Educators' Association

PO Box 242
New Hartford, CT 06057

PHONE: (203) 781-8569
WEBSITE: www.cthomeschoolers.com
EMAIL: cheachea@juno.com
FOCUS: Inclusive homeschooling

The Education Association of Christian Homeschoolers

363 Carriage Drive
Southbury, CT 06488

PHONE: (860) 677-4538 or (800) 205-7844
WEBSITE: www.teachct.org
EMAIL: teach.info@pobox.com
FOCUS: Christian homeschooling

Convention

The Education Association of Christian Homeschoolers Annual Conference and Curriculum Fair

363 Carriage Drive
Southbury, CT 06488

PHONE: (860) 677-4538 or (800) 205-7844
WEBSITE: www.teachct.org
EMAIL: teach.info@pobox.com
DATE: Held in June
FOCUS: Christian homeschooling

State Contact

Connecticut Department of Education

Room 246-A
165 Capitol Avenue
Hartford, CT 06106

PHONE: (860) 566-8263
WEBSITE: www.state.ct.us/sde
EMAIL: thomas.murphy@po.state.ct.us
COMPULSORY ATTENDANCE: Ages five to sixteen; 180 days per year.
TEACHING QUALIFICATIONS: None.
SCHOOL SETUP OPTIONS: Establish/operate a homeschool.
SUBJECTS REQUIRED: Reading, writing, spelling, English, grammar, arithmetic, geography, U.S. history, and citizenship.

Delaware

Organization

Delaware Home Education Association

500 North Dual Highway
PMB 415
Feaford, DE 19973

PHONE: (302) 337-0990
WEBSITE: www.dheaonline.org
EMAIL: info@dheaonline.org
FOCUS: Inclusive homeschooling

Convention

Delaware Home Education Association Conference

500 North Dual Highway
PMB 415
Feaford, DE 19973

PHONE: (302) 337-0990
WEBSITE: www.dheaonline.org
EMAIL: info@dheaonline.org
DATE: Held every other April in Wilmington
FOCUS: Inclusive homeschooling

State Contact

Delaware State Department of Education

John G. Townsend Building
PO Box 1402
Dover, DE 19903

PHONE: (302) 739-4583
WEBSITE: www.doe.state.de.us
COMPULSORY ATTENDANCE: Ages five through sixteen; 180 days per year.
TEACHING QUALIFICATIONS: None.
SCHOOL SETUP OPTIONS: Establish or enroll in a home-school association; establish a homeschool.
SUBJECTS REQUIRED: Same as public schools.

District of Columbia

Organization

Bolling Area Home Educators

PO Box 8401
Washington, DC 20336

PHONE: (202) 562-3952
WEBSITE: http://bahedc.org
FOCUS: Inclusive homeschooling

Convention

Interested parties must attend homeschool conventions in adjoining states.

District Contact

District of Columbia Public Schools

825 North Capitol Street NE, Seventh Floor
Washington, DC 20002

PHONE: (202) 724-4222
WEBSITE: www.k12.dc.us/dcps/home.html
EMAIL: webmaster@k12.dc.us
COMPULSORY ATTENDANCE: Ages five through eighteen; school attendance required when public schools in session.
TEACHING QUALIFICATIONS: None.
SCHOOL SETUP OPTIONS: Provide private instruction not related to any educational institution.
SUBJECTS REQUIRED: None.

Florida

Organization

Florida Parent Educators Association

PO Box 50684
Jacksonville Beach, FL 32240

PHONE: (877) 275-3732
WEBSITE: www.fpea.com
EMAIL: office@fpea.com
FOCUS: Inclusive homeschooling

Convention

Florida Parent Educators Association Annual Homeschool Conference

Orlando, FL 32240

PHONE: (877) 275-3732
WEBSITE: www.fpea.com
EMAIL: convention@fpea.com
DATE: Held in May
FOCUS: Inclusive homeschooling

State Contact

Florida Department of Education

325 West Gaines Street, Suite 532
Tallahassee, FL 32399

PHONE: (850) 487-8428
WEBSITE: www.fldoe.org
COMPULSORY ATTENDANCE: Ages six to sixteen; 180 days if a private school.
TEACHING QUALIFICATIONS: None.
SCHOOL SETUP OPTIONS: Establish/operate a homeschool; establish a private school corporation.
SUBJECTS REQUIRED: None.

Georgia

Organizations

Georgia Home Education Association

141 Massengale Road
Brooks, GA 30205

PHONE: (770) 461-3657
FAX: (770) 461-9053
WEBSITE: www.ghea.org
EMAIL: info@ghea.org
FOCUS: Christian homeschooling

Home Educators Information Resource

PO Box 2111
Roswell, GA 30077

PHONE: (404) 861-4347
WEBSITE: www.heir.org
EMAIL: info@heir.org
FOCUS: Inclusive homeschooling

Convention

Georgia Home Education Association Annual Homeschool Conference

141 Massengale Road
Brooks, GA 30205

PHONE: (770) 461-3657
FAX: (770) 461-9053
WEBSITE: www.ghea.org
EMAIL: info@ghea.org
DATE: Held in April
FOCUS: Christian homeschooling (but open to all)

State Contact

Georgia Department of Education

205 Butler Street
Atlanta, GA 30334

PHONE: (404) 656-2800
WEBSITE: www.doe.k12.ga.us/index.asp
EMAIL: help.desk@doe.k12.ga.us
COMPULSORY ATTENDANCE: Ages six to sixteen; 180 days per year.
TEACHING QUALIFICATIONS: High school diploma or GED if the parent; college degree if a private tutor.
SCHOOL SETUP OPTIONS: Establish a home-study program.
SUBJECTS REQUIRED: Reading, language arts, math, social studies, and science.

Hawaii

Organizations

The Hawaii Homeschool Association

PO Box 893513
Mililani, HI 96789

PHONE: (808) 944-3339
WEBSITE: www.hawaiihomeschoolassociation.org
EMAIL: hawaiihomeschoolers@hotmail.com
FOCUS: Inclusive homeschooling

Christian Homeschoolers of Hawaii

91-824 Oama Street
Ewa Beach, HI 96706

PHONE: (808) 689-6398
WEBSITE: www.christianhomeschoolersofhawaii.org
FOCUS: Christian homeschooling

Convention

Christian Homeschoolers of Hawaii Homeschool Conference

91-824 Oama Street
Ewa Beach, HI 96706

PHONE: (808) 689-6398
WEBSITE: www.christianhomeschoolersofhawaii.org
DATE: Held in March
FOCUS: Christian homeschooling

State Contact

Hawaii Department of Education

641 18th Avenue, Building V, Room 201
Honolulu, HI 96816
Phone (808) 733-9895

FAX: (808) 586-3234
WEBSITE: http://doe.k12.hi.us
COMPULSORY ATTENDANCE: Ages six to seventeen.
TEACHING QUALIFICATIONS: None for home school; college degree for alternative educational program.
SCHOOL SETUP OPTIONS: Establish/operate a homeschool; alternative educational program (approved by school superintendent).
SUBJECTS REQUIRED: Curriculum should be structured and based on educational objectives and the needs of the child.

Idaho

Organization

Idaho Coalition of Home Educators

5415 Kendall Street
Boise, ID 83706

WEBSITE: www.iche-idaho.org
EMAIL: listkeeper@iche-idaho.org
FOCUS: Inclusive homeschooling

Convention

Christian Home Educators of Idaho State Annual Conference

PHONE: (208) 322-4270
CONTACT: Becky Livingstone
DATE: Held in spring
FOCUS: Christian homeschooling

State Contact

Idaho Department of Education

PO Box 83720
Boise, ID 83720

PHONE: (208) 332-6800
WEBSITE: www.sde.state.id.us/dept
COMPULSORY ATTENDANCE: Ages seven to fifteen; same as public schools.
TEACHING QUALIFICATIONS: None.
SCHOOL SETUP OPTIONS: Alternate educational experience/comparable instruction to public schools.
SUBJECTS REQUIRED: Same as public schools.

Illinois

Organization

Home Oriented Unique Schooling Experience

2508 East 222 Place
Sauk Village, IL 60411

PHONE: (708) 758-7374
WEBSITE: www.illinoishouse.org
EMAIL: illinois_house@hotmail.com
CONTACT: Chuck Stoeckel
FOCUS: Inclusive homeschooling

Convention

Illinois Christian Home Educators Conference (ICHE)

PO Box 775
Harvard, IL 60033

PHONE: (815) 943-7882
WEBSITE: www.iche.org
EMAIL: info@iche.org
DATE: Held in May
FOCUS: Christian homeschooling

State Contact

Illinois State Board of Education

100 North First Street
Springfield, IL 62777

PHONE: (217) 782-3950
WEBSITE: www.isbe.state.il.us
COMPULSORY ATTENDANCE: Ages seven to sixteen; a non-mandated 176 days per year.
TEACHING QUALIFICATIONS: None.
SCHOOL SETUP OPTIONS: Operate a homeschool as a private school.
SUBJECTS REQUIRED: Biological science, physical science, math, language arts, social sciences, fine arts, health/physical development, and character education (honesty, justice, kindness, moral courage).

Indiana

Organization

Indiana Association of Home Educators

8106 Madison Avenue
Indianapolis, IN 46227

PHONE: (317) 859-1202
FAX: (317) 859-1204
WEBSITE: www.inhomeeducators.org
EMAIL: iahe@inhomeeducators.org
FOCUS: Christian homeschooling

Convention

Home Educators Conference

c/o Indiana Association of Home Educators
8106 Madison Avenue
Indianapolis, IN 46227

PHONE: (317) 859-1202
FAX: (317) 859-1204
WEBSITE: www.inhomeeducators.org
EMAIL: iahe@inhomeeducators.org
DATE: Held in June
FOCUS: Christian homeschooling

State Contact

Indiana Department of Education

State House, Room 229
Indianapolis, IN 46204

PHONE: (317) 232-6610
FAX: (317) 232-8004
WEBSITE: www.doe.state.in.us
EMAIL: webmaster@doe.state.in.us
COMPULSORY ATTENDANCE: Ages seven to eighteen; 180 days per year.
TEACHING QUALIFICATIONS: None.
SCHOOL SETUP OPTIONS: Operate a homeschool as a private school.
SUBJECTS REQUIRED: None.

Iowa

Organization

Network of Iowa Christian Home Educators

PO Box 158
Dexter, IA 50070

PHONE: (515) 830-1614 or (800) 723-0438
WEBSITE: www.the-niche.org
EMAIL: niche@netins.net
FOCUS: Christian homeschooling

Convention

Annual Christian Homeschool Conference

c/o Network of Iowa Christian Home Educators
PO Box 158
Dexter, IA 50070

PHONE: (515) 830-1614 or (800) 723-0438
WEBSITE: www.the-niche.org
EMAIL: niche@netins.net
DATE: Held in June
FOCUS: Christian homeschooling

State Contact

Iowa Department of Education

Grimes State Office Building
Des Moines, IA 50319

PHONE: (515) 281-5001
WEBSITE: www.state.ia.us/educate
EMAIL: webmaster@ed.state.ia.us
COMPULSORY ATTENDANCE: Ages six to sixteen; 148 days per year.
TEACHING QUALIFICATIONS: None for a teaching parent; teaching license required for private tutors or other teachers.

SCHOOL SETUP OPTIONS: Establish/operate a homeschool; establish a homeschool operated by licensed teacher; private tutor.
SUBJECTS REQUIRED: None.

Kansas

Organization

Christian Home Educators Confederation of Kansas

PO Box 1332
Topeka, KS 66601

PHONE: (785) 272-6655
WEBSITE: www.kansashomeschool.org
EMAIL: info@kansashomeschool.org
FOCUS: Christian homeschooling

Convention

Teaching Parents Associaton

PO Box 3968
Wichita, KS 67202

PHONE: (316) 945-0810
WEBSITE: www.wichitahomeschool.org
DATE: Held in May
FOCUS: Inclusive homeschooling

State Contact

Kansas State Department of Education

120 Southeast Tenth Avenue
Topeka, KS 66612

PHONE: (785) 296-3201
WEBSITE: www.ksbe.state.ks.us
COMPULSORY ATTENDANCE: Ages seven to seventeen; 186 days per year (or 1,116 hours per year).
TEACHING QUALIFICATIONS: Teacher must be "competent." However, the local school board is not allowed to determine competency of private school teachers.
SCHOOL SETUP OPTIONS: Operate a homeschool (as unaccredited private school); homeschool as satellite campus of an accredited private school; state board of education religious exemption for high school grades only.
SUBJECTS REQUIRED: None (except those prescribed by the private school or the state board of education).

Kentucky

Organizations

Christian Home Educators of Kentucky

691 Howardstown Road
Hodgensville, KY 42748

PHONE: (270) 358-9270
WEBSITE: www.chek.org
EMAIL: information@chek.org
FOCUS: Christian homeschooling

Kentucky Home Education Association

PO Box 81
Winchester, KY 40392

PHONE: (859) 737-3338
WEBSITE: www.khea.8k.com
EMAIL: katy@mis.net
FOCUS: Inclusive homeschooling

Convention

Annual Christian Homeschooling Conference

c/o Christian Home Educators of Kentucky
691 Howardstown Road
Hodgensville, KY 42748

PHONE: (270) 358-9270
WEBSITE: www.chek.org
EMAIL: information@chek.org
DATE: Held in June
FOCUS: Christian homeschooling

State Contact

Kentucky Department of Education

500 Mero Street, Eighth Floor
Capitol Plaza Tower
Frankfort, KY 40601

PHONE: (502) 564-3791
FAX: (502) 564-6470
WEBSITE: www.kde.state.ky.us
EMAIL: webmaster@kde.state.ky.us
COMPULSORY ATTENDANCE: Ages six to sixteen; 185 days per year (or 175 six-hour days).
TEACHING QUALIFICATIONS: None.
SCHOOL SETUP OPTIONS: Operate a homeschool as a private school.
SUBJECTS REQUIRED: Writing, spelling, reading, grammar, history, civics, and math.

Louisiana

Organizations

Christian Home Educators Fellowship of Louisiana

PO Box 74292
Baton Rouge, LA 70874

PHONE: (888) 876-2433
WEBSITE: www.chefofla.org
EMAIL: amedees@bellsouth.net
FOCUS: Christian homeschooling

Louisiana Home Education Network

PMB 700
602 West Prien Lake Road
Lake Charles, LA 70601

WEBSITE: www.la-home-education.com
EMAIL: webmaster@la-home-education.com
FOCUS: Inclusive homeschooling

Convention

Annual Christian Homeschool Conference

c/o Christian Home Educators Fellowship of Louisiana
PO Box 74292
Baton Rouge, LA 70874

PHONE: (888) 876-2433
WEBSITE: www.chefofla.org
EMAIL: amedees@bellsouth.net
DATE: Held in the spring
FOCUS: Christian homeschooling

State Contact

Louisiana Department of Education

Home Study Program
PO Box 94064
Baton Rouge, LA 70804

PHONE: (225) 342-3473
WEBSITE: www.doe.state.la.us
COMPULSORY ATTENDANCE: Ages seven to seventeen; 180 days per year.
TEACHING QUALIFICATIONS: None.
SCHOOL SETUP OPTIONS: Establish/operate a homeschool; operate a homeschool as a private school.
SUBJECTS REQUIRED: Must be at least the same subjects as the public schools and must include the Declaration of Independence and the Federalist Papers.

Maine

Organization

Maine Home Education Association

PO Box 421
Topsham, ME 04039

PHONE: (207) 657-6018
WEBSITE: www.geocities.com/mainehomeed
EMAIL: mainehomeed@yahoo.com
FOCUS: Inclusive homeschooling

Convention

Homeschoolers of Maine

19 Willowdale Drive
Gorham, ME 04038

PHONE: (207) 763-2880
WEBSITE: www.homeschoolersofmaine.org
EMAIL: homeschl@midcoast.com
DATE: Held in May
FOCUS: Christian homeschooling

State Contact

Maine Department of Education

23 State House Station
Augusta, ME 04333

PHONE: (207) 287-5922
WEBSITE: www.state.me.us/education
EMAIL: joyce.mazerolle@maine.gov
COMPULSORY ATTENDANCE: Ages seven to sixteen; 175 days per year.
TEACHING QUALIFICATIONS: None.
SCHOOL SETUP OPTIONS: Establish/operate a homeschool; operate a homeschool as a private school (in contrast to other states, you must have at least two unrelated students for this option).
SUBJECTS REQUIRED: Maine studies, English, language arts, science, math, social studies, health and physical education, library skills, fine arts, and computers.

Maryland

Organization

Maryland Home Education Association

9085 Flamepool Way
Columbia, MD 21045

PHONE: (410) 730-0073
WEBSITE: www.mhea.com
EMAIL: mhea@mac.com
FOCUS: Inclusive homeschooling

Conventions

Maryland Association of Christian Home Educators Annual Conference

PO Box 417
Clarksburg, MD 20871

PHONE: (301) 607-4284
WEBSITE: www.machemd.org
EMAIL: info@machemd.org
DATE: Held in April
FOCUS: Christian homsechooling

Maryland Home Education Association Annual Homeschool Conference

9085 Flamepool Way
Columbia, MD 21045

PHONE: (410) 730-0073
WEBSITE: www.mhea.com
EMAIL: mhea@mac.com
DATE: Held in April
FOCUS: Inclusive homeschooling

State Contact

Maryland State Department of Education

Director, Student Services
200 West Baltimore Street
Baltimore, MD 21201

PHONE: (410) 767-0288
WEBSITE: www.msde.state.md.us
COMPULSORY ATTENDANCE: Ages five to fifteen (with exemption possible for children aged five).
TEACHING QUALIFICATIONS: None.
SCHOOL SETUP OPTIONS: Establish/operate a homeschool; home instruction through a church school or a correspondence course. Contact the state for a list of approved courses.
SUBJECTS REQUIRED: Same as public schools for homeschool and the standard curriculum for the state-approved correspondence courses.

Massachusetts

Organization

Massachusetts Home Learning Association

PO Box 1558
Marstons Mills, MA 02648

PHONE: (508) 420-3673
WEBSITE: www.mhla.org
EMAIL: lisawood@aol.com
FOCUS: Inclusive homeschooling

Convention

Growing without Schooling Conference

c/o Holt Associates
2380 Mass Avenue, Suite 104
Cambridge, MA 02140

PHONE: (617) 864-3100
WEBSITE: www.holtgws.com
EMAIL: info@holtgws.com
DATE: Held each fall in Great Barrington
FOCUS: Unschooling

State Contact

State Department of Education

350 Main Street
Malden, MA 02148

PHONE: (781) 388-3300
WEBSITE: www.doe.mass.edu
EMAIL: www@doe.mass.edu
COMPULSORY ATTENDANCE: Ages six to sixteen; 990 hours per year at the secondary level.
TEACHING QUALIFICATIONS: None.
SCHOOL SETUP OPTIONS: Establish/operate a homeschool. It has to be approved by the superintendent or the local school committee.
SUBJECTS REQUIRED: Reading, writing, English language and grammar, mathematics, drawing, music, history, U.S. Constitution, health, duties of citizenship, physical education, and good behavior.

Michigan

Organization

Homeschool Support Network

PO Box 2457
Riverview, MI 48192

PHONE: (734) 284-1249
WEBSITE: www.homeeducator.com/HSN
EMAIL: hsnmom@aol.com
FOCUS: Inclusive homeschooling

Convention

Information Network for Christian Homes

4934 Cannonsburg Road
Belmont, MI 49306

PHONE: (616) 874-5656
FAX: (616) 874-5577
WEBSITE: www.inch.org
EMAIL: inch@inch.org
DATE: Held in May in Lansing
FOCUS: Christian homeschooling

State Contact

Michigan Department of Education

PO Box 30009
Lansing, MI 48909

PHONE: (517) 335-4074
WEBSITE: www.michigan.gov/mde
EMAIL: mdeweb@michigan.gov
COMPULSORY ATTENDANCE: Ages six to fifteen; no days-per-year requirement.
TEACHING QUALIFICATIONS: None for the home education program, but teacher certification is required if set up as a homeschool operating as a non-public school.
SCHOOL SETUP OPTIONS: Establish/operate a home education program; operate a home school as non-public school.
SUBJECTS REQUIRED: Reading, spelling, mathematics, history, science, civics, literature, writing, and English grammar.

Minnesota

Organization

Minnesota Homeschoolers' Alliance

PO Box 23072
Richfield, MN 55423

PHONE: (612) 288-9662
WEBSITE: www.homeschoolers.org
EMAIL: mha@homeschoolers.org
FOCUS: Inclusive homeschooling

Convention

Minnesota Association of Christian Home Educators

PO Box 32308
Fridley, MN 55432

PHONE: (763) 717-9070
WEBSITE: www.mache.org
EMAIL: mache@isd.net
DATE: Held in April
FOCUS: Christian homeschooling

State Contact

Department of Children, Families and Learning

1500 Highway 36 West
Roseville, MN 55113

PHONE: (651) 582-8246
WEBSITE: www.educ.state.mn.us
EMAIL: children@state.mn.us
COMPULSORY ATTENDANCE: Ages seven to sixteen; no days-per-year requirement.
TEACHING QUALIFICATIONS: None.
SCHOOL SETUP OPTIONS: Establish/operate a qualified homeschool.
SUBJECTS REQUIRED: Reading, writing, literature, fine arts, math, history, science, geography government, health, and physical education.

Mississippi

Organization

Mississippi Home Educators Association

PO Box 945
Brookhaven, MS 39602

PHONE: (601) 833-9110
WEBSITE: www.mhea.net
EMAIL: mhea@mhea.net
FOCUS: Christian homeschooling

Convention

Spring Conference and Curriculum Fair

c/o Mississippi Home Educators Association
PO Box 945
Brookhaven, MS 39602

PHONE: (601) 833-9110
WEBSITE: www.mhea.net
EMAIL: mhea@mhea.net
CONTACT: Jack Rutland
DATE: Held in May
FOCUS: Christian homeschooling

State Contact

Mississippi Department of Education

PO Box 771
Jackson, MS 39205

PHONE: (601) 359-2098
WEBSITE: www.mde.k12.ms.us
COMPULSORY ATTENDANCE: Ages six to sixteen; days per year same as public school.
TEACHING QUALIFICATIONS: None.
SCHOOL SETUP OPTIONS: Establish/operate a homeschool.
SUBJECTS REQUIRED: None.

Missouri

Organizations

Families for Home Education

PO Box 800
Platte City, MO 64079

PHONE: (816) 767-9825
WEBSITE: www.fhe-mo.org
EMAIL: 1983@fhe-mo.org
FOCUS: Inclusive homeschooling

Missouri Association of Teaching Christian Homes

2203 Rhonda Drive
West Plains, MO 65775

PHONE: (417) 255-2824
WEBSITE: www.match-inc.org
EMAIL: information@match-inc.org
FOCUS: Christian homeschooling

Conventions

Annual Christian Homeschool Conference

Missouri Association of Teaching Christian Homes
2203 Rhonda Drive
West Plains, MO 65775

PHONE: (417) 255-2824
WEBSITE: www.match-inc.org
EMAIL: information@match-inc.org
DATE: Held in March
FOCUS: Christian homeschooling

LEARN's Annual Inclusive State Convention

c/o Families for Home Education
PO Box 800
Platte City, MO 64079

PHONE: (816) 767-9825
WEBSITE: www.fhe-mo.org
EMAIL: 1983@fhe-mo.org
DATE: Held in June
FOCUS: Inclusive homeschooling

State Contact

Missouri Department of Elementary and Secondary Education

PO Box 480
Jefferson City, MO 65102

PHONE: (573) 751-3527
FAX: (573) 751-8613
WEBSITE: www.dese.state.mo.us
COMPULSORY ATTENDANCE: Ages seven to sixteen; a thousand hours per year.
TEACHING QUALIFICATIONS: None.
SCHOOL SETUP OPTIONS: Establish/operate a homeschool.
SUBJECTS REQUIRED: Reading, math, science, social studies, and language arts.

Montana

Organization

Montana Coalition of Home Educators

PO Box 43
Gallatin Gateway, MT 59730

PHONE: (406) 587-6163
WEBSITE: www.mtche.org
EMAIL: white@gomontana.com
FOCUS: Inclusive homeschooling

Convention

No information available.

State Contact

Montana Office of Public Instruction

1227 11th Street
Helena, MT 59602

PHONE: (406) 444-3095
WEBSITE: www.opi.state.mt.us
COMPULSORY ATTENDANCE: Ages seven to fifteen; 180 days per year (six hours per day).
TEACHING QUALIFICATIONS: None.
SCHOOL SETUP OPTIONS: Establish/operate a homeschool.
SUBJECTS REQUIRED: Same program as the public schools.

Nebraska

Organization

Nebraska Christian Home Education Association

PO Box 57041
Lincoln, NE 68505

PHONE: (402) 432-4297
WEBSITE: www.nchea.org
EMAIL: nchea@alltel.net
FOCUS: Christian homeschooling

Convention

HEN's Annual Christian Homeschool Conference

c/o Home Educators Network
PO Box 641978
Omaha, NE 68164

PHONE: (402) 451-3459
WEBSITE: www.mitec.net/~rkdick/HEN/HENhome.htm
EMAIL: mpantitus@tconl.com
CONTACT: Lori Darby
DATE: Held in the spring
FOCUS: Christian homeschooling

State Contact

Nebraska Department of Education

301 Centennial Mall
Lincoln, NE 68509

PHONE: (402) 471-2784
WEBSITE: www.nde.state.ne.us
COMPULSORY ATTENDANCE: Ages seven to sixteen; 1,080 hours per year for high school.
TEACHING QUALIFICATIONS: None. The only exception is if the family hires a teacher, in which case the teacher must be certified.
SCHOOL SETUP OPTIONS: Establish/operate a homeschool as a private school.
SUBJECTS REQUIRED: Language arts, math, science, social studies, and health.

Nevada

Organization

Home Schools United

PO Box 93564
Las Vegas, NV 89193

PHONE: (702) 870-9566
WEBSITE: http://homeschool8.tripod.com
EMAIL: homeschoolsunited.vv@juno.com
FOCUS: Inclusive homeschooling

Convention

Northern Nevada Homeschools

PO Box 21323
Reno, NV 89515

PHONE: (775) 852-6647
WEBSITE: www.nnhs.org
EMAIL: NNHS@aol.com
DATE: Held in May
FOCUS: Christian homeschooling

State Contact

Nevada Department of Education

700 East Fifth Street
Carson City, NV 89701

PHONE: (775) 687-9160
WEBSITE: www.nde.state.nv.us
EMAIL: warensd@nsn.k12.nv.us
COMPULSORY ATTENDANCE: Ages seven to seventeen; 180 days per year (330 minutes per day).
TEACHING QUALIFICATIONS: 1) teaching certificate; 2) consulting with licensed teacher or experienced homeschooling parent (with three or more years' experience); 3) approved correspondence course; 4) obtaining a waiver.
SCHOOL SETUP OPTIONS: Establish/operate a homeschool.
SUBJECTS REQUIRED: Same as public schools.

New Hampshire

Organization

New Hampshire Homeschooling Coalition

PO Box 2224
Concord, NH 03304

PHONE: (603) 539-7233
WEBSITE: www.nhhomeschooling.org
EMAIL: webmaster@NHHomeschooling.org
FOCUS: Inclusive homeschooling

Conventions

Annual Christian Homeschooling Conference

c/o Christian Home Educators of New Hampshire
PO Box 961
Manchester, NH 03105

WEBSITE: www.mv.com/ipusers/chenh
DATE: Held in April
FOCUS: Christian homeschooling

Annual Homeschooling Panel Workshop

c/o New Hampshire Homeschooling Coalition
PO Box 2224
Concord, NH 03304

PHONE: (603) 539-7233
WEBSITE: www.nhhomeschooling.org
EMAIL: webmaster@NHHomeschooling.org
DATE: Held in May
FOCUS: Inclusive homeschooling

State Contact

New Hampshire Department of Education

State Office Park South
101 Pleasant Street
Concord, NH 03301

PHONE: (603) 271-3144
FAX: (603) 271-1953
WEBSITE: www.ed.state.nh.us
EMAIL: llovering@ed.state.nh.us
COMPULSORY ATTENDANCE: Ages six to fifteen; no days-per-year requirement.
TEACHING QUALIFICATIONS: None.
SCHOOL SETUP OPTIONS: Establish/operate a homeschool.
SUBJECTS REQUIRED: Language, science, mathematics, government, history, health, reading, writing, spelling, U.S. Constitution, New Hampshire Constitution, art, and music appreciation.

New Jersey

Organization

Educational Network of Christian Homeschoolers

PO Box 308
Atlantic Highlands, NJ 07716

PHONE: (732) 291-7800
WEBSITE: www.enochnj.org
EMAIL: office@enochnj.org
CONTACT: Margaret Reed
FOCUS: Christian homeschooling

Convention

Annual Christian Homeschooling Conference

c/o Educational Network of Christian Homeschoolers
PO Box 308
Atlantic Highlands, NJ 07716

PHONE: (732) 291-7800 or (609) 222-4283
WEBSITE: www.enochnj.org
EMAIL: office@enochnj.org
DATE: Held in June
FOCUS: Christian homeschooling

State Contact

New Jersey Department of Education

100 Riverview Plaza
PO Box 500
Trenton, NJ 08625

PHONE: (609) 292-1126
WEBSITE: www.state.nj.us/education
COMPULSORY ATTENDANCE: Ages six to sixteen; no days-per-year requirement.
TEACHING QUALIFICATIONS: None.
SCHOOL SETUP OPTIONS: Establish/operate a homeschool.
SUBJECTS REQUIRED: U.S. history, New Jersey history, civics, citizenship, geography, health, safety, sexual assault prevention, and physical education. Parents/students can opt out of sexual assault prevention and health.

New Mexico

Organizations

Christian Association of Parent Educators—New Mexico

PO Box 25046
Albuquerque, NM 87125

PHONE: (505) 898-8548
WEBSITE: www.cape-nm.org
EMAIL: cape-nm@juno.com
FOCUS: Christian homeschooling

New Mexico Family Educators

PO Box 92276
Albuquerque, NM 87199

PHONE: (505) 275-7053
FOCUS: Inclusive homeschooling

Convention

Christian Homeschool Convention of New Mexico

c/o Christian Association of Parent Educators
PO Box 25046
Albuquerque, NM 87125

PHONE: (505) 425-8874
WEBSITE: www.cape-nm.org
EMAIL: cape-nm@juno.com
CONTACT: Ed and Sue Tsyitee
DATE: Held in April
FOCUS: Christian homeschooling

State Contact

New Mexico Department of Education

Management Support and Intervention
300 Don Gaspar
Santa Fe, NM 87501

PHONE: (505) 827-6582
WEBSITE: www.sde.state.nm.us
EMAIL: sperea@sde.state.nm.us
COMPULSORY ATTENDANCE: Ages five to eighteen; same as public schools.
TEACHING QUALIFICATIONS: High school diploma or equivalent.
SCHOOL SETUP OPTIONS: Establish/operate a homeschool.
SUBJECTS REQUIRED: Social studies, mathematics, science, reading, and language arts.

New York

Organizations

New York Home Education Network

30 North Street
Saratoga Springs, NY 12866

PHONE: (518) 584-9110
WEBSITE: www.nyhen.org
EMAIL: nyhen@juno.com
FOCUS: Inclusive homeschooling

NYS Loving Education at Home

PO Box 438
Fayetteville, NY 13066-0438

PHONE: (315) 637-4525
FAX: (315) 637-4525
WEBSITE: www.leah.org
EMAIL: info@leah.org
FOCUS: Christian homeschooling

Convention

Annual New York State LEAH Convention

c/o NYS Loving Education at Home
PO Box 438
Fayetteville, NY 13066-0438

PHONE: (315) 637-4525
FAX: (315) 637-4525
WEBSITE: www.leah.org
EMAIL: info@leah.org
DATE: Held in May
FOCUS: Christian homeschooling

State Contact

New York State Education Department

Office for Nonpublic School Services
Room 481 EBA
Albany, NY 12234

PHONE: (518) 474-3879
WEBSITE: www.nysed.gov
EMAIL: emscgen@mail.nysed.gov
COMPULSORY ATTENDANCE: Ages six to sixteen; 180 days per year.
TEACHING QUALIFICATIONS: The only requirement is "competency."
SCHOOL SETUP OPTIONS: Establish/operate a homeschool.

SUBJECTS REQUIRED: Patriotism and citizenship, substance abuse, traffic and fire safety, English, social studies, U.S. history (government, economics), math, science, art or music, health, physical education, and various electives.

North Carolina

Organization

North Carolinians for Home Education

419 North Boylan Avenue
Raleigh, NC 27603

PHONE: (919) 834-6243
FAX: (919) 834-6241
WEBSITE: www.nche.com
EMAIL: nche@mindspring.com
FOCUS: Inclusive homeschooling

Convention

Annual Christian Homeschool Conference

c/o North Carolinians for Home Education
419 North Boylan Avenue
Raleigh, NC 27603

PHONE: (919) 834-6243
FAX: (919) 834-6241
WEBSITE: www.nche.com
EMAIL: nche@mindspring.com
DATE: Held in May
FOCUS: Christian homeschooling

State Contact

North Carolina Division of Non-Public Education

1309 Mail Service Center
Raleigh, NC 27699

PHONE: (919) 733-4276
WEBSITE: www.ncdnpe.org
COMPULSORY ATTENDANCE: Ages seven to sixteen; nine calendar months per year.
TEACHING QUALIFICATIONS: High school diploma or GED.
SCHOOL SETUP OPTIONS: Establish/operate a homeschool.
SUBJECTS REQUIRED: None. However, the required standardized tests will cover math, spelling, English grammar, and reading.

North Dakota

Organization

North Dakota Homeschool Association

PO Box 7400
Bismarck, ND 58507

PHONE: (701) 223-4080
WEBSITE: www.ndhsa.org
EMAIL: ndhsa@riverjordan.com
FOCUS: Christian homeschooling

Convention

North Dakota Homeschool Association

PO Box 7400
Bismarck, ND 58507

PHONE: (701) 223-4080
WEBSITE: www.ndhsa.org
EMAIL: ndhsa@riverjordan.com
CONTACT: Gail Bilby
DATE: Held in March
FOCUS: Christian homeschooling

State Contact

North Dakota Department of Public Instruction

600 East Boulevard
Bismarck, ND 58505

PHONE: (701) 328-4572
FAX: (701) 328-2461
WEBSITE: www.dpi.state.nd.us
COMPULSORY ATTENDANCE: Ages seven to sixteen; 175 days per year (four hours per day).
TEACHING QUALIFICATIONS: Teacher certification or bachelor's degree or a high school diploma or GED, and must be monitored by a certified teacher for the first two years of homeschooling. Another possibility is to pass the National Teacher's Exam.
SCHOOL SETUP OPTIONS: Establish/operate a homeschool; operate a homeschool as a private school (which must be approved by both the state and county).
SUBJECTS REQUIRED: Language arts (reading, composition, grammar, spelling, creative writing), social studies (U.S. Constitution, U.S. history, geography, and government), mathematics, science (including agriculture), physical education, health (including physiology, hygiene, disease control, and the nature and effects of alcohol, tobacco, and narcotics).

Ohio

Organization

Christian Home Educators of Ohio (CHEO)

117 West Main Street, Suite 103
Lancaster, OH 43130

PHONE: (740) 654-3331
FAX: (740) 654-3337
WEBSITE: www.cheohome.org
EMAIL: cheoorg@usa.net
FOCUS: Christian homeschooling

Convention

Christian Home Educators of Ohio (CHEO)

117 West Main Street, Suite 103
Lancaster, OH 43130

PHONE: (740) 654-3331
FAX: (740) 654-3337
WEBSITE: www.cheohome.org
EMAIL: cheoorg@usa.net
CONTACT: Bruce Purdy
DATE: Held in June
FOCUS: Christian homeschooling

State Contact

Ohio Department of Education

65 Front Street
Columbus, OH 43215

PHONE: (614) 466-2937
WEBSITE: www.ode.state.oh.us
COMPULSORY ATTENDANCE: Ages six to eighteen; nine hundred hours per year.
TEACHING QUALIFICATIONS: High school diploma; GED; supervision by person with college degree.
SCHOOL SETUP OPTIONS: Establish/operate a homeschool.
SUBJECTS REQUIRED: U.S. history, Ohio history, language arts, geography, government, math, health, physical education, fine arts, science, and first aid.

Oklahoma

Organization

Home Educator's Resource Organization of Oklahoma

302 North Coolidge
Enid, OK 73703

PHONE: (580) 446-5679
WEBSITE: www.oklahomahomeschooling.org
EMAIL: HERO@oklahomahomeschooling.org
FOCUS: Inclusive homeschooling

Convention

Christian Home Educators Fellowship (CHEF) of Oklahoma

PO Box 471363
Tulsa, OK 74147

PHONE: (918) 583-7323
FAX: (918) 357-2016
WEBSITE: www.chefok.org
EMAIL: staff@chefok.org
DATE: Held in June
FOCUS: Christian homeschooling

State Contact

Oklahoma State Department of Education

2500 North Lincoln Boulevard
Oklahoma City, OK 73105

PHONE: (405) 521-3301
FAX: (405) 521-6205
WEBSITE: www.sde.state.ok.us
COMPULSORY ATTENDANCE: Ages five to seventeen; 180 days per year.
TEACHING QUALIFICATIONS: None.
SCHOOL SETUP OPTIONS: Establish/operate a homeschool.
SUBJECTS REQUIRED: Reading, writing, science, math, citizenship, U.S. Constitution, health, safety, physical education, and conservation.

Oregon

Organization

Oregon Home Education Network

PO Box 218
Beaverton, OR 97075

PHONE: (503) 321-5166
WEBSITE: www.home.teleport.com/~ohen
EMAIL: ohen@teleport.com
FOCUS: Inclusive homeschooling

Convention

Annual All-Inclusive Conference

c/o Oregon Home Education Network
PO Box 218
Beaverton, OR 97075

PHONE: (503) 321-5166
WEBSITE: www.home.teleport.com/~ohen
EMAIL: ohen@teleport.com
DATE: Held in April
FOCUS: Inclusive homeschooling

State Contact

Oregon Department of Education

255 Capitol Street NE
Salem, OR 97310

PHONE: (503) 378-3569
FAX: (503) 378-5156
WEBSITE: www.ode.state.or.us
EMAIL: ode.webmaster@state.or.us
COMPULSORY ATTENDANCE: Ages seven to eighteen; no days-per-year requirement.
TEACHING QUALIFICATIONS: None.
SCHOOL SETUP OPTIONS: Establish/operate a homeschool.
SUBJECTS REQUIRED: None.

Pennsylvania

Organizations

Catholic Homeschoolers of Pennsylvania

101 South College Street
Myerstown, PA 17067

PHONE: (717) 866-5425
FAX: (717) 866-9383
WEBSITE: www.catholichomeschoolpa.org
EMAIL: cathhmschpa@ihs2000.com
FOCUS: Catholic homeschooling

PA Homeschoolers

RR 2, Box 117
Kittanning, PA 16201

PHONE: (724) 783-6512
WEBSITE: www.pahomeschoolers.com
EMAIL: richmans@pahomeschoolers.com
FOCUS: Inclusive homeschooling

Pennsylvania Home Education Network

285 Allegheny Street
Meadville, PA 16335

PHONE: (412) 561-5288
WEBSITE: www.phen.org
EMAIL: Jsk8@juno.com
FOCUS: Inclusive homeschooling

Conventions

High School at Home Conference

PA Homeschoolers
RR 2, Box 117
Kittanning, PA 16201

PHONE: (724) 783-6512
WEBSITE: www.pahomeschoolers.com
EMAIL: richmans@pahomeschoolers.com
DATE: Held in July
FOCUS: Inclusive homeschooling

Christian Homeschool Association of Pennsylvania

PO Box 115
Mount Joy, PA 17552

PHONE: (717) 661-2428
WEBSITE: www.chapboard.org
CONTACT: Kim Huber
DATE: Held in May
FOCUS: Christian homeschooling

State Contact

Pennsylvania Department of Education

School Services Unit
333 Market Street, Fifth Floor
Harrisburg, PA 17126

PHONE: (717) 787-4860
WEBSITE: www.pde.state.pa.us
EMAIL: spearce@state.pa.us
COMPULSORY ATTENDANCE: Ages eight to seventeen; 180 days per year (or 990 hours per year).
TEACHING QUALIFICATIONS: High school diploma for parents and teacher certification for private tutors.
SCHOOL SETUP OPTIONS: Establish/operate a home education program; private tutor; establish/operate a homeschool as the satellite campus of a religious day school.
SUBJECTS REQUIRED: English language, literature, speech, composition, science, geography, civics, the world, U.S. history, Pennsylvania history, algebra, geometry, art, music, physical education, health, safety, and fire prevention.

Rhode Island

Organization

Rhode Island Guild of Home Teachers

PO Box 11
Hope, RI 02831

PHONE: (401) 821-7700
WEBSITE: www.rihomeschool.com
EMAIL: right_right@mail.excite.com
FOCUS: Christian homeschooling

Convention

No information available.

State Contact

Rhode Island Department of Education

225 Westminster Street, Fourth Floor
Providence, RI 02903

PHONE: (401) 222-4600, ext. 2503
WEBSITE: www.ridoe.net
COMPULSORY ATTENDANCE: Ages six to sixteen; same as public schools.
TEACHING QUALIFICATIONS: None.
SCHOOL SETUP OPTIONS: Establish/operate a homeschool. Local school board must approve it.
SUBJECTS REQUIRED: Reading, writing, mathematics, U.S. history, Rhode Island history, geography, American government principles, English, health, physical education, U.S. Constitution, and Rhode Island Constitution.

South Carolina

Organizations

South Carolina Association of Independent Homeschools

930 Knox Abbott Drive
Cayce, SC 29033

PHONE: (803) 454-0427
FAX: (803) 454-0428
WEBSITE: www.scaihs.org
EMAIL: scaihs@scaihs.org
FOCUS: Christian homeschooling

South Carolina Home Educators Association

PO Box 3231
Columbia, SC 29230

PHONE: (803) 772-2330
WEBSITE: www.christianity.com/schea (Coming soon: www.schea.org)
EMAIL: schea1@aol.com
FOCUS: Christian homeschooling

Convention

SC Home School Convention and Vendor Book Fair

c/o South Carolina Home Educators Association
PO Box 3231
Columbia, SC 29230

PHONE: (803) 772-2330
WEBSITE: www.christianity.com/schea (Coming soon: www.schea.org)
EMAIL: schea1@aol.com
DATE: Held in June
FOCUS: Christian homeschooling

State Contact

South Carolina Department of Education

1429 Senate Street
Columbia, SC 29201

PHONE: (803) 734-8493
WEBSITE: www.myscschools.com
EMAIL: slindsay@sde.state.sc.us
COMPULSORY ATTENDANCE: Ages five to seventeen (or graduation from high school); 180 days per year (4.5 hours per day).
TEACHING QUALIFICATIONS: High school diploma, GED, or college degree.
SCHOOL SETUP OPTIONS: Establish/operate a homeschool approved by local school board; establish/operate a homeschool as member of South Carolina Association of Independent Home Schools (SCAIHS); establish/operate a homeschool as part of an association with at least fifty members.
SUBJECTS REQUIRED: Reading, writing, science, social studies, composition, and literature.

South Dakota

Organization

South Dakota Christian Home Educators (SDCHE)

PO Box 9571
Rapid City, SD 57709-9571

PHONE: (605) 348-2001
FAX: (605) 341-2447
WEBSITE: www.sdche.org
EMAIL: sdche@christianemail.com
FOCUS: Christian homeschooling

Convention

Western Dakota Christian Home Schools

Box 528
Black Hawk, SD 57718

PHONE: (605) 923-1893
DATE: Held in the spring
FOCUS: Christian homeschooling

State Contact

South Dakota Department of Education

700 Governor's Drive
Pierre, SD 57501

PHONE: (605) 773-6934
FAX: (605) 773-3782
WEBSITE: www.state.sd.us/deca
EMAIL: wade.pogany@state.sd.us
COMPULSORY ATTENDANCE: Ages six to sixteen; 175 days per year.
TEACHING QUALIFICATIONS: None.
SCHOOL SETUP OPTIONS: Establish/operate a homeschool.
SUBJECTS REQUIRED: Math and language arts.

Tennessee

Organization

Tennessee Home Education Association

PO Box 681652
Franklin, TN 37068

PHONE: (858) 623-7899
FAX: (615) 834-3529
WEBSITE: www.tnhea.org
EMAIL: jcthornton3@earthlink.net
FOCUS: Inclusive homeschooling

Convention

Bill Rice Ranch Home School Conference

627 Bill Rice Ranch Road
Murfreesboro, TN 37128-4555

PHONE: (800) 253-7423
WEBSITE: www.billriceranch.org
EMAIL: BillRiceRanch@att.net
DATE: Held in April
FOCUS: Christian homeschooling

State Contact

Tennessee State Department of Education

2730 Island Home Boulevard
Knoxville, TN 37920

PHONE: (865) 579-3749
WEBSITE: www.state.tn.us/education
COMPULSORY ATTENDANCE: Ages six to seventeen; 180 days per year.
TEACHING QUALIFICATIONS: College degree or be granted an exemption by the Commissioner of Education.
SCHOOL SETUP OPTIONS: Establish/operate a homeschool; establish/operate a homeschool connected with a church-related school; operate as satellite campus of a church-related school; operate as satellite campus of a non-recognized religious school.
SUBJECTS REQUIRED: Either college-preparatory courses (for those seeking college admission) or general studies courses (for those only seeking to graduate from high school).

Texas

Organizations

Texas Homeschool Coalition

PO Box 6747
Lubbock, TX 79493

PHONE: (806) 744-4441
FAX: (806) 744-4446
WEBSITE: www.thsc.org
EMAIL: staff@thsc.org
CONTACT: Tim Lambert
FOCUS: Christian homeschooling

Home School Texas (HOST)

PO Box 29307
Dallas, TX 75229

PHONE: (214) 358-5723
FAX: (214) 358-2996
WEBSITE: www.homeschooltexas.com
EMAIL: info@homeschooltexas.com
CONTACT: Phillip and Betty May
FOCUS: Christian homeschooling

Convention

Texas Home School Coalition State Convention and Family Conference

c/o Texas Homeschool Coalition
PO Box 6747
Lubbock, TX 79493

PHONE: (806) 744-4441
FAX: (806) 744-4446
WEBSITE: www.thsc.org
EMAIL: staff@thsc.org
DATE: Held in April
FOCUS: Christian homeschooling

State Contact

Texas Education Agency

1701 Congress Avenue
Austin, TX 78701

PHONE: (512) 463-9630
WEBSITE: www.tea.state.tx.us
COMPULSORY ATTENDANCE: Ages six to seventeen; no days-per-year requirement.
TEACHING QUALIFICATIONS: None.
SCHOOL SETUP OPTIONS: Establish/operate a homeschool as a private school.
SUBJECTS REQUIRED: Reading, spelling, grammar, math, and citizenship.

Utah

Organizations

Utah Home Education Association

PO Box 1492
Riverton, UT 84065

PHONE: (888) 887-8432
WEBSITE: www.uhea.org
FOCUS: Inclusive homeschooling

Utah Christian Home School Association

PO Box 3942
Salt Lake City, UT 84110

PHONE: (801) 296-7198
WEBSITE: www.utch.org
EMAIL: utch@utch.org
FOCUS: Christian homeschooling

Conventions

Annual Convention and Curriculum Fair

c/o Utah Home Education Association
PO Box 1492
Riverton, UT 84065

PHONE: (888) 887-8432
WEBSITE: www.uhea.org
EMAIL: JYarrington@uhea.org
DATE: Held in June
FOCUS: Inclusive homeschooling

UTCH Home School Convention

c/o Utah Christian Home School Association
PO Box 3942
Salt Lake City, UT 84110

PHONE: (801) 296-7198
WEBSITE: www.utch.org
EMAIL: utch@utch.org
DATE: Held in March
FOCUS: Christian homeschooling

State Contact

Utah State Office of Education

250 East 500 South
Salt Lake City, UT 84111

PHONE: (801) 538-7801
WEBSITE: www.usoe.k12.ut.us
COMPULSORY ATTENDANCE: Ages six to eighteen; same as the public schools.
TEACHING QUALIFICATIONS: None, but local school board can consider someone's ability or inability to be the teacher.
SCHOOL SETUP OPTIONS: Establish/operate a homeschool approved by local school board; establish a group of homeschool families as a standard private school.
SUBJECTS REQUIRED: Language arts, math, science, social studies, arts, health, computer literacy, and vocational education.

Vermont

Organization

Vermont Association of Home Educators

214 VT Route 11 West
Chester, VT 05143

PHONE: (802) 875-1699
FAX: (802) 875-1689
WEBSITE: www.vermonthomeschool.org
EMAIL: otworks@vermontel.net
CONTACT: Sara Gagnon
FOCUS: Inclusive homeschooling

Convention

No information available. It appears that the nearest conferences are in Massachusetts.

State Contact

Vermont Department of Education

120 State Street
Montpelier, VT 05620

PHONE: (802) 828-5406
WEBSITE: www.state.vt.us/educ
COMPULSORY ATTENDANCE: Ages six to sixteen; no days-per-year requirement, but public schools require 175 days per year.
TEACHING QUALIFICATIONS: None.
SCHOOL SETUP OPTIONS: Establish/operate a homeschool.
SUBJECTS REQUIRED: Reading, writing, literature (English/American/other), history, citizenship, U.S. government, Vermont government, science, physical education, health, and fine arts.

Virginia

Organizations

Virginia Home Education Association

PO Box 5131
Charlottesville, VA 22905

PHONE: (540) 832-3578
WEBSITE: www.vhea.org
EMAIL: president@vhea.org
FOCUS: Inclusive homeschooling

Home Educators Association of Virginia

1900 Byrd Avenue, Suite 201
Richmond, VA 23230

PHONE: (804) 288-1608
FAX: (804) 288-6962
WEBSITE: www.heav.org
EMAIL: heav33@aol.com
FOCUS: Christian homeschooling

Convention

Annual HEAV State Convention and Educational Fair

c/o Home Educators Association of Virginia
1900 Byrd Avenue, Suite 201
Richmond, VA 23230

PHONE: (804) 288-1608
FAX: (804) 288-6962
WEBSITE: www.heav.org
EMAIL: heav33@aol.com
DATE: Held in June
FOCUS: Christian homeschooling (but all are welcome)

State Contact

Virginia Department of Education

PO Box 2120
Richmond, VA 23218

PHONE: (804) 786-9421
WEBSITE: www.pen.k12.va.us
COMPULSORY ATTENDANCE: Ages five to seventeen (with possible exemption for five-year-olds); 180 days for homeschool option.
TEACHING QUALIFICATIONS: Four options: 1) college degree; 2) teacher certification; 3) approved correspondence course; 4) show evidence parent can teach/use curriculum with Virginia state objectives for language arts and math.
SCHOOL SETUP OPTIONS: Establish/operate a homeschool; operate homeschool with religious exemption; private tutor.
SUBJECTS REQUIRED: None (unless using fourth option above).

Washington

Organization

Washington Homeschool Organization

6632 South 191st Place, Suite E-100
Kent, WA 98032

PHONE: (425) 251-0439
FAX: (425) 251-6984
WEBSITE: www.washhomeschool.org
EMAIL: WHOoffice@foxinternet.net
FOCUS: Inclusive homeschooling

Convention

Annual WHO Conference

c/o Washington Homeschool Organization
6632 South 191st Place, Suite E-100
Kent, WA 98032

PHONE: (425) 251-0439
FAX: (425) 251-6984
WEBSITE: www.washhomeschool.org
EMAIL: WHOoffice@foxinternet.net
DATE: Held in June
FOCUS: Inclusive homeschooling

State Contact

Office of Superintendent of Public Instruction

Old Capitol Building
PO Box 47200
Olympia, WA 98504

PHONE: (360) 664-3574
WEBSITE: www.k12.wa.us
EMAIL: webmaster@ospi.wednet.edu
COMPULSORY ATTENDANCE: Ages eight to seventeen; a thousand hours per year.
TEACHING QUALIFICATIONS: Three options: 1) certified teacher provides supervision; 2) have completed either forty-five quarter credit hours of college or an approved course in home education; 3) approval of local schools superintendent.
SCHOOL SETUP OPTIONS: Establish/operate a homeschool; operate as satellite of an approved private school with a home education focus.
SUBJECTS REQUIRED: Science, math, occupational education, language, social studies, history, health, reading, writing, spelling, music, and art appreciation.

West Virginia

Organizations

West Virginia Home Educators Association

PO Box 3707
Charleston, WV 25337

PHONE: (800) 736-9843
WEBSITE: www.wvheahome.homestead.com
EMAIL: lyvonbeth@people.com
FOCUS: Inclusive homeschooling

Christian Home Educators of West Virginia

Route 1, Box 122A
Buckhannon, WV 26201

WEBSITE: www.chewv.org
EMAIL: administrator@chewv.org
FOCUS: Christian homeschooling

Convention

Annual Christian Homeschool Conference

Christian Home Educators of West Virginia
Route 1, Box 122A
Buckhannon, WV 26201

WEBSITE: www.chewv.org
EMAIL: conference@chewv.org
DATE: Held in May
FOCUS: Christian homeschooling

State Contact

West Virginia Department of Education

1900 Kanawha Boulevard East
Building 6, Room 262
Charleston, WV 25305

PHONE: (304) 558-2118
FAX: (304) 558-6268
WEBSITE: http://wvde.state.wv.us
COMPULSORY ATTENDANCE: Ages six to sixteen; 180 days per year (if using local school board approved homeschool option).
TEACHING QUALIFICATIONS: Approval of local superintendent and school board for local school board approval option or high school diploma and four years higher education than the oldest child to be taught. For high-school-aged children, this would mean some college to ultimately four years of college.
SCHOOL SETUP OPTIONS: Homeschool approved by local school board; establish/operate a homeschool.
SUBJECTS REQUIRED: Math, social studies, science, English, grammar, and reading.

Wisconsin

Organization

Wisconsin Parents Association

PO Box 2502
Madison, WI 53701

PHONE: (608) 283-3131
WEBSITE: www.homeschooling-wpa.org
FOCUS: Inclusive homeschooling

Convention

Annual Home Education Conference

c/o Wisconsin Parents Association
PO Box 2502
Madison, WI 53701

PHONE: (608) 283-3131
WEBSITE: www.homeschooling-wpa.org
DATE: Held in May
FOCUS: Inclusive homeschooling

State Contact

Wisconsin Department of Public Instruction

125 South Webster Street
PO Box 7841
Madison, WI 53707

PHONE: (608) 266-3390 or (800) 441-4563
WEBSITE: www.dpi.state.wi.us
COMPULSORY ATTENDANCE: Ages six to eighteen years; 875 hours per year.
TEACHING QUALIFICATIONS: None.
SCHOOL SETUP OPTIONS: Establish/operate a home-based private educational program.
SUBJECTS REQUIRED: Language arts, reading, math, social studies, science, and health. Instruction of these subjects can be influenced by religious doctrine.

Wyoming

Organization

Homeschoolers of Wyoming

PO Box 3151
Jackson, WY 83001

PHONE: (307) 733-2834
WEBSITE: www.freewebz.com/basedintheword/how
EMAIL: contact@homeschoolersofwy.cjb.net
FOCUS: Christian homeschooling

Convention

HOW Convention

c/o Homeschoolers of Wyoming
PO Box 3151
Jackson, WY 83001

PHONE: (307) 733-2834
WEBSITE: www.freewebz.com/basedintheword/how
EMAIL: contact@homeschoolersofwy.cjb.net

DATE: Held in May
FOCUS: Christian homeschooling

State Contact

Wyoming Department of Education

Hathaway Building, Second Floor
2300 Capitol Avenue
Cheyenne, WY 82002

PHONE: (307) 777-7670
WEBSITE: www.k12.wy.us
COMPULSORY ATTENDANCE: Ages seven to sixteen (or completion of the tenth grade); 175 days per year.
TEACHING QUALIFICATIONS: None.
SCHOOL SETUP OPTIONS: Establish/operate a homeschool.
SUBJECTS REQUIRED: Reading, writing, math, civics, history, literature, and science.

Magazines and Other Periodicals

Adventist Home Educator

PO Box 936
Camino, CA 95709

WEBSITE: www.adventisthomeeducator.org
FOCUS: Seventh Day Adventist homeschoolers
COST: $12 per year

Back Home

PO Box 70
Hendersonville, NC 28793

PHONE: (828) 696-3838
FOCUS: Independent family living
COST: $21.97 per year

Backwoods Home Magazine

PO Box 712
Gold Beach, OR 97444

PHONE: (800) 835-2418
FAX: (541) 247-8600
WEBSITE: www.backwoodshome.com
FOCUS: Self-reliant living (including homeschooling)
COST: $21.95 per year

Tom Head was homeschooled from kindergarten through high school. After high school, he earned bachelor's and master's degrees nontraditionally. He is the author or co-author of eleven books on a wide range of topics, including *Get Your IT Degree and Get Ahead.* He can be found on the Web at www.tomhead.net.

Bears' Guide: Please describe why you decided to pursue an alternate route for your high school education.

Tom Head: I was homeschooled from day one, and never really gave serious thought to doing a traditional high school program; homeschooling gave me so much more academic freedom than any structured, institution-based high school program could offer.

Of course, these academic reflections could also be written off as sour grapes. I'd been diagnosed with chronic fatigue syndrome, and five days a week in crowded classrooms would have probably done me in, or close enough to send my grades through the floor.

BG: Please describe your particular homeschooling situation. Include the strengths and weaknesses that you perceived then and now.

TH: Up until I was fourteen or so, my mother took care of all the academics, my brother handled physics and taught me how to work on computers, and my local YWCA took care of the socialization and physical education. Then we ran into a problem.

Because my mother had been willing to drop everything and do a new curriculum from scratch whenever the situation called for it, I was doing twelfth grade English and tenth grade math. When you finish twelfth grade English, and English is your best subject, the prospects don't look all that interesting. (It's worth mentioning here that Mississippi state law prevents anyone under seventeen from taking the GED, a policy that was presumably introduced to prevent people like me from graduating early.) It was about that time that we discovered that Ole Miss offered English 101 by correspondence, and those wacky Bear [of the *Bears' Guides*] and Thorson [Marcie Thorson of *Campus Free College Degrees*] people said you could do a whole degree that way. So I signed up and did college English (English 101 and 102 from Ole Miss, creative writing from Penn State) alongside the last two years of my high school curriculum.

BG: Do you feel you missed out on anything by not participating in a traditional high school?

TH: I'm sure I must have, but I've always hated competitive power structures and I think the high school social environment would have created more problems than it would have solved for me. People always bring up socialization when they talk about homeschooling, but I wasn't starving for it, and as an adult I'm a lot more assertive than the norm. I'm not even scared of public speaking. Never have been, near as I can remember.

As homeschoolers, we're saying that an untrained parent and an undisciplined kid can go through a high school curriculum and do as well as (or better than) a well-tested, theory-based, tried-and-true organized education structure. Homeschooling is to education what anarchy is to government; it throws the whole problem in the hands of individual human beings, and the vast majority of them aren't trained to handle it. But homeschooling works, and it nearly always works better than institutional schools do.

BG: Please describe your background since finishing homeschooling.

TH: I attended Regents College (now Excelsior College) and was never even asked for a GED score. I'd already earned more than enough credits by then to qualify as a transfer student. I earned my B.A. a month before my eighteenth birthday. I went on to do a master's degree at California State University, Dominguez Hills; now I'm twenty-four, doing my Ph.D. from Edith Cowan University in Australia, and writing books. This year, many of those books seem to be grade-seven-to-twelve library-resource volumes, so, in a way, I'm going to high school after all.

Homeschooling is perfect preparation for distance learning, and distance learning is perfect preparation for a writing career. If you tell yourself, "I have to write something and mail it out in an envelope tomorrow morning," that works whether you're taking History 101 or plotting the Great American Novel. Self-discipline doesn't come overnight; it's really more of a habit than a virtue. Over time, it builds itself. If you do a nontraditional high school program, and you come out on the other side knowing what a high schooler knows, you'll have worked the mental muscles that many people never get the opportunity to work.

Catholic Home Educator

PO Box 787
Montrose, AL 36559

WEBSITE: www.nache.org/che.html
EMAIL: che@nache.org
FOCUS: Catholic homeschooling
COST: $15 per year

The Education Revolution

c/o Alternative Education Resource Organization
417 Roslyn Road
Roslyn Heights, NY 11577

PHONE: (516) 769-4171
WEBSITE: www.educationrevolution.org
FOCUS: Alternative education
COST: $15 per year

Feed My Lambs

909 North Ranney Street
Craig, CO 81625

PHONE: (970) 824-2845
FOCUS: Lutheran homeschooling
COST: $15 per year

Home Education Learning Magazine (HELM)

PO Box 1159
Tallevast, FL 34270

WEBSITE: www.helmonline.com
EMAIL: helm@helmonline.com
FOCUS: Independent learning/self-directed education
COST: $24.95 per year (be careful because they will renew your subscription unless you specifically cancel it)

Home Education Magazine

PO Box 1083
Tonasket, WA 98855

PHONE: (509) 486-1351 or (800) 236-3278
FAX: (509) 486-2753
WEBSITE: www.home-ed-magazine.com
EMAIL: HEM@home-ed-magazine.com
FOCUS: Inclusive homeschooling
COST: $26 per year

Home School Digest

c/o Wisdom Publications
PO Box 374
Covert, MI 49043

WEBSITE: www.homeschooldigest.com
EMAIL: subs@homeschooldigest.com
FOCUS: Christian homeschooling
COST: $18 per year

Home School Researcher

c/o National Home Education Research Institute
PO Box 13939
Salem, OR 97309

PHONE: (503) 364-1490
WEBSITE: www.nheri.org
EMAIL: mail@nheri.org
FOCUS: Research on the efficacy of homeschooling
COST: $25 per year

Homefires

180 El Camino Real, Suite 10
Millbrae, CA 94030

PHONE: (888) 446-6333
WEBSITE: www.homefires.com
EMAIL: editor@homefires.com
FOCUS: Homeschooling ideas
COST: None; Internet-based

Homeschooling Today

PO Box 1608
Fort Collins, CO 80522

PHONE: (954) 962-1930
WEBSITE: www.homeschooltoday.com
EMAIL: subscriptions@homeschooltoday.com
FOCUS: Christian homeschooling
COST: $14.99 per year

HSLDA Court Report

c/o Home School Legal Defense Association
PO Box 3000
Purcellville, VA 20134

PHONE: (540) 338-5600
FAX: (540) 338-2733
WEBSITE: www.hslda.org/courtreport
FOCUS: Homeschooling laws
COST: None; Internet-based

The Link

PMB 911
587 North Ventu Park Road, Suite F
Newbury Park, CA 91230

PHONE: (805) 492-1373 or (888) 470-4513
FAX: (805) 492-1373
WEBSITE: www.homeschoolnewslink.com
FOCUS: Inclusive homeschooling
COST: None; Internet-based

Practical Homeschooling Magazine

PO Box 1250
Fenton, MO 63026

PHONE: (800) 346-6322
WEBSITE: www.home-school.com/catalog/pages/phs.php3
FOCUS: Christian home education
COST: $19.95

Right at Home

PO Box 1703
Diamond Springs, CA 95619

WEBSITE: http://pages.ivillage.com/4rightathome
FOCUS: Ideas and support for homeschooling parents
COST: $18 per year (free subscription if you write articles for them)

Shining Star

PO Box 299
Carthage, IL 62321

PHONE: (800) 264-9873
FOCUS: Activities and ideas for Christian homeschoolers
COST: Unknown

Teaching Home

PO Box 20219
Portland, OR 97294

PHONE: (503) 253-9633
WEBSITE: www.teachinghome.com
EMAIL: tth@teachinghome.com
FOCUS: Christian homeschooling
COST: $5 for sample issue and trial subscription

Internet

About.com's About Homeschooling Website

WEBSITE: http://homeschooling.about.com

Beverly Hernandez provides links to everything within homeschooling as well as informative articles about how to get started and how to be successful.

Cafi Cohen's Homeschool Teens and College

WEBSITE: www.homeschoolteenscollege.net

Cafi Cohen has written some of the better books on homeschooling teens, including *Homeschooling the Teen Years: Your Complete Guide to Successfully Homeschooling the 13- to 18-Year-Old.* This website is an extension of the work already done by Cohen.

Home School Legal Defense Association

WEBSITE: www.hslda.org

This site provides legal information and support for homeschooling families. Run by a lawyer, the Home School Legal Defense Association (HSLDA) vigorously defends homeschooling wherever it sees encroachment on the rights of parents.

Homeschooling Links and More

WEBSITE: http://hometown.aol.com/sitnbquiet

This site provides links to homeschooling resources. Of particular interest are the links to curricular areas (math, language arts, and so on).

National Home Education Research Institute

WEBSITE: www.nheri.org

NHERI has a twofold approach: one, to act as a clearinghouse for research on home education and, two, to conduct research on homeschooling. It provides thoughtful analysis of the research and philosophy behind homeschooling.

CHAPTER 4

Private Tutoring

"It is a rare thing for a student to be taught by only one tutor. If he should by rare chance have been indoctrinated by Mr. A., he will certainly be liberated by Mr. B."

—*C. A. Simpson, Dean, Christ Church College, Oxford, 1963*

Some states, as part of the homeschooling law, allow for the use of private tutors. Tutors are almost always subject-specific, while teachers instruct in all areas. Within this context, the tutor may either be a parent or someone from outside the family. This chapter provides information for both new parent-tutors and non–family member tutors.

Most of the states that allow tutors prefer local tutors, but this may not be a requirement. Often education requirements are more stringent for non-parent tutors than they are for parents. For example, some states require tutors to have a bachelor's degree, but only require high school graduation for parents.

What to Look For

I would suggest looking for a tutor from the teaching profession—someone with experience in tutoring or in teaching. A retired teacher might work. A certified teacher who is staying at home to raise children is another possibility. Professional tutors can also be found—people who make their entire (or most of their) income from tutoring, either by working for a public entity or as a freelancer. Your tutor should be able to commit to seeing you at appointed times every week (or day or month, depending on your situation).

Frequently Asked Questions

What is the function of a tutor?
A tutor serves as a private teacher, ususally on a specific subject. Some students prefer to learn independently, without the aid of a teacher or the classroom experience, while others require/desire instruction. Working with a tutor puts you somewhere in the middle. You are not completely independent, but you are also not in a classroom.

What qualifications should a tutor have?
While backgrounds can vary widely, it seems reasonable to expect that a tutor would have at least a bachelor's degree in the subject being offered. Tutors should preferably have some experience at tutoring. The latter isn't absolutely necessary, but you will discover that experience does make teachers and tutors better at teaching and tutoring.

Is a tutor only for someone who is homeschooling?
Absolutely not. You could just as easily use a tutor for GED instruction. A tutor could also help you with online or correspondence high school courses when you come across information you don't understand. This would work particularly well with a tutoring company such as www.tutor.com (see page 67).

How much should I pay a tutor?

This is a difficult question because it depends on so many variables. Is this someone that you are seeing face-to-face, five days a week? Or is this someone that you are meeting online one hour a week? For a one-hour-a-week tutor, something around $20 to $50 would be acceptable. The fee will often be dependent on supply and demand for the subject being taught. An English teacher could easily be in the $20 range. A physics teacher, a much rarer commodity, would likely be more expensive.

If someone is committing to a longer term relationship, a monthly fee would probably be more appropriate as long as both sides live up to their part of the bargain.

Where should I meet with my tutor?

Here the relationship is the key factor. If this is someone that you do not know, choose a public place, such as a library, school, community center, or local restaurant for at least the first several meetings. If you are a minor, have your parent come with you at the beginning. Eventually you may decide that it would be okay to meet in your home. Clear this with parents, spouses, and anyone else who lives with you. Some tutors may prefer to meet in public. Please respect this wish; it's similar to public school teachers never shutting the classroom door when alone with one student.

National Organization

The National Tutoring Association (NTA) is a nonprofit membership-supported association formed in 1992. Members represent colleges, universities, school districts, and literacy programs. It has an annual conference where tutors can receive additional training. In addition, it offers ongoing training and recognizes training certifications from other organizations.

The NTA offers certification for tutors. While certification is far from mandatory for a tutor, it does show that a prospective tutor has at least some basic knowledge in tutoring techniques. If a tutor tells you that he or she is certified by the NTA, be sure to confirm this with the national office.

The NTA offers certification in several different areas: peer tutor, paraprofessional, professional tutor, and tutor trainer/administrator. In addition, the NTA offers three levels of certification: basic, advanced, and master.

For additional information on tutors or to check the certification status of a tutor, the NTA can be contacted at:

National Tutoring Association

3719 Washington Boulevard
Indianapolis, IN 46205

PHONE: (866) 311-6630
FAX: (317) 927-0789
WEBSITE: www.ntatutor.org
EMAIL: ntatutor@aol.com
CONTACT: Sandi Ayaz, Executive Director

Online Tutoring

Online tutoring can be one way to find a tutor in harder-to-find subject areas. Unless you are particularly talented at online learning through email or a web-based service, however, you should consider getting assistance from a local tutor.

While some states allow a non-parental tutor to serve as a homeschool teacher, this person must be local. It is therefore important to understand that an online tutor will not satisfy the homeschooling tutor requirement for any state. You can use an online tutor for learning purposes only.

Tutor.com provides this sort of service, for a fee, and you don't have to worry about where to meet the tutor. This is an exceptionally good way to get good tutoring without having to commit to a long-term relationship with one person (unless that is what you want). The cost is in the neighborhood of $20 per hour. Often an hour or two of tutoring in a week will be sufficient.

Tutor.com offers tutoring in a wide variety of courses. Here is a relevant sampling:

Middle School/Junior High

Grades 7–9 English
Creative Writing
Essay Writing
General English
Grammar
Literature

Grades 7–9 Math
Algebra
Fractions
General Math
Pre-Algebra

Grades 7–9
General History
General Social Sciences
Social Studies and History

Grades 7–9 Science
Biology
Earth Science
General Science
Physical Science

High School

Grades 10–12 English
Creative Writing
English as a Second Language (ESL)
Essay Writing
General English
Grammar
Literature

Grades 10–12 Science
Astronomy
Biology
Chemistry
Earth Science
General Science
Physics

Grades 10–12 Math
Algebra
Calculus
General Math
Geometry
Pre-Calculus
Trigonometry

Grades 10–12
Ancient History
Art History
European History
General History
General Social Science
Geography
Global Studies
Music History
Social Studies and History
U.S. History

Grades 10–12
Advanced Placement
Art History
Biology
Calculus AB

Grades 10–12, *continued*

Calculus BC
Chemistry
Computer Science
English
Environmental Science
European History
French
Human Geography
German
International English Language

Latin
Macroeconomics/Microeconomics
Music Theory
Physics
Psychology
Spanish
Statistics
Studio Art
U.S. Government and Politics
U.S. History
World History

Part II: Diplomas through Onsite Programs

CHAPTER 5

Alternative High Schools

"Our highest endeavor must be to develop free human beings, who are able of themselves to impart purpose and direction to their lives."

—Rudolf Steiner

Best of luck to anyone attempting to pigeonhole alternative high schools into a particular category. Alternative high schools can be as different as night and day. Want a conservative one? Plenty of them. Liberal? Yup. Religious? Certainly.

In this book, my definition of alternative high schools falls in line with a group of schools promoting nontraditional education, usually based on a particular philosophy, such as the Sudbury model. A second group of "alternative" schools is for at-risk students, who have had discipline or academic problems. For this second group, contact your local school district. Also, many charter schools offer education for at-risk youth.

While there are many possible alternative high schools, the largest "franchises" are the Sudbury Valley and Waldorf schools. Both are quite good, challenging school approaches. You will work hard!

Sudbury Schools in the United States

The Sudbury Valley School in Framingham, Massachusetts, has developed an educational model that has proven popular throughout the United States. The teaching theory is based on a philosophy of self-governance and democracy. Sudbury Valley schools encourage curiosity. The theory is that all people are by nature curious and that education should be founded on that premise. In other words, students should learn about what excites them.

California

Cedarwood Sudbury School

2545 Warburton Avenue
Santa Clara, CA 95051

PHONE: (408) 296-2072
WEBSITE: www.cedarwoodsudbury.org
EMAIL: freekids@aol.com

Diablo Valley School

2924 Clayton Road
Concord, CA 94519

PHONE: (925) 676-2982
FAX: (925) 676-2983
WEBSITE: www.dvschool.org
EMAIL: dvschool@earthlink.net

Marin Sudbury School

PO Box 6431
San Rafael, CA 94903

PHONE: (415) 258-4830
WEBSITE: www.marinsudbury.org
EMAIL: info@marinsudbury.org

Sacramento Valley School

2791 24th Street, Room 9
Sacramento, CA 95818

PHONE: (916) 452-2203
FAX: (916) 731-4386
WEBSITE: www.sacval.org
EMAIL: info@sacval.org

Colorado

Alpine Valley School

4501 Parfet Street
Wheat Ridge, CO 80033

PHONE: (303) 271-0525
WEBSITE: www.alpineval.org
EMAIL: alpineval@attbi.com

Connecticut

Greenwood Sudbury School

164 Main Street, Route 97
Hampton, CT 06247

PHONE: (860) 455-0505
FAX: (860) 455-0505
WEBSITE: www.greenwood.nu
EMAIL: info@greenwood.nu

Mountain Laurel Sudbury School

PO Box 40
Woodbury, CT 06798

PHONE: (860) 651-9854
WEBSITE: www.mountainlaurelsudbury.org
EMAIL: info@mountainlaurelsudbury.org

Delaware

The New School

PO Box 947
Newark, DE 19715

PHONE: (302) 456-9838
FAX: (302) 456-0921
WEBSITE: www.thenewschool.com
EMAIL: info@thenewschool.com

Florida

The Freedom School

PO Box 1513
Bonita Springs, FL 34133

PHONE: (941) 495-6743
FAX: (941) 495-6296
WEBSITE: www.thefreedomschool.com
EMAIL: mrbuyer@peganet.net

Full Circle Community School

1901 E. Robinson Street
Orlando, FL 32803

PHONE: (407) 365-6519
FAX: (407) 359-4087
EMAIL: fullcircleschool@aol.com

Illinois

The Chicago Sudbury School

PO Box 57737
Chicago, IL 60657

PHONE: (773) 348-4575
WEBSITE: www.chicagosudburyschool.org
EMAIL: info@chicagosudburyschool.org

Prairie Sage Sudbury School

PO Box 4185
Joliet, IL 60434

PHONE: (815) 730-0030
WEBSITE: www.prairiesage.org
EMAIL: melissa@prairiesage.org

Kansas

Four Winds Village School

PO Box 613
Kechi, KS 67067

PHONE: (316) 744-9402
EMAIL: fourwindsvillageschool@hotmail.com

Maine

Evergreen Sudbury School

Route 1, Box 1265-L
Hallowell, ME 04347

PHONE: (207) 622-9790
FAX: (207) 622-9790
WEBSITE: www.powerlink.net/evergreen
EMAIL: evergreens@adelphia.net.

Maryland

Fairhaven School

17900 Queen Anne Road
Upper Marlboro, MD 20774

PHONE: (301) 249-8060
WEBSITE: www.fairhavenschool.com
EMAIL: staff@fairhavenschool.com

New York

Hudson Valley Sudbury School

PO Box 159
West Hurley, NY 12491

PHONE: (845) 679-1002
FAX: (845) 679-1019
WEBSITE: www.hudsonvalleyschool.org
EMAIL: info@hudsonvalleyschool.org

Oregon

The Blue Mountain School

76132 Blue Mountain School Road
Cottage Grove, OR 97424

PHONE: (541) 942-7764
FAX: (541) 942-7957
WEBSITE: www.bluemountain-school.org
EMAIL: admissions@bluemountain-school.org

Pennsylvania

The Circle School

210 Oakleigh Avenue
Harrisburg, PA 17111

PHONE: (717) 564-6700
FAX: (717) 564-6570
WEBSITE: www.circleschool.org
EMAIL: info@circleschool.org

Texas

Brazos Valley Sudbury School

38110 Donigan Road
Brookshire, TX 77423

PHONE: (281) 375-7900
FAX: (281) 375-7900
WEBSITE: www.houstonsudbury.org
EMAIL: info@houstonsudbury.org

Washington

The Clearwater School

11006 34th Avenue NE
Seattle, WA 98125

PHONE: (206) 306-0060
WEBSITE: www.clearwaterschool.com
EMAIL: info@clearwaterschool.com

Waldorf Schools in the United States

The work in child development by Rudolph Steiner was the impetus for the Waldorf method. In the Waldorf method, children work toward balancing all the parts of schooling—artistic, academic, and practical work—and creating a cohesive whole. Waldorf students focus on relating what they learn to their own experience. By relating what they learn, they achieve ownership of the knowledge.

California

East Bay Waldorf School—High School

3800 Clark Road
El Sobrante, CA 94803

PHONE: (510) 223-3570
FAX: (510) 222-3141
WEBSITE: www.eastbaywaldorf.org
EMAIL: admin@eastbaywaldorf.org

Highland Hall Waldorf School

17100 Superior Street
Northridge, CA 91325

PHONE: (818) 349-1394, ext. 201
FAX: (818) 349-2390
WEBSITE: www.highlandhall.org/index_ctl.php
EMAIL: highlandhall@highlandhall.org

Mariah Bear, in addition to being one of the namesakes of the *Bears' Guides,* is the publisher of HowNow PocketPals, a division of Worldwise, Inc. As part of her quite nontraditional high school experience, she went to an alternative high school.

Bears' Guide: Please briefly describe your background prior to this educational experience.

Mariah Bear: I was, almost literally, born to pursue a nontraditional educational path. My father, Dr. John Bear, is widely acknowledged as one of the world's experts on nontraditional methods of obtaining an education. And by the time I was in high school, he was already supporting the family with his book (which went through a number of titles over the years, but is now called *Bears' Guide to Earning Degrees by Distance Learning*), his educational consulting business, and a range of related ventures, such as advising the FBI and the media on educational matters.

I consider myself lucky to have grown up in a family that valued education and intellectual curiosity over conformity, allowing me to follow my own path rather than fitting into the expected mold. While my parents were certainly not hippie dropouts by any stretch of the imagination, they were products of the sixties in that they appreciated alternative and unusual ways of looking at the world, and were not quick to judge. This allowed me a lot of latitude in how and what I studied—for better or worse!

BG: Please describe why you decided to pursue an alternate route for your high school education.

MB: The main reason was simply that I was bored. While my hometown's schools were/are better than many small-town schools, there were no Advanced Placement opportunities and no independent study available. I was able to talk some wonderful, supportive teachers into creative, special independent-study opportunities in the regular school, but they had no support from the administration. Of course at the time, being a teenager, I didn't realize what a great favor they were doing me, or how much work I was loading onto them. I was just glad that I didn't have to be bored in the more slowly paced classes. I figured that an even more alternative option would allow me to work at my own pace, learn everything I wanted, and not be bored anymore.

A secondary reason was that I was really not enjoying many of the social aspects of high school. As a "brain" and a "nerd," and a punk rocker at a time when that was fairly uncommon, I was the target for a lot of tormenting. Kids wanted to copy my homework or for me to help them during tests, and then would turn around and threaten to beat me and my friends up after school for being weirdos. It wasn't a scene I wanted to participate in for four years.

BG: Please describe the program in which you participated. Include the strengths and weaknesses that you perceived then and now.

MB: I didn't really participate in a program, so much as kind of drift into a mix-and-match thing, wherein I attended the local alternative school, created some independent-study projects for myself, took courses at a local community college, and did some summer courses at a university. The teachers at the alternative school were great about mentoring independent study and/or helping set me up with members of the community who had the knowledge and/or commitment they lacked.

At the time, I thought this was a fabulous scheme. I got to do what I wanted when I wanted, jam through high school on an accelerated schedule, and get to university, which was where I wanted to be.

In retrospect, I think I was given too much latitude and not enough structure. I skated through a lot, as smart kids do, with teachers assuming that, because I was smart, I was learning in my own way. But I was still a fifteen-year-old kid pumped up on hormones and eager to slack off and party, just as much as any other kid, so I think I could have used a bit more discipline. Easy to say now.

It was also disappointing that a number of the casual independent study arrangements didn't work out, as there was no formal contract and the expectations weren't clearly spelled out. For example, my sister, another girl, and I got a teacher at the alternative school to agree to teach us Latin. However, he was clearly not committed to the process and eventually stopped showing up for classes.

I think that the sort of crazy-quilt approach I took—some college courses, some traditional high school courses, some independent study with parents in a homeschooling scenario, some with community members—was a surprisingly good one. But it would have been better with a firmer plan and more accountability from both myself and the education providers.

BG: Do you feel you missed out on anything by not participating in a traditional high school? If so, what?

MB: Since I had access to not just one but two high schools (the traditional one and the alternative one), as well as the community college, I really don't feel that I missed out on any of the intangibles, such as the company of other people my age or the chance to do P.E. If I hadn't had some courses with others, I do think I would have felt their absence, as it is important for kids to have a gang at that age.

BG: What, if anything, did you gain by not participating in a traditional high school?

MB: I gained self-confidence and a healthy wariness about authority figures. In the example of the Latin class, my friends and I (the "irresponsible" kids) were on track, and the teacher let us down. The framework I was working in—designing my own program, evaluating how it was working for me, defending these choices to my parents, the school officials, and concerned community members—allowed me to see this in context. While the short-term disappointment was real, the long-term effect was that of confirming that I was capable of making mature, adult choices and sticking by them, and that's a powerful tool for a young person.

Indeed, when I got to university, I was surprised at how young and immature the students seemed. We were the same age, but they were accustomed to being told what to do, having choices made for them, and regarding teachers as unapproachable authority figures. My self-confidence and ability to work with professors as peers (more knowledgeable peers, of course, but not godlike creatures on a pedestal) stood me in good stead.

BG: Please describe your background since completing your high school education.

MB: I initially went to Evergreen State College in Olympia, Washington, because I liked the alternative nature of their programs and, perhaps more importantly, they would accept me without a high school diploma. (I returned home for a couple of days at the end of my first quarter of college to get my diploma, as a sort of courtesy from the high school—my college professors found that amusing.) However, I soon realized that I'd had enough of designing my own programs and being with immature students for a while, and decided I wanted something a bit more challenging and structured. So, after my first semester, I transferred to UC Berkeley. I graduated with a 4.0 in my field, mass communications and, a few years later, went to New York University for an M.A. in journalism, on the prestigious McCracken Fellowship.

BG: If you had it to do all over again, would you make the same choices? What would you do differently?

MB: I would ask for (demand!) more assistance from my parents or an educational counselor in putting together a more structured independent program that would better meet normal future adult needs (more community college courses in analytical writing, less independent study in music performance!). That said, it worked amazingly well, and I really can't complain. I had a lot of fun, did some really neat things, and went on to successful and rewarding undergraduate and graduate degrees, and a career I love.

Rudolf Steiner College

9200 Fair Oaks Boulevard
Fair Oaks, CA 95628

PHONE: (800) 515-8203
FAX: (916) 961-8731
WEBSITE: www.steinercollege.org
EMAIL: rsc@steinercollege.org

Sacramento Waldorf School

3750 Bannister Road
Fair Oaks, CA 95628

PHONE: (916) 961-3900
FAX: (916) 961-3970
WEBSITE: www.sacwaldorf.org
EMAIL: smack@sacwaldorf.org

San Francisco Waldorf School

245 Valencia Street
San Francisco, CA 94102

PHONE: (415) 431-2736
FAX: (415) 431-1712
WEBSITE: www.sfwaldorf.org
EMAIL: highschool@sfwaldorf.org

Summerfield Waldorf School

655 Willowside Road
Santa Rosa, CA 95401

PHONE: (707) 575-7194
FAX: (707) 575-3217
WEBSITE: www.summerfieldwaldorf.org
EMAIL: sws@summerfieldwaldorf.org

Colorado

Denver Waldorf School

735 East Florida Avenue
Denver, CO 80210

PHONE: (303) 777-0531, ext. 106
FAX: (303) 744-1216
WEBSITE: www.denverwaldorf.org
EMAIL: enroll@denverwaldorf.org

Shining Mountain Waldorf School

4301 Broadway
Boulder, CO 80304

PHONE: (303) 447-1973
FAX: (303) 447-1917
WEBSITE: www.shiningmountain.boulder.net
EMAIL: smws@dnvr.uswest.net

Hawaii

Honolulu Waldorf School

1339 Hunakai Street
Honolulu, HI 96816

PHONE: (808) 735-9311
FAX: (808) 735-5292
WEBSITE: www.honoluluwaldorf.org
EMAIL: hwscoll@lava.net

Kula Makua-Adult Waldorf Education

350 Ulua Street
Honolulu, HI 96821

PHONE: (808) 259-5407
FAX: (808) 373-2040
EMAIL: kulamakua@juno.com

Illinois

Arcturus Rudolf Steiner Education Program

PO Box 607116
6531 North Lakewood
Chicago, IL 60626

PHONE: (773) 761-3026
FAX: (773) 761-6652
WEBSITE: www.arcturus.info
EMAIL: arcturus23@hotmail.com

Chicago Waldorf School

1300 West Loyola Avenue
Chicago, IL 60626

PHONE: (773) 465-2662
FAX: (773) 465-6648
WEBSITE: www.chicagowaldorf.org
EMAIL: info@chicagowaldorf.org

Maryland

Washington Waldorf School

4800 Sangamore Road
Bethesda, MD 20816-3501

PHONE: (301) 229-6107
FAX: (301) 229-9379
WEBSITE: www.washingtonwaldorf.org
EMAIL: info@washingtonwaldorf.org

Massachusetts

Waldorf School, Lexington

703 Massachusetts Avenue
Lexington, MA 02420

PHONE: (781) 860-7430
FAX: (781) 863-7221
WEBSITE: www.thewaldorfschool.org
EMAIL: contact@thewaldorfschool.org

Michigan

Rudolf Steiner School of Ann Arbor

2309 Packard Road
Ann Arbor, MI 48104

PHONE: (734) 669-9394
FAX: (734) 669-9396
EMAIL: rshs@wwnet.net

New Hampshire

High Mowing School

PO Box 850
Abbot Hill Road
Wilton, NH 03086

PHONE: (603) 654-2391
FAX: (603) 654-6588
WEBSITE: www.highmowing.org
EMAIL: highmowing@highmowing.org

New Mexico

Santa Fe Waldorf School

310 West Zia Road
Santa Fe, NM 87505

PHONE: (505) 992-0566
FAX: (505) 992-0568
EMAIL: rswing@aol.com

New York

Green Meadow Waldorf School

307 Hungry Hollow Road
Chestnut Ridge, NY 10977

PHONE: (845) 356-2514
FAX: (845) 356-2921
WEBSITE: www.gmws.org
EMAIL: info@gmws.org

Hawthorne Valley School—High School

330 Route 21C
Ghent, NY 12075

PHONE: (518) 672-7092
FAX: (518) 672-0181
WEBSITE: www.hawthornevalleyschool.org
EMAIL: hawthornevalley@taconic.net

Rudolf Steiner School

15 East 78th Street
New York, NY 10021

PHONE: (212) 879-1101
FAX: (212) 794-1554
WEBSITE: www.steiner.edu
EMAIL: info@steiner.edu

Waldorf School of Garden City

Cambridge Avenue
Garden City, NY 11530

PHONE: (516) 742-3434, ext. 119
FAX: (516) 742-3457
WEBSITE: www.waldorfgarden.org
EMAIL: admissions@waldorfgarden.org

Waldorf School of Sarasota Springs

122 Regent Street
Saratoga Springs, NY 12866

PHONE: (518) 587-2224
WEBSITE: www.waldorf.saratoga.ny.us
EMAIL: thewaldorfschool@yahoo.com

Oregon

Portland Waldorf School

215 SE Ninth Avenue
Portland, OR 97202

PHONE: (503) 234-9660
FAX: (503) 234-6206
WEBSITE: www.portlandwaldorfschool.org
EMAIL: info@portlandwaldorfschool.org

Pennsylvania

Camphill Special School

1784 Fairview Road
Glenmoore, PA 19343

PHONE: (610) 469-9236
FAX: (610) 469-9758
WEBSITE: www.camphillfoundation.org
EMAIL: bvrrn@aol.com

Kimberton Waldorf School

PO Box 350
410 West Seven Stars Road
Kimberton, PA 19442

PHONE: (610) 933-3635
FAX: (610) 917-3805
WEBSITE: www.kimberton.org
EMAIL: admissions@kimberton.org

Texas

Austin Waldorf School

8700 South View Road
Austin, TX 78737

PHONE: (512) 301-9550
FAX: (512) 301-9566
WEBSITE: www.austinwaldorf.org
EMAIL: awsmail@texas.net

Vermont

Lake Champlain Waldorf School

PO Box 250
359 Turtle Lane
Shelburne, VT 05482

PHONE: (802) 985-2827
FAX: (802) 985-2834
WEBSITE: www.lcwaldorf.org
EMAIL: lcwald@together.net

Washington

Sound Circle Center

16054 32nd Avenue NE
Lake Forest Park, WA 98155

PHONE: (206) 361-5931
FAX: (206) 361-5931
EMAIL: dmm@soundcircle.org

CHAPTER 6

Charter Schools

"More than 1.8 million people [are] involved in charter schools—showing strong grassroots support—proof positive that charter schools have become a vibrant part of communities nationwide."

—Jeanne Allen, President, Center for Education Reform

Charter schools are founded with the idea of providing a different kind of education than most students can get within the traditional high school environment. Although public, they do not have to follow many of the state's administrative rules. In addition, they have one thing over most other methods of earning a high school diploma non-traditionally—they are free. Like other public schools, they are funded with tax dollars.

While cost alone should not be the determining factor in the alternative education you choose, charter schools might be a good place to start your search. Charter schools run the gamut from site-based to independent study, from online to home-based.

There is no one specific type of charter school. This is one of the many reasons why charter schools have succeeded; there are few rules governing what they can or cannot do. While a public school that wants to hire someone to teach six hours of music a week must deal with many rules, including union regulations, a charter school can just hire the person, pay them an hourly wage, and be done with it.

What to Look For

Look for local control of the school. While in theory all charter schools have local control, some school districts have had trouble letting go. The advantage to site-based control and fewer regulations is that there could very well be less bureaucracy.

The Center for Education Reform, the nation's leading charter school organization, regularly ranks state charter laws in terms of "how each encourages or inhibits the development of autonomous charter schools." In addition, the center groups states in a report card format. Those states with the most charter-friendly laws get an A. Those with the least friendly laws earn an F. Why should this be important to you, the consumer? Simply put, the stronger the charter school law, the more possibility for innovation in programs. It's no surprise that Arizona, ranked number one, also has more charter schools than any other state in the country.

These are the rankings as of 2003. There are no charter school laws, and thus no charter schools, in Alabama, Kentucky, Maryland, Maine, Montana, Nebraska, North Dakota, South Dakota, Vermont, Washington, or West Virginia.

Ranking: A

1. Arizona
2. Minnesota
3. District of Columbia
4. Delaware
5. Michigan
6. Indiana
7. Massachusetts

Ranking: B

8. Florida
9. Colorado
10. New York
11. Ohio
12. North Carolina
13. Pennsylvania
14. Missouri

15. California
16. Oregon
17. New Jersey
18. Wisconsin
19. Texas
20. New Mexico

Ranking: C

21. Illinois
22. Oklahoma
23. South Carolina
24. Louisiana
25. Georgia
26. Utah
27. Idaho

28. Connecticut
29. Nevada
30. Wyoming
31. New Hampshire (no high schools)
32. Tennessee
33. Hawaii

Ranking: D

34. Alaska
35. Arkansas
36. Rhode Island

37. Virginia
38. Kansas

Ranking: F

39. Iowa
40. Mississippi

Frequently Asked Questions

What is a charter school?

Contrary to the beliefs of many, charter schools are not private schools run with state money. Charter schools are public schools subject to some, but not all, of the same rules that guide public education. Where the rules are different, it is specifically to create a different model from the typical public school. In addition, while many charter schools are site-based, there are charter schools that are solely online or available through independent study. Some charter schools were set up specifically to provide resources for homeschooling families.

Charter schools are operated under performance contracts. If they don't meet certain goals, they can be shut down. This provides a powerful impetus for them to succeed.

How much does it cost to attend a charter school?

Charter schools are free. Or rather, as free as any public school can be. In other words, they are paid for with your tax dollars, but you don't have any up-front costs. This is what can make charter schools a good choice for many seeking an alternative education.

School Information

The number of charter schools in the United States is growing exponentially, and it would be impossible to list all of the available charter schools. Instead, I attempt to provide a wide range of possibilities, factoring in diversity of curriculum, location, the range of programs offered, and other variables.

School Types

Site-based refers to those schools that are structured similarly to traditional high schools (you go to a place to learn). *Online* refers to those schools that are completely or mostly delivered over the Internet. *Independent study,* commonly called correspondence study, are programs completed through the mail with pen and paper. *Homeschool resource* programs offer curriculum and other support for students being taught at home by their parents or other adults.

It can sometimes be difficult to distinguish between independent study programs and homeschool resource programs. Wherever possible, it's best to let the schools speak for themselves. In fact, there is little to distinguish the two programs, and the terms are often used interchangeably when the homeschooling student is using independent study materials. The difference lies most often in who is running the program and their particular philosophy of education. Both are excellent opportunities; which is better is up to you.

School Size

Although I have arbitrarily divided the schools into small, medium, large, and very large, readers should not surmise that this in any way refers to the quality of the program. Some of the smaller schools are quite good precisely because they are small. Some of the larger schools are also quite good because of the number of programs that they can offer. My rough categories are

> Small = up to 150 students
> Medium = 151 to 300 students
> Large = 300 to 600 students
> Very Large = 601 and above

This scale is based on the sizes of most charter schools—very few charter schools have eight hundred students. Typically these schools are quite small compared to regular public schools, which is one of charter schools' key advantages.

School Age

The first thing that you may notice is that very few of these charter schools are even ten years old. Charter schools are a new phenomenon; the first, City Academy, started in Minnesota only in 1992. While it is certainly a good idea to wait a year or two to see if a new charter school will survive, the majority of schools have only come into being within the last five years. Some schools have been in existence much longer, but they were formerly alternative schools. The advent of charters brought the possibility of financial stability, so these alternative schools opted to convert to the charter system.

For detailed descriptions of each school listed below, the best resource is the *National Charter School Directory* (Center for Education Reform [202] 822-9000). Melanie Looney, the editor, does a superior job of providing comprehensive information on the many thousands of charter schools, both elementary and secondary, which is an almost insurmountable task.

Schools

The schools listed below offer a wide variety of programs, from military school to performing arts academies, from online schools to schools for at-risk youth. Which will work best for you depends upon your personal life circumstances, but you certainly have a wide variety to choose from.

Alaska

Delta Cyber School

PO Box 1672
Delta Junction, AK 99737

PHONE: (907) 895-1043 or (877) 895-1043
FAX: (907) 895-5198
WEBSITE: www.dcSouthk12.ak.us:8001
EMAIL: mary.corcoran@dgsdmail.dgsd.k12.ak.us
YEAR FOUNDED: 1997
SPONSOR: Delta/Greely School District
TYPE: Online
SIZE: Small

Offers a challenging curriculum entirely online.

Family Partnership Charter School

3339 Fairbanks Street
Anchorage, AK 99503

PHONE: (907) 742-3700
FAX: (907) 742-3710
WEBSITE: www.fpcs.org
EMAIL: fpcsoffice@alaskalifenet
YEAR FOUNDED: 1997
SPONSOR: Anchorage School District
TYPE: Homeschool resource
SIZE: Large

Family Partnership provides resources and teachers for homeschooling families.

New Beginnings Charter School

609 Third Street
Fairbanks, AK 99707

PHONE: (907) 456-2807
FAX: (907) 456-2849
YEAR FOUNDED: 1997
SPONSOR: Fairbanks North Star School District
TYPE: Site-based
SIZE: Small

Focuses on children with substance abuse problems.

Arizona

Accelerated Learning Center

4101 East Shea Boulevard
Phoenix, AZ 85028

PHONE: (602) 485-0309
FAX: (602) 485-9356
YEAR FOUNDED: 1997
SPONSOR: State Board of Education
TYPE: Site-based
SIZE: Medium

A school-to-work program.

Air Academy Charter High School

7544 West Indian School Road
Phoenix, AZ 85033

PHONE: (623) 247-4100
FAX: (623) 247-4101
YEAR FOUNDED: 2001
SPONSOR: State Board for Charter Schools
TYPE: Site-based
SIZE: Medium

Focuses on aviation industry careers.

Alternative Computerized Education Charter School

1929 North Stone
Tucson, AZ 85705

PHONE: (520) 623-5843
FAX: (520) 791-9893
YEAR FOUNDED: 1996
SPONSOR: State Board of Education
TYPE: Self-directed, resident
SIZE: Medium

Its curriculum revolves around technology and business.

AmeriSchools Academy #001

1333 West Camelback Road
Phoenix, AZ 85013

PHONE: (602) 532-0100
FAX: (602) 326-7452
WEBSITE: www.amerischools.org
YEAR FOUNDED: 1998
SPONSOR: State Board for Charter Schools
TYPE: Site-based
SIZE: Small

A college-prepatory program.

AmeriSchools Academy #003

7444 East Broadway
Tucson, AZ 85364

PHONE: (520) 722-1200
FAX: (520) 624-4376
WEBSITE: www.amerischools.org
YEAR FOUNDED: 1998
SPONSOR: State Board for Charter Schools
TYPE: Site-based
SIZE: Small

A college-preparatory program.

Arizona Academy of Science and Technology

1111 North First Street
Phoenix, AZ 85004

PHONE: (602) 937-4017
FAX: (602) 707-5962
YEAR FOUNDED: 1998
SPONSOR: State Board for Charter Schools
TYPE: Site-based
SIZE: Small

Emphasizes science and technology in the curriculum, but provides a well-rounded course of study.

Arizona Agribusiness and Equine Center

7050 South 24th Street
Phoenix, AZ 85040

PHONE: (602) 297-8500
FAX: (602) 297-8540
YEAR FOUNDED: 1997
SPONSOR: State Board for Charter Schools
TYPE: Site-based
SIZE: Small

Special features include programs in equine science, animal science, veterinarian technology, biotechnology, ecology/conservation, and business.

Arizona Agribusiness and Equine Center #2

18401 North 32nd Street
Phoenix, AZ 85032

PHONE: (602) 243-8004
FAX: (602) 243-8001
YEAR FOUNDED: 1998
SPONSOR: State Board for Charter Schools
TYPE: Site-based
SIZE: Small

Special features include programs in equine science, animal science, veterinarian technology, biotechnology, ecology/conservation, and business.

Arizona Agribusiness and Equine Center #3

6000 West Olive Avenue
Glendale, AZ 85302

PHONE: (623) 243-8004
YEAR FOUNDED: 2001
SPONSOR: State Board for Charter Schools
TYPE: Site-based
SIZE: Medium

Special features include programs in equine science, animal science, veterinarian technology, biotechnology, ecology/conservation, and business.

Arizona School for the Arts

1313 North Second Street
Phoenix, AZ 85004

PHONE: (602) 257-1444
FAX: (602) 257-7795
YEAR FOUNDED: 1995
SPONSOR: State Board for Charter Schools
TYPE: Site-based
SIZE: Medium

The curriculum fuses fine and performing arts with a traditional course of study.

Capitol High School

1650 Willow Creek Road
Prescott, AZ 86301

PHONE: (928) 778-1422
FAX: (928) 778-1756
YEAR FOUNDED: 2001
SPONSOR: State Board for Charter Schools
TYPE: Site-based
SIZE: Small

Although site-based, students are able to work at their own pace to complete graduation requirements.

Career Success High School

1777 West Camelback Road, N-100
Phoenix, AZ 85015

PHONE: (602) 285-5525
FAX: (602) 285-0026
YEAR FOUNDED: 2000
SPONSOR: State Board of Education
TYPE: Site-based
SIZE: Large

The focus is on careers and job readiness.

Carmel Community Arts and Technology School

97 West Oakland Avenue
Chandler, AZ 85225

PHONE: (480) 899-6600
FAX: (480) 899-4122
YEAR FOUNDED: 1999
SPONSOR: State Board for Charter Schools
TYPE: Site-based
SIZE: Small

Offers programs in the arts, technology, and career preparation.

Center for Academic Success #1

650 East Wilcox
Sierra Vista, AZ 85635

PHONE: (520) 417-9913
FAX: (520) 417-9910
YEAR FOUNDED: 1996
SPONSOR: State Board for Charter Schools
TYPE: Site-based
SIZE: Medium

The spotlight is on career preparation.

Center for Academic Success #2

510 G Avenue
Douglas, AZ 85607

PHONE: (520) 364-8906
FAX: (520) 417-9910
YEAR FOUNDED: 1996
SPONSOR: State Board for Charter Schools
TYPE: Site-based
SIZE: Small

The spotlight is on career preparation.

Center for Academic Success #3

1400 B San Antonio
Douglas, AZ 85607

PHONE: (520) 458-4200
FAX: (520) 458-1409
YEAR FOUNDED: 2000
SPONSOR: State Board for Charter Schools
TYPE: Site-based
SIZE: Small

The spotlight is on career preparation.

Clear View Charter School (Springerville)

20725 East Main
Springerville, AZ 85938

PHONE: (928) 634-7320
FAX: (928) 634-7494
YEAR FOUNDED: 2000
SPONSOR: Peach Springs Unified District
TYPE: Site-based
SIZE: Small

This school's program is for at-risk youth.

Clear View Charter School (St. John's)

205 South First Street West
St. Johns, AZ 85936

PHONE: (928) 634-7320
FAX: (928) 634-7494
YEAR FOUNDED: 2000
SPONSOR: Peach Springs Unified District
TYPE: Site-based
SIZE: Small

This school's program is for at-risk youth.

Compass High School

8250 East 22nd Street
Tucson, AZ 85710

PHONE: (520) 296-4070
FAX: (520) 296-4103
YEAR FOUNDED: 2001
SPONSOR: State Board for Charter Schools
TYPE: Site-based
SIZE: Small

The curriculum is based on the Arizona State Standards.

Desert Eagle Secondary School

3191 North Longmore
Scottsdale, AZ 85256

PHONE: (480) 850-8335
FAX: (480) 941-7207
YEAR FOUNDED: 1996
SPONSOR: State Board of Education
TYPE: Site-based
SIZE: Medium

The Pima-Maricopa Native American culture provides the framework for this school.

Desert Rose Academy Charter School

40 West Fort Lowell
Tucson, AZ 85705

PHONE: (520) 696-0819
FAX: (520) 696-1743
YEAR FOUNDED: 2001
SPONSOR: State Board for Charter Schools
TYPE: Site-based
SIZE: Medium

The goal is that no discipline problems exist in order to better enhance learning.

Desert Technology High School

2818 Sweetwater Avenue
Lake Havasu City, AZ 86406

PHONE: (520) 453-3383
FAX: (520) 453-3886
YEAR FOUNDED: 1997
SPONSOR: Higley Unified School District
TYPE: Site-based
SIZE: Small

Special features include programs in technology and career preparation.

E.A.G.L.E. Academy

423 South Colorado Road
Golden Valley, AZ 86413

PHONE: (520) 565-3400
FAX: (520) 565-3454
YEAR FOUNDED: 1999
SPONSOR: Higley Unified School District
TYPE: Site-based
SIZE: Medium

An added enhancement is a 144-day school year (but same number of minutes as traditional schools). This could increase the likelihood of school attendance for some students.

E-Institute

4744 West Grovers Avenue
Glendale, AZ 85308

PHONE: (623) 547-8806
FAX: (623) 547-2841
YEAR FOUNDED: 2000
SPONSOR: State Board for Charter Schools
TYPE: Site-based
SIZE: Small

Special focus is on technology and career preparation.

El Dorado High School

2200 North Arizona Avenue, #17
Chandler, AZ 85224

PHONE: (480) 726-9536
FAX: (480) 726-9543
YEAR FOUNDED: 1999
SPONSOR: State Board for Charter Schools
TYPE: Site-based
SIZE: Medium

All subjects are taught in an interdisciplinary manner.

Excalibur Charter School

10839 East Apache Trail
Apache Junction, AZ 85220

PHONE: (480) 373-9575
FAX: (480) 373-9576
YEAR FOUNDED: 1999
SPONSOR: Higley Unified School District
TYPE: Site-based
SIZE: Medium

Emphasis is on careers.

Excel Education Centers (Chino Valley)

1985 North Road 1 West
Chino Valley, AZ 86323

PHONE: (928) 636-1444
FAX: (928) 636-1414
WEBSITE: www.exceleducationcenters.org/chino.htm
YEAR FOUNDED: 1999
SPONSOR: State Board for Charter Schools
TYPE: Site-based (computer-assisted instruction, small classes)
SIZE: Small

Provides a combination of training in job readiness and independent living skills.

Excel Education Centers (Cottonwood)

1229 East Cherry Street
Cottonwood, AZ 86326

PHONE: (928) 634-2065
FAX: (928) 639-2952
WEBSITE: www.exceleducationcenters.org/cottonwoodhomepage.htm
YEAR FOUNDED: 1995
SPONSOR: State Board for Charter Schools
TYPE: Site-based (computer-assisted instruction, small classes)
SIZE: Small

Provides a combination of training in job readiness and independent living skills.

Excel Education Centers (Flagstaff)

2229 East Spruce Street
Flagstaff, AZ 86001

PHONE: (928) 214-7442
FAX: (928) 214-7256
WEBSITE: www.exceleducationcenters.org/flagstaf2.htm
YEAR FOUNDED: 1996
SPONSOR: State Board for Charter Schools
TYPE: Site-based (computer-assisted instruction, small classes)
SIZE: Medium

Provides a combination of training in job readiness and independent living skills.

Excel Education Centers (Fort Mohave)

1385 Gemini Street
Fort Mohave, AZ 86426

PHONE: (928) 758-5472
FAX: (928) 758-2821

WEBSITE: www.exceleducationcenters.org/fort_mohave.htm
YEAR FOUNDED: 2001
SPONSOR: State Board for Charter Schools
TYPE: Site-based (computer-assisted instruction, small classes)
SIZE: Small

Provides a combination of training in job readiness and independent living skills.

Excel Education Centers (Prescott)

1040 Whipple Street, Suite 401
Prescott, AZ 86305

PHONE: (928) 541-1701
FAX: (928) 778-5766
WEBSITE: www.exceleducationcenters.org/prescotthomepage.htm
YEAR FOUNDED: 1995
SPONSOR: State Board for Charter Schools
TYPE: Site-based (computer-assisted instruction, small classes)
SIZE: Medium

Provides a combination of training in job readiness and independent living skills.

Excel Education Centers (Prescott Valley)

7515 Long Look Drive
Prescott Valley, AZ 86314

PHONE: (928) 775-6681
FAX: (928) 775-6691
WEBSITE: www.exceleducationcenters.org/PVhomepage.htm
YEAR FOUNDED: 1996
SPONSOR: State Board for Charter Schools
TYPE: Site-based (computer-assisted instruction, small classes)
SIZE: Medium

Provides a combination of training in job readiness and independent living skills.

Excel Education Centers (San Carlos)

Moon Base Road, Highway 70
Peridot, AZ 85542

PHONE: (928) 475-2292
FAX: (928) 475-2441
WEBSITE: www.exceleducationcenters.org/SChomepage.htm
YEAR FOUNDED: 1996
SPONSOR: State Board for Charter Schools

TYPE: Site-based (computer-assisted instruction, small classes)
SIZE: Medium

Provides a combination of training in job readiness and independent living skills.

Flagstaff Arts and Leadership Academy

3100 North Fort Valley Road, #41
Flagstaff, AZ 86001

PHONE: (928) 779-7223
FAX: (928) 779-7041
WEBSITE: www.fala.apscc.k12.az.us
YEAR FOUNDED: 1996
SPONSOR: State Board of Education
TYPE: Site-based
SIZE: Small

Provides a combination of training in fine arts education and leadership.

Foothills Academy

6424 East Cave Creek Road
Cave Creek, AZ 85331

PHONE: (480) 488-5583
FAX: (480) 488-6902
WEBSITE: www.foothillsacademy.com
YEAR FOUNDED: 1997
SPONSOR: State Board of Education
TYPE: Site-based
SIZE: Small

Offers several different tracks, including environment and the arts, technical, cultural, and aesthetic literacy.

Gateway Community High School

108 North 40th Street
Phoenix, AZ 85034

PHONE: (602) 392-5466
FAX: (602) 392-5410
WEBSITE: www.gwc.maricopa.edu/high_school
YEAR FOUNDED: 1995
SPONSOR: State Board of Education
TYPE: Site-based
SIZE: Medium

The focus is on technical and health-care careers.

Genesis Academy

640 North First Avenue
Phoenix, AZ 85003

PHONE: (602) 223-4200
FAX: (602) 223-4210

WEBSITE: www.genesisacademy.com
YEAR FOUNDED: 1997
SPONSOR: State Board for Charter Schools
TYPE: Site-based
SIZE: Small

Genesis serves high-risk youth with a focus on academic rigor.

Ha:sañ Preparatory and Leadership Charter School

1333 East Tenth Street
Tucson, AZ 85719

PHONE: (520) 882-8826
FAX: (520) 882-8651
WEBSITE: www.hasanprep.org
YEAR FOUNDED: 1999
SPONSOR: State Board for Charter Schools
TYPE: Site-based
SIZE: Medium

The Tohono O'odham Himdag culture provides the curriculum framework.

Heritage Academy, Inc.

32 South Center
Mesa, AZ 85210

PHONE: (480) 969-5641
FAX: (480) 686-6972
YEAR FOUNDED: 1995
SPONSOR: State Board for Charter Schools
TYPE: Site-based
SIZE: Large

The great men and women of history provide the framework for instruction.

Humanities and Sciences Academy

Dine College, Building AJ
Tsaile, AZ 86556

PHONE: (800) 762-0010
FAX: (928) 650-1777
WEBSITE: www.humsci.org
YEAR FOUNDED: 1999
SPONSOR: State Board for Charter Schools
TYPE: Site-based
SIZE: Small

The precepts of the program include the teaching of the humanities and sciences, social responsibility, employability preparation, and college preparation.

Humanities and Sciences Academy

1105 East Broadway Road
Tempe, AZ 85282

PHONE: (480) 317-5900
FAX: (480) 829-4999
WEBSITE: www.humsci.org
YEAR FOUNDED: 2001
SPONSOR: State Board for Charter Schools
TYPE: Site-based
SIZE: Small

The precepts of the program include the teaching of the humanities and sciences, social responsibility, employability preparation, and college preparation.

Humanities and Sciences Academy

5201 North Seventh Street
Phoenix, AZ 85014

PHONE: (602) 650-1333
FAX: (602) 650-1881
WEBSITE: www.humsci.org
YEAR FOUNDED: 1997
SPONSOR: State Board for Charter Schools
TYPE: Site-based
SIZE: Medium

The precepts of the program include the teaching of the humanities and sciences, social responsibility, employability preparation, and college preparation.

Integrity Education Centre, Inc.

1290 North Scottsdale Road, #122
Tempe, AZ 85281

PHONE: (480) 731-4829
FAX: (480) 731-6380
YEAR FOUNDED: 1998
SPONSOR: Higley Unified School District
TYPE: Site-based
SIZE: Small

Special features include wellness training for mind and body and character education.

Intelli-School (Glendale)

13806 North 51st Avenue
Glendale, AZ 85306

PHONE: (623) 564-7220
FAX: (623) 564-7301
WEBSITE: www.intellischool.org
EMAIL: info@intellischool.org
YEAR FOUNDED: 1999

SPONSOR: State Board for Charter Schools
TYPE: Self-paced resident
SIZE: Small

Clientele includes special-needs students and nontraditional learners.

Intelli-School (Metro Center)

3101 West Peoria Avenue, #B305
Phoenix, AZ 85029

PHONE: (602) 564-7220
FAX: (602) 564-7301
WEBSITE: www.intellischool.org
EMAIL: info@intellischool.org
YEAR FOUNDED: 1996
SPONSOR: State Board for Charter Schools
TYPE: Self-paced resident
SIZE: Small

Clientele includes special-needs students and nontraditional learners.

Intelli-School (Paradise Valley)

1107 East Bell Road, #109A
Phoenix, AZ 85022

PHONE: (602) 564-7208
FAX: (602) 564-7301
WEBSITE: www.intellischool.org
EMAIL: info@intellischool.org
YEAR FOUNDED: 1999
SPONSOR: State Board for Charter Schools
TYPE: Self-paced resident
SIZE: Small

Clientele includes special-needs students and nontraditional learners.

International Commerce Institute

5201 North Seventh Street
Phoenix, AZ 85014

PHONE: (602) 650-1116
FAX: (602) 650-1881
WEBSITE: www.humsci.org
YEAR FOUNDED: 1997
SPONSOR: State Board for Charter Schools
TYPE: Site-based
SIZE: Very large

Special features include occupational education, social responsibility, and employability training.

International Commerce Institute (Tempe)

1105 East Broadway Road
Tempe, AZ 85282

PHONE: (800) 762-0010
FAX: (480) 650-1777
WEBSITE: www.internationalstudies.org
YEAR FOUNDED: 2000
SPONSOR: State Board for Charter Schools
TYPE: Site-based
SIZE: Small

Special features include occupational education, social responsibility, and employability training.

International Commerce Institute (Tsaile)

Dine College, Building AJ
Tsaile, AZ 86556

PHONE: (800) 762-0010
FAX: (928) 650-1777
WEBSITE: www.humsci.org
YEAR FOUNDED: 1999
SPONSOR: State Board for Charter Schools
TYPE: Site-based
SIZE: Small

Special features include occupational education, social responsibility, and employability training.

International Studies Academy

4744 West Grovers Avenue
Glendale, AZ 85308

PHONE: (623) 547-8806
FAX: (623) 547-2841
WEBSITE: www.internationalstudies.org
EMAIL: info@internationalstudies.org
YEAR FOUNDED: 1996
SPONSOR: State Board of Education
TYPE: Site-based
SIZE: Medium

Has a special focus on international studies and offers intensive language studies.

Ira H. Hayes High School

PO Box 10899
Bapchule, AZ 85221

PHONE: (520) 315-3496
FAX: (520) 315-1199
WEBSITE: www.cbcschools.com
EMAIL: irah.hayes@cbcschools.com
YEAR FOUNDED: 2000

SPONSOR: State Board for Charter Schools
TYPE: Site-based
SIZE: Small

Preparation for higher education, technical schools, and life.

Isaac Charter School

4006 West Osborn Road
Phoenix, AZ 85019

PHONE: (602) 731-8050
FAX: (602) 791-8061
YEAR FOUNDED: 2000
SPONSOR: State Board for Charter Schools
TYPE: Site-based
SIZE: Small

Emphasis is on math, science, and technology, but provides a solid grounding in all the core subjects.

Juniper Canyon Alternative School

221 Brewer Road
Sedona, AZ 86336

PHONE: (928) 204-6830
FAX: (928) 282-0232
YEAR FOUNDED: 1997
SPONSOR: Sedona-Oak Creek Joint Unified School District
TYPE: Site-based
SIZE: Small

Goals are the teaching of personal life skills and intellectual growth.

Kachina Country Day School

8620 East McDonald Drive
Scottsdale, AZ 85251

PHONE: (480) 922-8751
FAX: (480) 922-5244
WEBSITE: www.kachina.org
EMAIL: chrisk@kachina.k12.az.us
YEAR FOUNDED: 1996
SPONSOR: State Board of Education
TYPE: Site-based
SIZE: Small

Has an emphasis on fitness, neuro-feedback, and college preparation.

Kestrel High School

325 North Washington Avenue
Prescott, AZ 86304

PHONE: (928) 541-1090
FAX: (928) 541-9939
YEAR FOUNDED: 2000
SPONSOR: State Board for Charter Schools
TYPE: Site-based
SIZE: Small

In addition to education, it places a premium on environmental stewardship, wellness, independent thinking, creativity, and community service.

Kino Academy

2055 North Grand Avenue
Nogales, AZ 85621

PHONE: (520) 218-5190
FAX: (520) 218-5132
YEAR FOUNDED: 2001
SPONSOR: State Board for Charter Schools
TYPE: Online
SIZE: Medium

Its focus is on offering the core academic subjects in a challenging and creative manner.

Lake Havasu Charter School

1055 Empire Drive
Lake Havasu City, AZ 86404

PHONE: (520) 505-5427
FAX: (520) 505-3533
YEAR FOUNDED: 1996
SPONSOR: State Board for Charter Schools
TYPE: Site-based
SIZE: Small

Its emphases are vocational and technology learning.

Liberty Academy

3015 South Power Road
Mesa, AZ 85212

PHONE: (480) 830-3444
FAX: (480) 830-4335
WEBSITE: www.liberty-academy.com
EMAIL: info@liberty-academy.com
YEAR FOUNDED: 1999
SPONSOR: State Board for Charter Schools
TYPE: Site-based
SIZE: Medium

Liberty Academy operates under the premise that all schools should be small. Strong parental involvement is actively encouraged. The student, parents, and instructor meet to construct an individualized learning plan.

Liberty High School

482 Hagen Road
Globe, AZ 85501

PHONE: (520) 402-8024
FAX: (520) 402-0038
YEAR FOUNDED: 1997
SPONSOR: State Board of Education
TYPE: Site-based
SIZE: Small

Major focal point is school-to-work training.

Life School College Preparatory Gold

2929 E. McKellips Road
Mesa, AZ 85213

PHONE: (480) 924-4396
FAX: (480) 632-2077
WEBSITE: www.lifeschoolgold.com
EMAIL: info@lifeschoolgold.com
YEAR FOUNDED: 1999
SPONSOR: State Board for Charter Schools
TYPE: Site-based
SIZE: Medium

Life School College Prep operates under the premise that all schools should be small. Strong parental involvement is actively encouraged. The student, parents, and instructor meet to construct an individualized learning plan.

Metropolitan Arts Institute

660 East Van Buren, Building #3
Phoenix, AZ 85004-2222

PHONE: (602) 252-2530
FAX: (602) 252-2540
WEBSITE: www.metro-arts.org
EMAIL: julie@metro-arts.org
YEAR FOUNDED: 1998
SPONSOR: State Board for Charter Schools
TYPE: Site-based
SIZE: Small

Melds visual and performing arts into a rigorous integrated academic program.

Mexicayotl Charter School

338 North Morley Avenue
Nogales, AZ 85621

PHONE: (520) 287-6790
FAX: (520) 287-9131
YEAR FOUNDED: 1998
SPONSOR: State Board of Education
TYPE: Site-based
SIZE: Medium

In contrast to some schools and some districts that seem to be running away from this powerful teaching philosophy, it offers a bilingual/bicultural education format.

Mountain Rose Academy

40 West Fort Lowell Road
Tucson, AZ 85705

PHONE: (520) 229-1777
FAX: (520) 229-1985
YEAR FOUNDED: 2000
SPONSOR: State Board for Charter Schools
TYPE: Site-based
SIZE: Medium

A self-paced program that offers gifted/honors classes. Inquiry fuels the learning.

Mountain Rose Academy

3686 West Orange Grove Road, #180
Tucson, AZ 85741

PHONE: (520) 930-9373
FAX: (520) 616-7431
YEAR FOUNDED: 1999
SPONSOR: State Board for Charter Schools
TYPE: Site-based
SIZE: Small

Offers a gifted/honors program. Instruction is inquiry based; discovery is the goal.

New School for the Arts

7475 East McDowell Road
Scottsdale, AZ 85257

PHONE: (480) 481-9235
FAX: (480) 481-6625
WEBSITE: www.aznsa.com
YEAR FOUNDED: 1995
SPONSOR: State Board of Education
TYPE: Site-based
SIZE: Medium

Emphasis is on the visual and performing arts as well as in providing a rigorous integrated academic program.

North Pointe Preparatory

4941 West Union Hills Drive
Glendale, AZ 85308

PHONE: (623) 896-1166
FAX: (623) 896-1164
WEBSITE: www.northpointeprep.org
YEAR FOUNDED: 2001
SPONSOR: State Board for Charter Schools
TYPE: Site-based
SIZE: Large

The focus is on Western civilization and analytical skills.

Northern Arizona Academy for Career Development (Florence)

350 South Main Street
Florence, AZ 85232

PHONE: (520) 868-2307
FAX: (520) 868-2308
YEAR FOUNDED: 1999
SPONSOR: State Board for Charter Schools
TYPE: Site-based
SIZE: Small

A computer-based learning environment with vocational, technical, and school-to-work programs.

Northern Arizona Academy for Career Development (Holbrook)

324 Navajo Boulevard
Holbrook, AZ 86025

PHONE: (928) 524-3838
FAX: (928) 524-3844
YEAR FOUNDED: 2000
SPONSOR: State Board for Charter Schools
TYPE: Site-based
SIZE: Small

A computer-based learning environment with vocational, technical, and school-to-work programs.

Northern Arizona Academy for Career Development (Show Low)

1233B Fawnbrook Drive
Show Low, AZ 85901

PHONE: (928) 537-4060
FAX: (928) 537-5356
YEAR FOUNDED: 1995

SPONSOR: State Board for Charter Schools
TYPE: Site-based
SIZE: Small

A computer-based learning environment with vocational, technical, and school-to-work programs.

Northern Arizona Academy for Career Development (Springerville)

1359 East Main Street
Springerville, AZ 85938

PHONE: (928) 333-3854
FAX: (928) 333-2903
YEAR FOUNDED: 1999
SPONSOR: State Board for Charter Schools
TYPE: Site-based
SIZE: Small

A computer-based learning environment with vocational, technical, and school-to-work programs.

Northern Arizona Academy for Career Development (Taylor)

333 West Paper Mill Road
Taylor, AZ 85939

PHONE: (928) 536-4222
FAX: (928) 537-5376
YEAR FOUNDED: 1996
SPONSOR: State Board for Charter Schools
TYPE: Site-based
SIZE: Small

A computer-based learning environment with vocational, technical, and school-to-work programs.

Northern Arizona Academy for Career Development (Winslow)

502 Airport; HC-62, Box 110
Winslow, AZ 86047

PHONE: (928) 289-3329
FAX: (928) 289-4485
YEAR FOUNDED: 1995
SPONSOR: State Board for Charter Schools
TYPE: Site-based
SIZE: Small

A computer-based learning environment with vocational, technical, and school-to-work programs.

Northland Preparatory Academy

2290 East Route 66
Flagstaff, AZ 86004

PHONE: (928) 214-8776
FAX: (928) 214-8778
WEBSITE: www.northlandprep.org/npa
YEAR FOUNDED: 1996
SPONSOR: State Board for Charter Schools
TYPE: Site-based
SIZE: Medium

Offers the prestigious International Baccalaureate. This is very rigorous academics and not for the faint of heart.

Ocotillo High School

2616 East Greenway Road
Phoenix, AZ 85032

PHONE: (602) 765-8470
FAX: (602) 765-8471
WEBSITE: www.leonagroupaz.com
EMAIL: tmartin@leonagroupaz.com
YEAR FOUNDED: 1999
SPONSOR: State Board for Charter Schools
TYPE: Site-based
SIZE: Large

The Leona Group runs some charter schools in Arizona and elsewhere. Its focus is interdisciplinary learning.

Ombudsman Learning Center

9163 West Union Hills Drive
Peoria, AZ 85382

PHONE: (800) 833-9235
FAX: (623) 367-0367
YEAR FOUNDED: 2002
SPONSOR: State Board of Education
TYPE: Site-based
SIZE: Small

Performance-based education and assistance for alternative education are the central missions of this school.

Ombudsman Learning Center (East)

3943 East Thomas Road
Phoenix, AZ 85018

PHONE: (602) 275-4815
FAX: (602) 840-1402
YEAR FOUNDED: 1998
SPONSOR: State Board of Education
TYPE: Site-based
SIZE: Small

Performance-based education and assistance for alternative education are the central missions of this school.

Ombudsman Learning Center (Metro)

4220 West Northern Avenue, #111
Phoenix, AZ 85031

PHONE: (623) 842-6157
FAX: (623) 842-6157
YEAR FOUNDED: 1999
SPONSOR: State Board of Education
TYPE: Site-based
SIZE: Small

Performance-based education and assistance for alternative education are the central missions of this school.

Ombudsman Learning Center (Northeast)

3242 East Bell Road, #10
Phoenix, AZ 85032

PHONE: (800) 833-9235
FAX: (602) 367-0367
YEAR FOUNDED: 2000
SPONSOR: State Board of Education
TYPE: Site-based
SIZE: Small

Performance-based education and assistance for alternative education are the central missions of this school.

Ombudsman Learning Center (West)

3618 West Bell Road, #2
Phoenix, AZ 85023

PHONE: (602) 564-8102
FAX: (602) 564-8102
YEAR FOUNDED: 1998
SPONSOR: State Board of Education
TYPE: Site-based
SIZE: Small

Performance-based education and assistance for alternative education are the central missions of this school.

Personalized Academies and Computer Education (PACE) Preparatory Academy

460 South Main Street
Camp Verde, AZ 86322

PHONE: (928) 567-1805
FAX: (928) 567-5913
WEBSITE: www.paceacademy.com
YEAR FOUNDED: 2000
SPONSOR: State Board for Charter Schools

TYPE: Site-based
SIZE: Small

This school has a computer-driven learning environment. Instruction is self-paced with a particular focus on special-needs students and nontraditional learners.

Personalized Academies and Computer Education (PACE) Preparatory Academy

12355 Iron King Road
Humboldt, AZ 86329

PHONE: (928) 632-0200
FAX: (928) 632-0330
WEBSITE: www.paceacademy.com
YEAR FOUNDED: 2000
SPONSOR: State Board for Charter Schools
TYPE: Site-based
SIZE: Small

This school has a computer-driven learning environment. Instruction is self-paced with a particular focus on special-needs students and nontraditional learners.

Pima Vocational High School

2805 East Ajo Way
Tucson, AZ 85713

PHONE: (520) 740-4626
FAX: (520) 740-4635
YEAR FOUNDED: 2000
SPONSOR: State Board of Education
TYPE: Site-based
SIZE: Small

Serves high-risk youth within a school-to-work model.

Pimeria Alta High School

52 West Calle de Las Tiendas
Green Valley, AZ 85614

PHONE: (520) 399-0135
FAX: (520) 287-7902
WEBSITE: www.pimeria.com
YEAR FOUNDED: 1995
SPONSOR: State Board for Charter Schools
TYPE: Site-based
SIZE: Medium

This school has a computer-driven environment. The learning, including technical training, is self-paced.

Pinnacle Education Inc. (Phoenix Challenge Academy)

2030 North 36th Street
Phoenix, AZ 85008

PHONE: (602) 275-3852
FAX: (602) 275-5685
YEAR FOUNDED: 2001
SPONSOR: State Board for Charter Schools
TYPE: Online
SIZE: Small

Offers an individualized program of study that challenges the student to succeed.

Pinnacle Education Inc. (South Mountain Academy)

749 East Baseline Road
Phoenix, AZ 85040

PHONE: (602) 323-2798
FAX: (602) 323-0417
YEAR FOUNDED: 2001
SPONSOR: State Board for Charter Schools
TYPE: Online
SIZE: Small

Offers an individualized program of study that challenges the student to succeed.

Pinnacle High School

409 West McMurray Boulevard
Casa Grande, AZ 85222

PHONE: (520) 423-2380
FAX: (520) 423-2383
WEBSITE: www.pin-ed.com
YEAR FOUNDED: 1999
SPONSOR: State Board of Education
TYPE: Site-based
SIZE: Small

In addition to the core academic subjects, it provides technical training for at-risk youth. Provides counseling where necessary.

Pinnacle High School (Mesa)

151 North Centennial Way
Mesa, AZ 85201

PHONE: (480) 668-5003
FAX: (480) 668-5003
WEBSITE: www.pin-ed.com
YEAR FOUNDED: 1995
SPONSOR: State Board of Education

TYPE: Site-based
SIZE: Medium

In addition to the core academic subjects, it provides technical training for at-risk youth. Provides counseling where necessary.

Pinnacle High School (Tempe)

2224 West Southern Avenue
Tempe, AZ 85282

PHONE: (480) 414-0950
FAX: (480) 414-0927
WEBSITE: www.pin-ed.com
YEAR FOUNDED: 1995
SPONSOR: State Board of Education
TYPE: Site-based
SIZE: Medium

In addition to the core academic subjects, it provides technical training for at-risk youth. Provides counseling where necessary.

PPEP TEC (Alice S. Paul Learning Center)

220 East Florence Boulevard
Casa Grande, AZ 85222

PHONE: (520) 836-1499
FAX: (520) 836-0290
WEBSITE: www.ppep.org
YEAR FOUNDED: 1995
SPONSOR: State Board for Charter Schools
TYPE: Site-based
SIZE: Small

The focus is on serving low-income families, migrant workers, American Indians, and Mexican Americans by providing learning that meets their needs.

PPEP TEC (Celestino Fernandez Learning Center)

1840 East Benson Highway
Tucson, AZ 85714

PHONE: (520) 294-6997
FAX: (520) 294-7738
WEBSITE: www.ppep.org
YEAR FOUNDED: 1998
SPONSOR: State Board for Charter Schools
TYPE: Site-based
SIZE: Small

The focus is on serving low-income families, migrant workers, American Indians, and Mexican Americans by providing learning that meets their needs.

PPEP TEC (Cesar Chavez Learning Center)

10455 West B Street
San Luis, AZ 85349

PHONE: (520) 627-8550
FAX: (520) 627-8980
WEBSITE: www.ppep.org
YEAR FOUNDED: 1995
SPONSOR: State Board for Charter Schools
TYPE: Site-based
SIZE: Small

The focus is on serving low-income families, migrant workers, American Indians, and Mexican Americans by providing learning that meets their needs.

PPEP TEC (Colin L. Powell Learning Center)

4116 Avenida Cochise, Suite F-H
Sierra Vista, AZ 85635

PHONE: (520) 458-8205
FAX: (520) 458-8293
WEBSITE: www.ppep.org
YEAR FOUNDED: 1995
SPONSOR: State Board for Charter Schools
TYPE: Site-based
SIZE: Small

The focus is on serving low-income families, migrant workers, American Indians, and Mexican Americans by providing learning that meets their needs.

PPEP TEC (Coy Payne Learning Center)

670 North Arizona Avenue
Chandler, AZ 85224

PHONE: (480) 857-1499
FAX: (480) 857-3186
WEBSITE: www.ppep.org
YEAR FOUNDED: 1995
SPONSOR: State Board for Charter Schools
TYPE: Site-based
SIZE: Small

The focus is on serving low-income families, migrant workers, American Indians, and Mexican Americans by providing learning that meets their needs.

PPEP TEC (Eugene Lopez Learning Center)

658 Bisbee Avenue
Wilcox, AZ 85643

PHONE: (520) 384-2050
FAX: (520) 384-2112
WEBSITE: www.ppep.org
YEAR FOUNDED: 1999

SPONSOR: State Board for Charter Schools
TYPE: Site-based
SIZE: Small

The focus is on serving low-income families, migrant workers, American Indians, and Mexican Americans by providing learning that meets their needs.

PPEP TEC (Jan Olsen Learning Center)

8822 East Broadway Boulevard
Tucson, AZ 85710

PHONE: (520) 751-9330
FAX: (520) 751-9450
WEBSITE: www.ppep.org
YEAR FOUNDED: 1995
SPONSOR: State Board for Charter Schools
TYPE: Site-based
SIZE: Small

The focus is on serving low-income families, migrant workers, American Indians, and Mexican Americans by providing learning that meets their needs.

PPEP TEC (John David Arnold Learning Center)

4140 West Ina Road, #118-122
Tucson, AZ 85741

PHONE: (520) 579-8560
FAX: (520) 579-8566
WEBSITE: www.ppep.org
YEAR FOUNDED: 1996
SPONSOR: State Board for Charter Schools
TYPE: Site-based
SIZE: Small

The focus is on serving low-income families, migrant workers, American Indians, and Mexican Americans by providing learning that meets their needs.

PPEP TEC (Jose Yepez Learning Center)

144 West Main Street
Somerton, AZ 85350

PHONE: (520) 627-9648
FAX: (520) 627-9197
WEBSITE: www.ppep.org
YEAR FOUNDED: 1995
SPONSOR: State Board for Charter Schools
TYPE: Site-based
SIZE: Small

The focus is on serving low-income families, migrant workers, American Indians, and Mexican Americans by providing learning that meets their needs.

PPEP TEC ("Lito" Pena Learning Center)

12 East Western Avenue
Avondale, AZ 85323

PHONE: (623) 925-2161
FAX: (623) 925-1035
WEBSITE: www.ppep.org
YEAR FOUNDED: 1995
SPONSOR: State Board for Charter Schools
TYPE: Site-based
SIZE: Small

The focus is on serving low-income families, migrant workers, American Indians, and Mexican Americans by providing learning that meets their needs.

PPEP TEC (Manuel Bojorquez Learning Center)

203 Bisbee Road
Bisbee, AZ 85603

PHONE: (520) 432-5445
FAX: (520) 432-5414
WEBSITE: www.ppep.org
YEAR FOUNDED: 1996
SPONSOR: State Board for Charter Schools
TYPE: Site-based
SIZE: Small

The focus is on serving low-income families, migrant workers, American Indians, and Mexican Americans by providing learning that meets their needs.

PPEP TEC (Raul H. Castro Learning Center)

1012 G Avenue
Douglas, AZ 85607

PHONE: (520) 364-4405
FAX: (520) 364-1405
WEBSITE: www.ppep.org
YEAR FOUNDED: 1995
SPONSOR: State Board for Charter Schools
TYPE: Site-based
SIZE: Small

The focus is on serving low-income families, migrant workers, American Indians, and Mexican Americans by providing learning that meets their needs.

PPEP TEC (Victor Soltero Learning Center)

8230 East 22nd Street
Tucson, AZ 85710

PHONE: (520) 290-9167
FAX: (520) 290-9220
WEBSITE: www.ppep.org

YEAR FOUNDED: 1995
SPONSOR: State Board for Charter Schools
TYPE: Site-based
SIZE: Small

The focus is on serving low-income families, migrant workers, American Indians, and Mexican Americans by providing learning that meets their needs.

PPEP TEC (Virtual Interactive Program)

1840 East Benson Highway
Tucson, AZ 85714

PHONE: (520) 682-4926
FAX: (520) 682-4106
WEBSITE: www.ppep.org
YEAR FOUNDED: 2001
SPONSOR: State Board for Charter Schools
TYPE: Online
SIZE: Small

The focus is on serving low-income families, migrant workers, American Indians, and Mexican Americans by providing learning that meets their needs. One unique feature of this campus of PPEP TEC is that instruction is online.

Precision Academy

2517 North 107th Avenue
Avondale, AZ 85323

PHONE: (623) 936-8682
FAX: (623) 936-8559
WEBSITE: www.precisionacademy.com
YEAR FOUNDED: 1999
SPONSOR: Higley Unified School District
TYPE: Site-based
SIZE: Small

Offers a high school completion program. In addition, it has advanced classes and provides hands-on training.

Precision Academy System Charter School

3906 East Broadway, #105
Phoenix, AZ 85040

PHONE: (602) 453-3661
FAX: (602) 453-3671
WEBSITE: www.precisionacademy.com
YEAR FOUNDED: 1998
SPONSOR: Higley Unified School District
TYPE: Site-based
SIZE: Large

Offers a high school completion program. In addition, it has advanced classes and provides hands-on training.

Premier Charter High School

7544 West Indian School Road
Phoenix, AZ 85033

PHONE: (623) 245-1500
FAX: (623) 245-1506
YEAR FOUNDED: 2001
SPONSOR: State Board for Charter Schools
TYPE: Site-based
SIZE: Large

Student empowerment, job-readiness, and lifelong learning are the primary goals of this school.

Presidio School

3225 North Martin Avenue
Tucson, AZ 85719

PHONE: (520) 881-5222
FAX: (520) 322-8128
YEAR FOUNDED: 1996
SPONSOR: State Board of Education
TYPE: Site-based
SIZE: Large

Offers education for homeless and adjudicated youth within an individualized course of instruction.

Primavera Technical Learning Center

3029 North Alma School Road
Chandler, AZ 85224

PHONE: (480) 695-7629
FAX: (480) 558-5373
YEAR FOUNDED: 2001
SPONSOR: State Board for Charter Schools
TYPE: Site-based
SIZE: Medium

Emphasis is on technical skills.

RCB High School (Mesa)

323 North Gilbert Road
Mesa, AZ 85203

PHONE: (480) 833-0024
FAX: (480) 833-1369
WEBSITE: www.rcbhighschool.org
YEAR FOUNDED: 2001
SPONSOR: State Board for Charter Schools
TYPE: Site-based
SIZE: Medium

This program is for students aged sixteen to twenty-one. It uses a computer-based curriculum in a block schedule format.

RCB High School (Phoenix)

6049 North 43rd Avenue
Phoenix, AZ 85019

PHONE: (602) 589-1322
FAX: (602) 589-1349
WEBSITE: www.rcbhighschool.org
YEAR FOUNDED: 2000
SPONSOR: State Board for Charter Schools
TYPE: Site-based
SIZE: Small

This program is for students aged sixteen to twenty-one. It uses a computer-based curriculum in a block schedule format.

Renaissance Academy (Anasazi Campus)

1450 East White Mountain Boulevard
Pinetop, AZ 85935

PHONE: (928) 367-3074
FAX: (928) 367-5307
YEAR FOUNDED: 1998
SPONSOR: State Board for Charter Schools
TYPE: Site-based
SIZE: Small

A computer-based, self-paced curriculum for at-risk students.

Renaissance Academy (Heber/Overgaard Campus)

3201 F.S. Road 504
Heber, AZ 85928

PHONE: (928) 535-3475
FAX: (928) 337-3479
YEAR FOUNDED: 2000
SPONSOR: State Board for Charter Schools
TYPE: Site-based
SIZE: Small

A computer-based, self-paced curriculum for at-risk students.

Renaissance Academy (Malpais Campus)

367 North Main Street
Eagar, AZ 85925

PHONE: (928) 333-1554
FAX: (928) 333-1555
YEAR FOUNDED: 1998
SPONSOR: State Board for Charter Schools
TYPE: Site-based
SIZE: Small

A computer-based, self-paced curriculum for at-risk students.

Renaissance Academy (San Juan Campus)

345 West Cleveland Avenue
St. Johns, AZ 85936

PHONE: (928) 337-3478
FAX: (928) 337-3479
YEAR FOUNDED: 1999
SPONSOR: State Board for Charter Schools
TYPE: Site-based
SIZE: Small

A computer-based, self-paced curriculum for at-risk students.

Richard Milburn Charter High School

415 West Grant Street
Phoenix, AZ 85003

PHONE: (602) 254-1844
FAX: (602) 254-1533
WEBSITE: www.rmhs.org
YEAR FOUNDED: 2000
SPONSOR: State Board of Education
TYPE: Site-based
SIZE: Large

A special feature is the academic, career, and life-skills program.

Scholars' Academy

Parker Poston Road
Ehrenberg, AZ 85334

PHONE: (928) 923-7907
FAX: (928) 923-8908
WEBSITE: www.scholarsacademy.net
YEAR FOUNDED: 1996
SPONSOR: State Board for Charter Schools
TYPE: Site-based
SIZE: Small

An academically rigorous program; students should come prepared to learn.

School for the Advancement of Gifted Education

3120 North 32nd Street
Phoenix, AZ 85018

PHONE: (602) 955-0355
FAX: (602) 508-0682
YEAR FOUNDED: 1998
SPONSOR: State Board for Charter Schools
TYPE: Site-based
SIZE: Medium

Focuses on at-risk students and students who are gifted, ADD, or ADHD.

School for Integrated Academics and Technologies

901 South Campbell Avenue
Tucson, AZ 85719

PHONE: (520) 726-6367
FAX: (520) 726-6424
YEAR FOUNDED: 2001
SPONSOR: State Board for Charter Schools
TYPE: Site-based
SIZE: Small

The school has a year-round calendar and has a focus on global society.

School for Integrated Academics and Technologies

518 South Third Street
Phoenix, AZ 85004

PHONE: (602) 258-3912
FAX: (602) 258-3985
YEAR FOUNDED: 2001
SPONSOR: State Board for Charter Schools
TYPE: Site-based
SIZE: Medium

The school has a year-round calendar and has a focus on global society.

Shonto Preparatory Technology High School

East Highway 160/98
Shonto, AZ 86054

PHONE: (928) 672-2652
FAX: (928) 672-2749
YEAR FOUNDED: 1999
SPONSOR: State Board for Charter Schools
TYPE: Site-based
SIZE: Small

Central focus is technology and learning.

Sonoran Desert School

4448 East Main Street
Mesa, AZ 85205

PHONE: (480) 396-5463
FAX: (480) 396-4980
WEBSITE: www.sdschool.org
YEAR FOUNDED: 1999
SPONSOR: State Board for Charter Schools
TYPE: Site-based
SIZE: Medium

Offers self-paced, individualized instruction.

South Mountain College Preparatory High School

2006 East Broadway
Phoenix, AZ 85040

PHONE: (602) 268-4508
FAX: (602) 730-9309
YEAR FOUNDED: 2001
SPONSOR: State Board for Charter Schools
TYPE: Site-based
SIZE: Large

Teaches workplace skills and emphasizes university preparation.

Southern Arizona Community High School

2470 North Tucson Boulevard
Tucson, AZ 85716

PHONE: (520) 319-6113
FAX: (520) 498-0265
YEAR FOUNDED: 2000
SPONSOR: State Board for Charter Schools
TYPE: Site-based
SIZE: Small

This school is for students aged sixteen to twenty-one. It has a focus on humanities and sciences.

Summit High School

728 East McDowell Road
Phoenix, AZ 85006

PHONE: (602) 258-8959
FAX: (602) 258-8953
WEBSITE: wwwleonagroupaz.com
EMAIL: info@leonagroup.com
YEAR FOUNDED: 1999
SPONSOR: State Board for Charter Schools
TYPE: Site-based
SIZE: Large

As with all Leona Group schools, the focal point is inter-disciplinary learning.

Sun Valley High School

1143 South Lindsay Road
Mesa, AZ 85204

PHONE: (480) 497-4800
FAX: (480) 497-1314
WEBSITE: www.leonagroupaz.com
EMAIL: info@leonagroup.com
YEAR FOUNDED: 1997
SPONSOR: State Board for Charter Schools

TYPE: Site-based
SIZE: Very large

As with all Leona Group schools, the focal point is inter-disciplinary learning.

Tempe Accelerated High School

5040 South Price Road
Tempe, AZ 85282

PHONE: (480) 831-6057
FAX: (480) 831-6095
WEBSITE: www.leonagroupaz.com
EMAIL: info@leonagroup.com
YEAR FOUNDED: 1997
SPONSOR: State Board for Charter Schools
TYPE: Site-based
SIZE: Large

As with all Leona Group schools, the focal point is inter-disciplinary learning. By accelerating the learning, students are able to graduate sooner.

Tri-City Prep High School

3200 Willow Creek
Prescott, AZ 86301

PHONE: (928) 708-3950
FAX: (928) 708-3951
EMAIL: tricityprephighschool@hotmail.com
YEAR FOUNDED: 1999
SPONSOR: State Board for Charter Schools
TYPE: Site-based
SIZE: Medium

The curriculum requires high academic standards.

Tucson Accelerated High School

7280 East Wrightstown Road
Tucson, AZ 85715

PHONE: (520) 722-4721
FAX: (520) 722-4785
WEBSITE: leonagroupaz.com
EMAIL: info@leonagroup.com
YEAR FOUNDED: 1997
SPONSOR: State Board for Charter Schools
TYPE: Site-based
SIZE: Large

As with all Leona Group schools, the focal point is inter-disciplinary learning. By accelerating the learning, students are able to graduate sooner.

Tucson Urban League Academy

2323 South Park Avenue
Tucson, AZ 85713

PHONE: (520) 622-3651
FAX: (520) 923-9364
YEAR FOUNDED: 1996
SPONSOR: State Board for Charter Schools
TYPE: Site-based
SIZE: Medium

Offers instruction in a four-hour block program with a low student-to-teacher ratio.

Victory High School

1650 West Southern Avenue
Phoenix, AZ 85041

PHONE: (602) 243-7583
FAX: (602) 243-7563
YEAR FOUNDED: 1996
SPONSOR: State Board for Charter Schools
TYPE: Site-based
SIZE: Small

The primary focus is on math, science, and technology.

The Village: High School for Pregnant and Parenting Teens

301 West Roosevelt
Phoenix, AZ 85003

PHONE: (602) 258-6990
FAX: (602) 258-6980
WEBSITE:
www.phoenixbirthingproject.org/village_high.html
EMAIL: contact@phoenixbirthingproject.org
YEAR FOUNDED: 1997
SPONSOR: State Board for Charter Schools
TYPE: Site-based
SIZE: Small

Specifically designed for pregnant/parenting teens.

Arkansas

Academics Plus Charter School

PO Box 13622
Maumelle, AR 72113

PHONE: (501) 851-8142
FAX: (501) 851-6347
WEBSITE: www.academicsplus.org
YEAR FOUNDED: 2001
SPONSOR: State Board of Education

TYPE: Site-based
SIZE: Small

A college-preparatory program.

Benton County School of the Arts

602 North 34th Street
Rogers, AR 72756

PHONE: (501) 636-2272
FAX: (501) 636-5547
WEBSITE: bcschoolofthearts.org
EMAIL: info@bcschoolofthearts.org
YEAR FOUNDED: 2001
SPONSOR: State Board of Education
TYPE: Site-based
SIZE: Large

The focal point is the arts, both fine and performing, but the school also provides an outstanding education in the core academic subjects.

Blytheville Charter School

1700 West McHaney Street
Blytheville, AR 72316

PHONE: (870) 763-7191
FAX: (870) 762-0141
YEAR FOUNDED: 2001
SPONSOR: Blytheville School District
TYPE: Site-based
SIZE: Small

Offers college-preparatory and vocational/technical programs.

California

Academic/Vocational Charter Institute

294 Green Valley Road
Watsonville, CA 95076

PHONE: (831) 728-2144
FAX: (831) 728-6230
YEAR FOUNDED: 1999
SPONSOR: Pajaro Valley Joint Unified School District
TYPE: Site-based
SIZE: Small

Its unique focus is on applied vocations (hospitality, culinary arts, mechanics, aeronautics, technology).

Academy for Career Education Charter School

801 Olive Street
Wheatland, CA 95692

PHONE: (530) 633-3113
FAX: (530) 633-3106
YEAR FOUNDED: 1999
SPONSOR: Wheatland Union School District
TYPE: Site-based
SIZE: Small

This school converted from an alternative high school. It offers applied academics (according to student's career interests).

Advanced Instructional Model (AIM) Charter School

9055 Locust Street
Elk Grove, CA 95624

PHONE: (916) 685-8303
FAX: (916) 685-8372
YEAR FOUNDED: 1999
SPONSOR: Elk Grove Unified School District
TYPE: Homeschool resource
SIZE: Large

Has a cooperative school program, providing resources for the homeschooling community through community-based education and distance learning.

Anderson Valley Charter Network

PO Box 457
Booneville, CA 95415

PHONE: (707) 895-3774
FAX: (707) 895-2665
YEAR FOUNDED: 1999
SPONSOR: Anderson Valley Unified School District
TYPE: Homeschool resource
SIZE: Small

Offers work experience, apprenticeships, and occupational and technical programs.

Animo Leadership Charter High School

1155 Arbor Vitae
Inglewood, CA 90301

PHONE: (310) 216-3277
FAX: (310) 216-7934
WEBSITE: www.animoleadership.org
EMAIL: aztecs@animoleadership.org
YEAR FOUNDED: 2000
SPONSOR: Lennox Elementary School District
TYPE: Site-based
SIZE: Medium

Advanced technology, multicultural sensitivity, and leadership development are the trademarks of this program.

Antelope View Home Charter School

8725 Watt Avenue
Antelope, CA 95843

PHONE: (916) 339-4690
FAX: (916) 339-4693
WEBSITE:
www.centerusd.k12.ca.us/antelopeview/index.html
EMAIL: pkeefer@centerusd.k12.ca.us
YEAR FOUNDED: 2000
SPONSOR: Center Joint Unified School District
TYPE: Homeschool resource
SIZE: Small

Has an ongoing relationship with Crocker Art Museum. Provides courses in web design. Students can attend Center High activities.

Art's Charter School

2350 Beverly Drive
Redding, CA 96002

PHONE: (530) 221-5284
FAX: (530) 221-8503
YEAR FOUNDED: 1999
SPONSOR: Shasta Union High School District
TYPE: Site-based
SIZE: Small

Offers career preparation as the model for education.

Bay Area School of Enterprise

2750 Todd Street
Alameda, CA 94501

PHONE: (510) 748-4314
FAX: (510) 748-4326
WEBSITE: www.homeproject.org
EMAIL: mail4home@aol.com
YEAR FOUNDED: 2001
SPONSOR: Alameda City Unified School District
TYPE: Site-based
SIZE: Small

Project-based, hands-on learning is the central tool for learning.

Bitney Springs Charter High School

13020 Bitney Springs Road, Building 4
Nevada City, CA 95959

PHONE: (530) 477-1235
FAX: (530) 272-1091
WEBSITE: www.bschs.net
EMAIL: BSCHS@tresd.k12.ca.us
YEAR FOUNDED: 1999
SPONSOR: Twin Ridges Elementary School District
TYPE: Site-based
SIZE: Small

Focus is on the arts and experiential learning.

California Charter Academy

12530 Hesperia Road, Suite 209
Victorville, CA 92392

PHONE: (760) 951-3575
FAX: (760) 951-2265
WEBSITE: www.cca2000.org
EMAIL: GHoffecker@tresd.k12.ca.us
YEAR FOUNDED: 1999
SPONSOR: Orange Unified School District
TYPE: Site-based
SIZE: Very large

Traditional classroom learning, plus a work experience program, makes this a well-rounded program.

California Charter Academy of Orange County

12530 Hesperia Road, Suite 209
Victorville, CA 92392

PHONE: (760) 951-3575
FAX: (760) 951-2265
YEAR FOUNDED: 2001
SPONSOR: Orange Unified School District
TYPE: Site-based
SIZE: Very large

Operates five campuses throughout Orange County.

Carter G. Woodson Public Charter School

3333 North Bond Avenue
Fresno, CA 93726

PHONE: (559) 229-3529
FAX: (559) 229-0459
YEAR FOUNDED: 2001
SPONSOR: Fresno Unified School District
TYPE: Site-based
SIZE: Medium

Challenging academics with a technology focus.

Center for Advanced Research and Technology (CART)

2555 Clovis Avenue
Clovis, CA 93612

PHONE: (559) 248-7400
FAX: (559) 248-7423
WEBSITE: www.cart.org
EMAIL: iolguin@cart.org
YEAR FOUNDED: 2000
SPONSOR: Fresno Unified School District and Clovis Unified School District
TYPE: Site-based
SIZE: Very large

An advanced technological model that offers truly unique career paths. This program offers a challenging education that surpasses much of the competition.

The Charter High School of San Diego

2245 San Diego Avenue, Suite 127
San Diego, CA 92110

PHONE: (619) 686-6666
FAX: (619) 686-6672
WEBSITE: www.charterschool-sandiego.net
YEAR FOUNDED: 1994
SPONSOR: San Diego City Unified School District
TYPE: Site-based
SIZE: Very large

Features active parental involvement.

Choice 2000 On-Line Charter School

155 East Fourth Street, Suite 100
Perris, CA 92570

PHONE: (909) 940-5700
FAX: (909) 940-5706
WEBSITE: www.choice2000.org
EMAIL: info@choice2000.org
YEAR FOUNDED: 1994
SPONSOR: Perris Union High School District (WASC-accredited)
TYPE: Online
SIZE: Medium

Unlike many alternative schools, Choice 2000 has WASC accreditation and its curriculum is based on California state standards.

Choices Charter School

3425 Arden Way
Sacramento, CA 95825

PHONE: (916) 575-4529
FAX: (916) 575-1935
YEAR FOUNDED: 1999
SPONSOR: San Juan Unified School District
TYPE: Site-based
SIZE: Small

Specializes in at-risk or out-of-school students.

Circle of Independent Learning

4210 Technology Drive
Fremont, CA 94538

PHONE: (510) 445-1545
FAX: (510) 445-0657
YEAR FOUNDED: 1998
SPONSOR: Fremont Unified School District
TYPE: Independent study
SIZE: Medium

Offers two options: independent study with enrichment classes or independent study with classroom-based learning two days a week.

The CORE @ Camptonville Academy

10094 Olympia Park Road
Grass Valley, CA 95922

PHONE: (530) 272-8619
FAX: (530) 272-8650
WEBSITE: www.camptonville.org
EMAIL: jjablecki@camptonville.org
YEAR FOUNDED: 1998
SPONSOR: Camptonville Elementary School District
TYPE: Independent study/online
SIZE: Large

Offers a distance-learning program for at-risk youth.

Cortez Hills Academy Charter School

1475 Sixth Avenue, Second Floor
San Diego, CA 92101

PHONE: (619) 338-9206
FAX: (619) 338-0448
YEAR FOUNDED: 2000
SPONSOR: San Diego Unified School District
TYPE: Site-based
SIZE: Small

Cortez Hills Academy has a project-based arts and technology focus. It offers a choice of college-prep or school-to-work programs. Public service work is required.

Crenshaw Learn Charter High School

5010 11th Avenue
Los Angeles, CA 90043

PHONE: (323) 296-5370
FAX: (323) 292-6712
YEAR FOUNDED: 1999
SPONSOR: Los Angeles Unified School District
TYPE: Site-based
SIZE: Very large

The curriculum is delivered through thematic units. It has after-school and Saturday programs.

Cypress Grove Charter High School for Arts and Sciences

225 Normandy Avenue
Seaside, CA 93955

PHONE: (831) 392-0200
FAX: (831) 392-0400
WEBSITE: www.cypressgrovechs.com
EMAIL: cypressgrove@redshift.com
YEAR FOUNDED: 2001
SPONSOR: Monterey Peninsula Unified School District
TYPE: Site-based/independent study
SIZE: Small

The program combines classes on the arts and sciences with experiential learning to create a demanding program. Well worth the effort.

Delta Charter High School

31400 South Koster Road
Tracy, CA 95304

PHONE: (209) 830-6789
FAX: (209) 830-9707
YEAR FOUNDED: 2001
SPONSOR: New Jerusalem Elementary School District
TYPE: Independent study
SIZE: Small

Individualized independent study plans provide the curricular focus.

Downtown College Preparatory

PO Box 90307
San Jose, CA 95109

PHONE: (408) 271-1730
FAX: (408) 271-1734
WEBSITE: www.downtowncollegeprep.org
EMAIL: info@downtowncollegeprep.org
YEAR FOUNDED: 2000

SPONSOR: San Jose Unified School District
TYPE: Site-based
SIZE: Small

Offers a small-school environment with Advanced Placement courses and an extended day.

Eagle Summit Academy

3850 Trinity Road
Phelan, CA 92329

PHONE: (760) 868-3442
FAX: (760) 868-4725
YEAR FOUNDED: 1994
SPONSOR: Snowline Joint Unified School District
TYPE: Site-based
SIZE: Small

This program for expelled and at-risk students offers an evening schedule.

East Bay Conservation Corps Charter School

1021 Third Street
Oakland, CA 94607

PHONE: (510) 992-7800
FAX: (510) 992-7950
WEBSITE: www.ebcc-school.org
EMAIL: info@ebcc-school.org
YEAR FOUNDED: 1996
SPONSOR: Oakland Unified School District
TYPE: Site-based
SIZE: Small

This at-risk youth program focuses on environmental stewardship.

Elise P. Buckingham Charter School

188 Bella Vista Road, Suite B
Vacaville, CA 95687

PHONE: (707) 453-7312
FAX: (707) 453-7303
WEBSITE:
www.vusd.solanocoEastk12.ca.us/Buck/index.htm
YEAR FOUNDED: 1994
SPONSOR: Vacaville Unified School District
TYPE: Site-based
SIZE: Very large

The program combines personalized learning plans with classroom and community-based instruction.

Escondido Charter High School

1845 East Valley Parkway
Escondido, CA 92927

PHONE: (760) 737-3154
FAX: (760) 738-8996
YEAR FOUNDED: 1996
SPONSOR: Escondido Union High School District
TYPE: Independent study
SIZE: Very large

This school utilizes personal education plans, which can include group work, tutoring, supervised study, and so on.

Excelsior Education Center

12217 Spring Valley Parkway
Victorville, CA 92392

PHONE: (760) 245-4448
FAX: (760) 245-4009
WEBSITE: www.eecweb.com
EMAIL: info@eecweb.com
YEAR FOUNDED: 1995
SPONSOR: Victor Valley Union High School District
TYPE: Homeschool resource
SIZE: Very large

Utilizes the California State Standards.

Fresno Prep Academy

3355 East Shields Avenue
Fresno, CA 93726

PHONE: (559) 222-3840
FAX: (559) 222-3540
YEAR FOUNDED: 1999
SPONSOR: Fresno Unified School District
TYPE: Site-based
SIZE: Small

Focuses on business and employment for at-risk students. Schedule includes extended day, evening, and weekend courses.

Gold Rush Home Study Charter School

14763 Mono Way
Sonora, CA 95370

PHONE: (209) 533-8644
FAX: (209) 586-1357
YEAR FOUNDED: 2001
SPONSOR: Keyes Union Elementary School District
TYPE: Independent study
SIZE: Large

A home-study program.

Grizzly Challenge Charter School

PO Box 8105
San Luis Obispo, CA 93403

PHONE: (805) 782-6882
FAX: (805) 782-6885
YEAR FOUNDED: 1998
SPONSOR: Paso Robles Joint Unified School District
TYPE: Site-based
SIZE: Small

Provides the educational component of the National Guard Youth Challenge Program.

Guajome Park Academy

135 East Broadway
Vista, CA 92084

PHONE: (760) 945-1227
FAX: (760) 945-1683
WEBSITE: www.gpa-inc.com
YEAR FOUNDED: 1994
SPONSOR: Vista Unified School District
TYPE: Site-based
SIZE: Very large

The curriculum is based on University of California entrance requirements and International Baccalaureate guides.

Heritage Family Academy

955 West Center Street, Suite 9
Manteca, CA 95337

PHONE: (209) 239-7306
FAX: (209) 823-7439
WEBSITE: www.hfac.org
YEAR FOUNDED: 1999
SPONSOR: Manteca Unified School District
TYPE: Homeschool resource/independent study
SIZE: Very large

Offers apprenticeships, co-op programs, community-based learning, and distance learning.

Horizon Instructional Systems

2800 Nicolaus Road, Suite 100
Lincoln, CA 95648

PHONE: (916) 408-5275
FAX: (916) 408-5223
WEBSITE: www.hiscs.org
YEAR FOUNDED: 1993
SPONSOR: Western Placer Unified School District
TYPE: Independent study/homeschool resource
SIZE: Very large

Has supplemental learning projects and cooperative schools. Resource teachers are available for assistance.

Julian Charter School

1704 Cape Horn
Julian, CA 92036

PHONE: (760) 765-3847
FAX: (760) 765-3849
WEBSITE: www.juliancharter.org
YEAR FOUNDED: 2000
SPONSOR: Julian Union Elementary School District
TYPE: Independent study
SIZE: Very large

In addition to the availability of traditional materials, it offers distance-learning courses.

Kern Workforce 2000 Academy Charter

5801 Sundale Avenue
Bakersfield, CA 93309

PHONE: (661) 827-3158
FAX: (661) 827-3320
WEBSITE: www.khsd.k12.ca.us/workforce
YEAR FOUNDED: 1995
SPONSOR: Kern High School District
TYPE: Site-based
SIZE: Large

A program for out-of-school and at-risk youth. It provides learning opportunities during off-peak hours.

La Sierra High School

1735 East Houston Avenue
Visalia, CA 93292

PHONE: (559) 733-6963
FAX: (559) 635-8754
YEAR FOUNDED: 2000
SPONSOR: Tulare County Office of Education
TYPE: Site-based
SIZE: Small

Offers certification programs in culinary arts, building trades, and graphic arts, as well as other areas.

Leadership High School

300 Seneca Avenue
San Francisco, CA 94112

PHONE: (415) 841-8910
FAX: (415) 841-8925
WEBSITE: www.leadershiphigh.org
EMAIL: gpeter@leadershiphigh.org
YEAR FOUNDED: 1997

SPONSOR: San Francisco Unified School District
TYPE: Site-based
SIZE: Large

This school seeks a diverse student body. The goal is to create effective community leaders.

Learning Community Charter School

1859 Bird Street
Oroville, CA 95965

PHONE: (530) 532-5665
FAX: (530) 532-5758
WEBSITE: www.bcoe.butte.k12.ca.us
YEAR FOUNDED: 1996
SPONSOR: Butte County Office of Education
TYPE: Site-based
SIZE: Large

The focus is on Native American culture, career preparation, and the use of technology.

Learning with a Purpose

6187 Pleasant Valley Road
El Dorado, CA 95623

PHONE: (530) 644-4100
FAX: (530) 647-8829
YEAR FOUNDED: 2000
SPONSOR: Pioneer Union Elementary School District
TYPE: Site-based
SIZE: Small

Teaching employability and work-readiness are essential elements of this program.

Liberty Family Academy

17782 Moro Road
Prunedale, CA 93907

PHONE: (831) 663-1777
FAX: (831) 663-3439
WEBSITE: www.lfacs.org
YEAR FOUNDED: 1998
SPONSOR: North Monterey County Unified School District
TYPE: Homeschool resource
SIZE: Large

Features integrated thematic instruction with a project emphasis.

Life Learning Academy

651 Eighth Street, Building 229
Treasure Island
San Francisco, CA 94130

PHONE: (415) 397-8957
FAX: (415) 512-5186
YEAR FOUNDED: 1998
SPONSOR: San Francisco Unified School District
TYPE: Site-based
SIZE: Small

Teaches youth involved in the juvenile justice system by using hands-on vocational projects.

Lubeles Academy Charter

85 Rose Avenue
Chico, CA 95928

PHONE: (530) 343-2041
FAX: (530) 343-2388
YEAR FOUNDED: 1999
SPONSOR: Gateway Unified School District
TYPE: Site-based/homeschool program
SIZE: Small

American Indian beliefs and individual learning styles provide the framework for instruction and learning.

Mare Island Technology Academy High School

611 Amador Street
Vallejo, CA 94590

PHONE: (707) 552-6482
FAX: (707) 552-0288
WEBSITE: www.mitacademy.org
YEAR FOUNDED: 2001
SPONSOR: Vallejo City Unified School District
TYPE: Site-based
SIZE: Large

A strong focus on technology and its uses.

Marysville Charter Academy for the Arts

1917 B Street
Marysville, CA 95901

PHONE: (530) 749-6157
FAX: (530) 741-7892
YEAR FOUNDED: 2000
SPONSOR: Marysville Joint Union School District
TYPE: Site-based
SIZE: Small

This college-preparatory program specializes in the teaching of literature and the visual and performing arts.

Modoc Charter School

1670 Market Street, #268
Redding, CA 96001

PHONE: (530) 229-0948
FAX: (530) 229-5986
YEAR FOUNDED: 2000
SPONSOR: Modoc Joint Union School District
TYPE: Independent study
SIZE: Medium

Curriculum-based materials are used in individualized academic programs.

Monterey County Home Charter School

PO Box 80851
Salinas, CA 93912

PHONE: (831) 755-6468
FAX: (831) 755-0837
YEAR FOUNDED: 2000
SPONSOR: Monterey County Office of Education
TYPE: Homeschool resource
SIZE: Large

Provides public support for homeschooling families

Moreno Valley Community Learning Center

13911 Parris Boulevard
Moreno Valley, CA 92553

PHONE: (909) 485-5771
FAX: (909) 485-5772
WEBSITE: www.mvusd.k12.ca.us
YEAR FOUNDED: 1994
SPONSOR: Moreno Valley Unified School District
TYPE: Site-based
SIZE: Small

An expelled-students program.

Muir Charter School

10031 Joerschke Drive, Suite D
Grass Valley, CA 95945

PHONE: (530) 477-7569
FAX: (530) 477-2114
YEAR FOUNDED: 1999
SPONSOR: Nevada County Office of Education
TYPE: Site-based (non-classroom based)
SIZE: Large

In this program of the California Conservation Corps, most students are over eighteen but without a high school diploma.

Multicultural Learning Center

7510 DeSoto Avenue
Canoga Park, CA 91303

PHONE: (818) 716-5789
FAX: (818) 716-7346
YEAR FOUNDED: 2001
SPONSOR: Los Angeles Unified School District
TYPE: Site-based
SIZE: Medium

This is a diverse community of learners with a focus on the differences that make us all special. This is a dual immersion program so instruction is offered in two languages.

Natomas Charter School

4600 Blackrock Drive
Sacramento, CA 95835

PHONE: (916) 928-5353
FAX: (916) 928-5333
WEBSITE: www.natomascharter.org
YEAR FOUNDED: 1993
SPONSOR: Natomas Unified School District
TYPE: Site-based
SIZE: Very large

Includes a fine and performing arts academy. It has a task-based curriculum that provides for different interests and learning styles.

New Millennium Institute of Education Charter School

830 Fresno Street
Fresno, CA 93706

PHONE: (559) 497-9331
FAX: (559) 497-9109
YEAR FOUNDED: 1999
SPONSOR: Fresno Unified School District
TYPE: Site-based
SIZE: Medium

Designed with Fresno Youth Opportunities Unlimited for at-risk and not-in-school youth.

Nexus Learning Community Charter School

1620 Sonoma Avenue
Santa Rosa, CA 95405

PHONE: (707) 545-8419
FAX: (707) 569-8819
YEAR FOUNDED: 2001

SPONSOR: Santa Rosa High School District
TYPE: Site-based
SIZE: Small

Offers a strong service-learning emphasis.

Oakdale Charter School

1235 East D Street
Oakdale, CA 95361

PHONE: (209) 848-4361
FAX: (209) 848-4363
YEAR FOUNDED: 1996
SPONSOR: Oakdale Unified School District
TYPE: Independent study
SIZE: Small

The student goal can be a high school diploma, GED, or an adult education diploma.

Oakland School for the Arts

1212 Broadway Avenue, Suite 730
Oakland, CA 94612

PHONE: (510) 763-7270
FAX: (510) 763-1155
WEBSITE: www.oakarts.org
EMAIL: info@oakarts.org
YEAR FOUNDED: 2001
SPONSOR: Oakland Unified School District
TYPE: Site-based
SIZE: Small

Oakland School for the Arts offers preprofessional training in creative writing, dance, theater, music, and visual arts.

Orange County High School of the Arts

1010 North Main Street
Santa Ana, CA 92701

PHONE: (714) 560-0900
FAX: (714) 664-0463
WEBSITE: www.ocsarts.net
EMAIL: pat.mcmaster@ocsarts.net
YEAR FOUNDED: 2000
SPONSOR: Santa Ana Unified School District
TYPE: Site-based
SIZE: Very large

Offers classes in the visual and performing arts; admissions are based on audition and portfolio. Orange County is well known for the quality and quantity of visual and performing arts.

Pacific Collegiate Charter Public School

PO Box 1701
Santa Cruz, CA 95061

PHONE: (831) 427-7785
FAX: (831) 427-5254
WEBSITE: www.pacificcollegiate.com
YEAR FOUNDED: 1999
SPONSOR: Santa Cruz County Office of Education
TYPE: Site-based
SIZE: Medium

AP classes, small class size, and high academic and behavioral standards can make this a good choice for high achievers.

Pacific Learning Center

780 Atlantic Avenue, Third Floor
Long Beach, CA 90813

PHONE: (562) 437-0681
FAX: (562) 591-4612
YEAR FOUNDED: 2000
SPONSOR: Long Beach Unified School District
TYPE: Site-based/independent study
SIZE: Medium

Gives credit for work experience and community service activities.

Palisades Charter High School and Math, Science, & Technology Magnet

15777 Bowdoin Street
Pacific Palisades, CA 90272

PHONE: (310) 454-0611
FAX: (310) 454-6076
YEAR FOUNDED: 1993
SPONSOR: Los Angeles Unified School District
TYPE: Site-based
SIZE: Very large

Utilizes interdisciplinary thematic instruction and block scheduling.

Paradise Charter Network/The Independent Learning Center

645 Pearson Road
Paradise, CA 95969

PHONE: (530) 872-6461
FAX: (530) 872-9708
WEBSITE: www.paradisedirect.com/pusd/ilc
YEAR FOUNDED: 1998
SPONSOR: Paradise Unified School District

TYPE: Independent study
SIZE: Medium

In addition to regular courses, it offers work experience, apprenticeships, and technical and trade programs.

Premiere Education Charter School

1140 East San Antonio Drive
Long Beach, CA 90807

PHONE: (562) 427-3802
FAX: (562) 427-6832
WEBSITE: www.pecs2000.com
YEAR FOUNDED: 2000
SPONSOR: Long Beach Unified School District
TYPE: Independent study
SIZE: Medium

Has special programs for pregnant teens, disabled students, and youth in house-arrest programs.

Promise Academy Charter School

11633 Buford Street
Cerritos, CA 90703

PHONE: (562) 818-8242
FAX: (562) 402-0946
YEAR FOUNDED: 2001
SPONSOR: Long Beach Unified School District
TYPE: Site-based/independent study
SIZE: Large

Provides a mixture of independent study and resident instruction.

Prosser Creek Charter School

12640 Union Mills Road
Truckee, CA 96161

PHONE: (530) 550-2305
FAX: (530) 550-2310
WEBSITE: www.prosser.net
YEAR FOUNDED: 1998
SPONSOR: Tahoe-Truckee Joint Unified School District
TYPE: Site-based
SIZE: Large

Offers developmentally appropriate education, including mentorships and apprenticeships, on multiple campuses.

Provisional Accelerated Learning Academy

PO Box 7100
San Bernardino, CA 92411

PHONE: (909) 887-7002
FAX: (909) 887-8942
YEAR FOUNDED: 2000
SPONSOR: San Bernardino City Unified School District
TYPE: Site-based
SIZE: Medium

Offers a GED or high school diploma track.

River Valley High Charter School

9797 Marilla Drive
Lakeside, CA 92040

PHONE: (619) 390-2579
FAX: (619) 390-2581
YEAR FOUNDED: 1997
SPONSOR: Lakeside Union Elementary School District
TYPE: Site-based/independent study
SIZE: Small

Parent involvement, core subject emphasis, and community involvement are three important precepts of this school.

Sacramento River Discovery Center Charter School

1000 Sale Lane
Red Bluff, CA 96080

PHONE: (530) 527-1196
FAX: (530) 527-1312
WEBSITE: www.srdc.tehama.k12.ca.us
EMAIL: lgreen@tehama.k12.ca.us
YEAR FOUNDED: 2001
SPONSOR: Red Bluff Union Elementary School District
TYPE: Site-based
SIZE: Small

Offers research opportunities related to natural resources and water conservation. (I think if I lived in Red Bluff, I'd check it out for my own children.)

Sanger Hallmark Charter School

1905 Seventh Street
Sanger, CA 93657

PHONE: (559) 875-6521
FAX: (559) 875-3152
YEAR FOUNDED: 1999
SPONSOR: Sanger Unified School District
TYPE: Homeschool resource
SIZE: Large

Individual learning programs, with some site-based classes available.

Santee Explorer Academy

1900 Joe Crosson Drive
El Cajon, CA 92020

PHONE: (619) 258-4945
FAX: (619) 258-8895
YEAR FOUNDED: 2000
SPONSOR: Santee Elementary School District
TYPE: Site-based
SIZE: Small

This school provides small classes, hands-on learning, and team projects.

School of Unlimited Learning

2336 Calaveras Street
Fresno, CA 93721

PHONE: (559) 498-8543
FAX: (559) 237-0956
YEAR FOUNDED: 1998
SPONSOR: Fresno Unified School District
TYPE: Site-based
SIZE: Medium

Special features include at-risk youth programs.

Shasta Secondary Home School

2200 Eureka Way
Redding, CA 96001

PHONE: (530) 245-2600
FAX: (530) 245-2347
WEBSITE: www.homeschool.suhsd.net
YEAR FOUNDED: 1999
SPONSOR: Shasta Union High School District
TYPE: Homeschool resource
SIZE: Medium

Its curriculum provides for diverse delivery and outcomes.

Sierra Charter School

1931 North Fine
Fresno, CA 93727

PHONE: (559) 490-4290
FAX: (559) 490-4292
WEBSITE: www.sierracharter.org
YEAR FOUNDED: 1998
SPONSOR: Eastern Sierra Unified School District
TYPE: Homeschool resource
SIZE: Large

Utilizes a computerized assessment system and individual education plans for instruction.

SLVUSD Charter School

6264B Highway 9
Felton, CA 95018

PHONE: (831) 335-8344
FAX: (831) 335-8346
WEBSITE: www.slv.k12.ca.us/CHARTER
YEAR FOUNDED: 1993
SPONSOR: San Lorenzo Valley Unified School District
TYPE: Homeschool resource/resident
SIZE: Large

Varied formats including distance learning, alternative high school, The Nature Academy, and so on.

Soledad Enrichment Action Charter School

3763 East Fourth Street
Los Angeles, CA 90063

PHONE: (323) 267-0321
FAX: (323) 262-8820
YEAR FOUNDED: 1997
SPONSOR: Los Angeles County Office of Education
TYPE: Site-based
SIZE: Large

Special features include an at-risk and high-risk youth program. The goal is the return of the students to their home schools.

Stanislaus Technical High School

250 Hinkley Avenue
Oakdale, CA 95361

PHONE: (209) 847-1735
FAX: (209) 847-9627
YEAR FOUNDED: 1999
SPONSOR: Oakdale Joint Unified School District
TYPE: Site-based
SIZE: Small

The three possible outcomes of this program are a high school diploma, GED certificate, or CHSPE certificate. The school achieves this through individualized learning and a school-to-work program.

Summit Charter School

47 Laurel Mount Road
Mammoth, CA 93546

PHONE: (760) 934-0031
FAX: (760) 934-1443
YEAR FOUNDED: 2000
SPONSOR: Mono County Office of Education

TYPE: Homeschool resource
SIZE: Small

Offers a cooperative education process between students and parents.

Temescal Canyon Continuation High School

777 Temescal Canyon Road
Pacific Palisades, CA 90272

PHONE: (310) 454-0315
FAX: (310) 459-8560
YEAR FOUNDED: 1995
SPONSOR: Los Angeles Unified School District
TYPE: Site-based
SIZE: Small

Specially focuses on at-risk youth and students short on credits for graduation.

University High School

College of Arts and Sciences
California State University, Fresno
2355 East Keats, MS-UH34
Fresno, CA 93740-8010

PHONE: (559) 278-8263
FAX: (559) 278-6758
WEBSITE: www.csufresno.edu/univhigh
EMAIL: uhs@listserv.csufresno.edu
YEAR FOUNDED: 2000
SPONSOR: Sierra Unified School District
TYPE: Site-based
SIZE: Small

Offers an accelerated college-preparatory curriculum. Requires a middle-school level of music education (instrumental or voice) and algebra prior to admittance.

University Preparatory Charter Academy

3030 75th Avenue
Oakland, CA 94605

PHONE: (510) 636-4082
FAX: (510) 238-8440
YEAR FOUNDED: 2001
SPONSOR: Oakland Unified School District
TYPE: Site-based
SIZE: Small

This college-preparatory program offers AP courses.

Valley Business High School

715 13th Street
Modesto, CA 95354

PHONE: (209) 558-4407
FAX: (209) 558-8741
YEAR FOUNDED: 1999
SPONSOR: Stanislaus County Office of Education
TYPE: Site-based
SIZE: Small

This is a school-to-career program.

Valley Oak Charter School

3501 Chester Avenue
Bakersfield, CA 93301

PHONE: (661) 633-5288
FAX: (661) 322-6415
YEAR FOUNDED: 2000
SPONSOR: Kern County Office of Education
TYPE: Site-based
SIZE: Small

The Kern County Museum and the California Living Museum collaborate on this program.

Vantage Point Charter School

10862 Spenceville Road
Penn Valley, CA 95946

PHONE: (530) 432-5312
FAX: (530) 432-8744
WEBSITE: www.cdlp.rssd.k12.ca.us
YEAR FOUNDED: 1993
SPONSOR: Ready Springs Union Elementary School District
TYPE: Homeschool resource or site-based
SIZE: Small

Offers an individualized curriculum.

View Park Continuation High School

4701 Rodeo Road
Los Angeles, CA 90016

PHONE: (323) 292-0331
FAX: (323) 292-7920
YEAR FOUNDED: 1999
SPONSOR: Los Angeles Unified School District
TYPE: Site-based
SIZE: Small

Schedule includes Saturday and after-school programs. Thematic units are used for instruction.

W.E.B. Dubois Charter School

302 Fresno Street, Suite 205
Fresno, CA 93706

PHONE: (559) 499-0799
FAX: (559) 442-5811
YEAR FOUNDED: 2000
SPONSOR: West Fresno Elementary School District
TYPE: Site-based
SIZE: Large

This program is specifically for young parents who have left school. In addition to the educational opportunities, day care, preschool, and kindergarten classes are available for the little ones.

West Fresno Performing Arts Academy

PO Box 1640
Fresno, CA 93716

PHONE: (559) 437-9954
FAX: (559) 447-0744
YEAR FOUNDED: 2001
SPONSOR: West Fresno Elementary School District
TYPE: Site-based
SIZE: Medium

In addition to the core academic subjects, this program has a performing arts focus.

West Park Charter Academy

2695 South Valentine Avenue
Fresno, CA 93706

PHONE: (559) 497-1779
FAX: (559) 497-1944
WEBSITE: www.westpark.k12.ca.us
YEAR FOUNDED: 1994
SPONSOR: West Park Elementary School District
TYPE: Site-based or homeschool resource
SIZE: Large

Special features include multi-age classrooms, an experiential program, distance learning, and an onsite small farm.

Whitney Young LEARN Charter High School

3051 West 52nd Street
Los Angeles, CA 90043

PHONE: (323) 296-3258
FAX: (323) 292-6595
YEAR FOUNDED: 1999
SPONSOR: Los Angeles Unified School District

TYPE: Site-based
SIZE: Small

This school offers Saturday and after-school programs using thematic instruction.

Wonder to Wisdom Charter Academy

PO Box 286
Shingletown, CA 96088

PHONE: (530) 474-4781
FAX: (530) 474-4820
YEAR FOUNDED: 2001
SPONSOR: Mineral Elementary School District
TYPE: Site-based and independent study
SIZE: Small

The structure is a combination of resident and independent study.

Yuba City Charter School

405 Center Street
Yuba City, CA 95991

PHONE: (530) 822-9667
FAX: (530) 822-9629
YEAR FOUNDED: 2000
SPONSOR: Yuba City Unified School District
TYPE: Site-based and homeschool resource
SIZE: Medium

The school guarantees that at least 75 percent of students will show one grade level's progress for each academic year. Students work on projects and are given multi-age instruction.

Colorado

Boulder Preparatory High School

1640 Range Street
Boulder, CO 80303

PHONE: (303) 545-6186
FAX: (303) 441-4716
YEAR FOUNDED: 1998
SPONSOR: Boulder Valley School District
TYPE: Site-based
SIZE: Small

A strength of this college-preparatory program is that it allows students to complete all high school requirements within two or three years. The student body is primarily at-risk youth.

Brighton Charter School

1931 East Bridge Street
Brighton, CO 80601

PHONE: (303) 655-0773
FAX: (303) 655-9155
WEBSITE: www.brightoncharter.org
YEAR FOUNDED: 1998
SPONSOR: Brighton School District No. 27J
TYPE: Site-based
SIZE: Large

This is a college- and career-preparatory school that delivers instruction in concert with the Front Range Community College.

Center for Discovery Learning

7700 West Woodard Drive
Lakewood, CO 80227

PHONE: (303) 985-7092
FAX: (303) 985-7721
WEBSITE: http://jeffcoweb.jeffco.k12.co.us/charter/cics
YEAR FOUNDED: 1994
SPONSOR: Jefferson County R-1
TYPE: Site-based
SIZE: Medium

The goal of this school is preparing students to succeed in college. Academics are presented through open and experiential learning.

Colorado High School

2651 11th Street Road
Greeley, CO 80634

PHONE: (970) 353-6132
FAX: (970) 392-2687
YEAR FOUNDED: 1998
SPONSOR: Weld County School District No. 6
TYPE: Independent study
SIZE: Small

Each student has his or her own self-directed learning plan that arises from the work of the student, staff, and parents.

Community of Learners

201 East 12th Street
Durango, CO 81301

PHONE: (970) 259-0328
FAX: (970) 259-1216

WEBSITE: www.durango.k12.co.us/animas/col/home.html
YEAR FOUNDED: 1994
SPONSOR: Durango 9-R School District
TYPE: Site-based
SIZE: Small

This school provides for self-direction and individual learning plans. Service learning and outdoor education play a vital role in the academic program.

Community Prep School

332 East Willamette Avenue
Colorado Springs, CO 80903

PHONE: (719) 227-8836
FAX: (719) 227-8897
YEAR FOUNDED: 1995
SPONSOR: Colorado Springs District 11
TYPE: Site-based
SIZE: Medium

After-school tutoring and counseling.

GLOBE Charter School

2132 E. Bijou Avenue
Colorado Springs, CO 80909

PHONE: (719) 630-0577
FAX: (719) 630-0395
YEAR FOUNDED: 1995
SPONSOR: Colorado Springs District 11
TYPE: Site-based
SIZE: Medium

Instruction revolves around world cultures, earth sciences, and global issues.

James Irwin Charter High School

1626 South Murray Boulevard
Colorado Springs, CO 80916

PHONE: (719) 576-8055
FAX: (719) 576-8071
YEAR FOUNDED: 2001
SPONSOR: Harrison School District
TYPE: Site-based
SIZE: Medium

This program, modeled on the U.S. Air Force Academy, provides a rigorous selection of courses in the core academic areas.

Jefferson Academy Senior High

9955 Yarrow Street
Broomfield, CO 80021

PHONE: (303) 469-4382
WEBSITE:
http://jeffconet.jeffco.k12/co.us/charter/jeffacademy
YEAR FOUNDED: 1999
SPONSOR: Jefferson County School District
TYPE: Site-based
SIZE: Small

The curriculum is humanities based.

P.S. 1

1062 Delaware Street
Denver, CO 80204

PHONE: (303) 575-6690
FAX: (303) 575-6661
YEAR FOUNDED: 1995
SPONSOR: Denver Public Schools
TYPE: Site-based
SIZE: Medium

Utilizes an extended day to better meet the needs of its students.

Passage Charter School

703 South Ninth Street
Montrose, CO 81401

PHONE: (970) 252-8066
FAX: (970) 252-2539
YEAR FOUNDED: 1998
SPONSOR: Montrose School district RE-IJ
TYPE: Site-based
SIZE: Small

This school only serves pregnant and parenting (male or female) teens.

Prairie Creeks Charter School

PO Box 889
Strasburg, CO 80136

PHONE: (303) 622-9211
FAX: (303) 622-9224
YEAR FOUNDED: 1998
SPONSORS: Bennett, Byers, Deer Trail, and Strasburg School Districts
TYPE: Site-based
SIZE: Small

Students can earn either a GED or a high school diploma. This program serves high-risk youth.

Pueblo School for the Arts and Sciences

University of Southern Colorado
1745 Acero Avenue
Pueblo, CO 81004

PHONE: (719) 549-2737
FAX: (719) 549-2725
WEBSITE: www.uscolo.edu
EMAIL: romanh@uscolo.edu
YEAR FOUNDED: 1994
SPONSOR: Pueblo 60 School District
TYPE: Site-based
SIZE: Large

The University of Southern Colorado operates this high-achieving school that focuses on the arts and sciences.

Southwest Open School

PO Box DD
Cortez, CO 81321

PHONE: (970) 565-1150
FAX: (970) 565-8770
YEAR FOUNDED: 1999
SPONSOR: Montezuma-Cortez School District
TYPE: Site-based
SIZE: Medium

Academics are strengthened with service learning and outdoor education. Staff and students jointly govern the program.

University Schools

University of Northern Colorado
6525 West 18th Street
Greeley, CO 80634

PHONE: (970) 330-2221
FAX: (970) 351-2064
WEBSITE: www.universityschools.com
EMAIL: gpierson@universityschools.com
YEAR FOUNDED: 1999
SPONSOR: Weld County School Board
TYPE: Site-based
SIZE: Large

Although it is now a charter school, this school has been on the University of Northern Colorado's campus for over one hundred years. Accredited by the North Central Association of Schools and Colleges.

West End Learning Center

PO Box 190
Naturita, CO 81422

PHONE: (970) 865-2290
FAX: (970) 865-2573
YEAR FOUNDED: 1999
SPONSOR: West End School District
TYPE: Site-based
SIZE: Small

This school for at-risk youth offers GED preparation courses.

Connecticut

Ancestors Community Charter High School

74 North Walnut Street
Waterbury, CT 06704

PHONE: (203) 597-5482
FAX: (203) 346-6966
YEAR FOUNDED: 1997
SPONSOR: State Board of Education
TYPE: Site-based
SIZE: Small

This school provides an alternative for at-risk youth that have not been able to succeed in more traditional schools.

Bridge Academy

510 Barnum Avenue
Bridgeport, CT 06608

PHONE: (203) 336-9999
FAX: (203) 336-9852
WEBSITE: http://brooklawn.k12.ct.us
YEAR FOUNDED: 1997
SPONSOR: State Board of Education
TYPE: Site-based
SIZE: Medium

This is a college-preparatory program. Parental involvement is seen as a necessary component of the education process. In addition, it has a mentoring program and a focus on the arts.

Common Ground High School

358 Springside Avenue
New Haven, CT 06515

PHONE: (203) 389-4333
FAX: (203) 389-0823
YEAR FOUNDED: 1997

SPONSOR: State Board of Education
TYPE: Site-based
SIZE: Small

The study of ecology interspersed with farm-based activities all within the city of New Haven makes for a unique and challenging approach to high school education.

Explorations

286 Main Street
Winsted, CT 06098

PHONE: (860) 738-9070
FAX: (860) 738-9092
YEAR FOUNDED: 1997
SPONSOR: State Board of Education
TYPE: Site-based
SIZE: Small

Offers many after-school programs as well as "adventure education."

Sport Sciences Academy

338 Asylum Street
Hartford, CT 06103

PHONE: (860) 722-8009
FAX: (860) 722-8017
YEAR FOUNDED: 1997
SPONSOR: State Board of Education
TYPE: Site-based
SIZE: Large

A truly exciting program for those interested in sports and perhaps a career in the sports industry.

Delaware

Positive Outcomes Charter School

193 South DuPont Highway
Camden, DE 19934

PHONE: (302) 697-8805
FAX: (302) 697-8813
YEAR FOUNDED: 1996
SPONSOR: State Board of Education
TYPE: Site-based
SIZE: Small

This school provides options for students who risk failure in the traditional school system.

Arts and Technology Academy

5300 Blaine Street NE
Washington, DC 20001

PHONE: (202) 398-6811
FAX: (202) 388-8567
WEBSITE: www.advantage-schools.com
YEAR FOUNDED: 1999
SPONSOR: D.C. Public Charter School Board
TYPE: Site-based
SIZE: Large

This school, run by Mosaica Advantage, is an academically rigorous program that focuses on the environment, the arts, and technology.

Booker T. Washington Public Charter School for Technical Arts

1348 Florida Avenue NW
Washington, DC 20009

PHONE: (202) 232-6090
FAX: (202) 232-6282
YEAR FOUNDED: 1999
SPONSOR: D.C. Public Charter School Board
TYPE: Site-based
SIZE: Large

This school uses a school-to-career framework and the goal is to prepare at-risk students (and others, including adults) for careers in the building and construction trades.

Cesar Chavez Public Charter High School for Public Policy

1346 Florida Avenue NE, Second Floor
Washington, DC 20009

PHONE: (202) 387-6980
FAX: (202) 387-7808
WEBSITE: www.cesarchavezhs.org
EMAIL: salcido@cesarchavezhs.org
YEAR FOUNDED: 1998
SPONSOR: D.C. Board of Education
TYPE: Site-based
SIZE: Medium

The curriculum is driven by public policy themes. Students are provided with ample opportunity to work with public interest organizations.

Hyde Leadership Charter School of Washington, D.C.

101 T Street NE, Third Floor
Washington, DC 20002

PHONE: (202) 529-4400
FAX: (202) 529-4500
YEAR FOUNDED: 1999
SPONSOR: D.C. Board of Education
TYPE: Site-based
SIZE: Large

This school is a college-preparatory program that utilizes a strong teacher-student-parent framework in devising its curriculum.

Integrated Design and Electronics Academy Public Charter School

1027 45th Street NE
Washington, DC 20019

PHONE: (202) 399-4750
FAX: (202) 399-4387
YEAR FOUNDED: 1998
SPONSOR: D.C. Board of Education
TYPE: Site-based
SIZE: Medium

The focus is on preparing students for employment within engineering-related fields (engineering, drafting, electronics). It also has a JROTC program for those interested in military careers.

Maya Angelou Public Charter School

1851 Ninth Street NW
Washington, DC 20009

PHONE: (202) 939-9080
FAX: (202) 939-9084
WEBSITE: www.seeforever.org/MAPCS/index.html
EMAIL: admin@seeforever.org
YEAR FOUNDED: 1998
SPONSOR: D.C. Public Charter School Board
TYPE: Site-based
SIZE: Small

This school not only provides students with the opportunity to learn academic skills but also has a strong emphasis on work-related skills.

School for Arts in Learning

1100 16th Street NW
Washington, DC 20036

PHONE: (202) 296-9100
FAX: (202) 261-0200
WEBSITE: www.wvsarts.org/sail.html
EMAIL: kmorton@wvsarts.org
YEAR FOUNDED: 1998
SPONSOR: D.C. Public Charter School Board
TYPE: Site-based
SIZE: Small

Provides an alternative education for students with various special needs. Its curriculum has an arts focus.

Washington Math, Science, Technology Public Charter High School

401 M Street SW, Second Floor
(Waterside Mall)
Washington, DC 20024

PHONE: (202) 488-1996
FAX: (202) 488-1997
WEBSITE: www.wmstpchs.net
EMAIL: principal@wmstpchs.net
YEAR FOUNDED: 1998
SPONSOR: D.C. Public Charter School Board
TYPE: Site-based
SIZE: Large

This school provides a challenging atmosphere that focuses on science, math, and technology.

Florida

Ed Venture Charter School

117 East Coast Avenue
Hypoluxo, FL 33462

PHONE: (561) 582-1454
FAX: (561) 582-0692
YEAR FOUNDED: 1998
SPONSOR: Palm Beach County School Board
TYPE: Site-based
SIZE: Small

This school is specifically for educationally handicapped and severely emotionally disturbed students. Students must be certified by the public school district in these special education categories.

Florida State University School

Florida High
3000 School House Road
Tallahassee, FL 32311

PHONE: (850) 245-3700
FAX: (850) 245-3737
WEBSITE: www.fsus.fsu.edu/index.asp
EMAIL: clane@mailer.fsu.edu
YEAR FOUNDED: 1922
SPONSOR: Leon County School Board
TYPE: Site-based
SIZE: Very large

Offers a guarantee that graduates will receive a career certificate and be college-ready. If not, it will pay for some of the remediation courses required. (I think standing behind your product, your student body, is admirable. It also appears that the school is unlikely to have to pay for very many classes.)

KOTA Charter School

1265 South Semoran Boulevard, Suite 1217
Winter Park, FL 32792

PHONE: (407) 671-2323
FAX: (407) 671-2012
EMAIL: Kotacharterschool@yahoo.com
YEAR FOUNDED: 2001
SPONSOR: Orange County School District
TYPE: Site-based
SIZE: Large

Provides an excellent opportunity for students who need less than seven credits of high school work to complete their education in a relatively short period of time.

New Dimensions Charter School

4900 Pleasant Hill Road
Kissimmee, FL 34759

PHONE: (407) 870-9949
FAX: (407) 870-8976
YEAR FOUNDED: 1998
SPONSOR: Osceola School Board
TYPE: Site-based
SIZE: Medium

The focus is on career and vocation programs that prepare students for the workforce.

North Lauderdale Academy High School

7101 Kimberly Boulevard
North Lauderdale, FL 33068

PHONE: (954) 720-0299
FAX: (954) 722-1508
YEAR FOUNDED: 1998
SPONSOR: Broward County School Board
TYPE: Site-based
SIZE: Large

Provides both a college-preparatory track and a career-vocational track.

Richard Milburn Academy

2207 Industrial Boulevard
Sarasota, FL 34234

PHONE: (941) 355-0835
FAX: (941) 355-4395
YEAR FOUNDED: 2001
SPONSOR: Sarasota County School District
TYPE: Site-based
SIZE: Small

By using an experiential approach, it provides at-risk youth with an opportunity to succeed academically and become upstanding citizens. It offers general and vocational programs with flexible scheduling options.

Ruby J. Gainer School for Reaching Your Dream

4000 West Fairfield Drive
Pensacola, FL 32505

PHONE: (850) 450-6905
FAX: (850) 458-0959
WEBSITE: www.escambia.k12.fl.us/instres/alted/
charter_school_programs.htm#gainer
YEAR FOUNDED: 2000
SPONSOR: Escambia County School Board
TYPE: Site-based
SIZE: Medium

This school views its role as reaching out to dropouts between the ages of sixteen and nineteen and pulling them back into school. It provides students with the opportunity to earn either a GED or a high school diploma.

S.T.A.R. Charter School

301 North Florida Avenue
Lakeland, FL 33802

PHONE: (863) 682-3777
FAX: (863) 682-9537
YEAR FOUNDED: 1999
SPONSOR: Polk County School Board
TYPE: Site-based
SIZE: Small

This program is solely for pregnant and parenting teens. It also provides a program for the children of these teens.

Westminster Academy

830 West 29th Street
Orlando, FL 32805

PHONE: (407) 841-6560
FAX: (407) 841-7311
YEAR FOUNDED: 2001
SPONSOR: Orange County School District
TYPE: Site-based
SIZE: Small

Serves medically fragile children in an environment that takes into account their special needs. One component of the school is a rehabilitation program.

Georgia

Central Educational Center (CEC)

160 Martin L. King, Jr. Drive
Newnan, GA 30263

PHONE: (678) 423-2000
FAX: (678) 423-2008
YEAR FOUNDED: 2000
SPONSOR: Coweta County School Board
TYPE: Site-based
SIZE: Large

Students who complete an approved course of study in conjunction with West Central Technical College at CEC will graduate with a technical certificate. It provides joint credit from several local post-secondary institutions that could give students a head start in life and in education. In addition to a GED program, it also offers a high school diploma program in the evening.

Savannah Arts Academy

500 Washington Avenue
Savannah, GA 31401

PHONE: (912) 201-5000
FAX: (912) 651-7064
YEAR FOUNDED: 1998
SPONSOR: Chatham County School Board
TYPE: Site-based
SIZE: Large

The school's central theme revolves around the visual and performing arts.

Hawaii

Ipu Ha'a Academy of Natural Science Public Charter School

4444 Hokualele Road
Anahola, HI 96703

PHONE: (808) 823-0927
FAX: (808) 823-6110
YEAR FOUNDED: 2002
SPONSOR: State Board of Education
TYPE: Site-based
SIZE: Small

Where better to study the natural sciences than in one of the most beautiful places on Earth? The focus is on providing students with a solid grounding in the sciences.

Kanu O Ka 'Aina New Century Public Charter School

PO Box 398
Kamuela, HI 96743

PHONE: (808) 887-8144
FAX: (808) 887-8146
WEBSITE: www.kalo.org
YEAR FOUNDED: 2000
SPONSOR: State Board of Education
TYPE: Site-based
SIZE: Medium

A program designed for native Hawaiians that focuses on rigorous academics.

Idaho

Coeur d'Alene Charter Academy

711 West Kathleen Avenue
Coeur d'Alene, ID 83815

PHONE: (208) 676-1667
FAX: (208) 676-8667
WEBSITE: www.cdacharter.org
EMAIL: info@cdacharter.org
YEAR FOUNDED: 1999
SPONSOR: Coeur d'Alene School District
TYPE: Site-based
SIZE: Medium

Has a particular focus on the visual and performing arts. High academic standards are emphasized as well as becoming better prepared for university studies.

Illinois

Global Villages Charter School

3737 South Paulina Avenue
Chicago, IL 60609

PHONE: (312) 849-8300
FAX: (312) 849-8309
YEAR FOUNDED: 2001
SPONSOR: Chicago Board of Education
TYPE: Site-based
SIZE: Medium

Music is the focus of this school; it is commonly called the Choir Academy.

Nuestra America Charter School

3814 West Iowa Street
Chicago, IL 60651

PHONE: (773) 235-6063
FAX: (773) 235-6436
YEAR FOUNDED: 1997
SPONSOR: Chicago Board of Education
TYPE: Site-based
SIZE: Small

Provides instruction in both English and Spanish.

Southern Illinois University East St. Louis Charter School

601 James R. Thompson Boulevard
East St. Louis, IL 62703

PHONE: (618) 482-8370
FAX: (618) 482-8372

YEAR FOUNDED: 1999
SPONSOR: East St. Louis School District #189
TYPE: Site-based
SIZE: Small

Located on the campus of Southern Illinois University and takes advantage of university resources.

Indiana

Burris Laboratory School

Teachers College 1003B
Ball State University
Muncie, IN 47306

PHONE: (765) 285-5251
FAX: (765) 285-5455
WEBSITE: www.bsu.edu/teachers/charter
EMAIL: askus@bsu.edu
YEAR FOUNDED: 2002
SPONSOR: Ball State University
TYPE: Site-based
SIZE: Medium

The Burris Laboratory School provides opportunities to teaching majors for classroom experience. Admissions criteria closely match those for other public schools.

Indiana Academy for Science, Mathematics, and Humanities

Teachers College 1003B
Ball State University
Muncie, IN 47306

PHONE: (765) 285-5251
FAX: (765) 285-5455
WEBSITE: www.bsu.edu/teachers/charter
EMAIL: askus@bsu.edu
YEAR FOUNDED: 2002
SPONSOR: Ball State University
TYPE: Site-based, residential
SIZE: Medium

The Indiana Academy is the only public residential high school in Indiana. Admissions selection is based on academic ability.

Options Charter High School

PO Box 3790
Carmel, IN 46082

PHONE: (317) 815-2098
FAX: (317) 846-3806
WEBSITE: http://optionsined.org
EMAIL: kdavis@optionsined.org

YEAR FOUNDED: 2002
SPONSOR: Carmel Clay School District
TYPE: Site-based
SIZE: Medium

Options Charter High School was converted into a charter school by the local school district. It was formed by a group of experienced teachers and parents as an alternative to the traditional high school format and environment.

Iowa

Although charter schools are technically legal in Iowa, the law was written in such a way as to discourage the actual formation of schools. As of March 2003, there are no charter schools in the state.

Kansas

Baldwin Experiential Learning Program (BELP)

415 Eisenhower Street
Baldwin City, KS 66006

PHONE: (785) 594-2725
FAX: (785) 594-2858
YEAR FOUNDED: 1998
SPONSOR: Baldwin City Unified School District
TYPE: Site-based
SIZE: Small

Using a thematic and experiential method, BELP provides an opportunity for students to learn through a hands-on approach to learning.

Basehor-Linwood Virtual Charter School

PO Box 282
Basehor, KS 66007

PHONE: (913) 724-1727
WEBSITE: vcs.usd458.k12.ks.us
EMAIL: Brenda_degroot@mail.usd458.k12.ks.us
YEAR FOUNDED: 1998
SPONSOR: Basehor-Linwood Unified School District
TYPE: Online
SIZE: Large

Provides an individualized curriculum accessed through students' home computers. Focus is on current and emerging technologies.

Cornerstone Alternative High School

720 East Seventh Street
Galena, KS 66739

PHONE: (316) 783-4499, ext. 40
FAX: (316) 783-1718
YEAR FOUNDED: 1998
SPONSOR: Galena Unified School District 499
TYPE: Site-based
SIZE: Small

Primarily for students that are at risk of not graduating, this school provides vocational preparation.

Electronic Charter School

150 Wildcat Avenue
Elkhart, KS 67950

PHONE: (620) 697-1166
FAX: (620) 697-2607
WEBSITE: www.onlineecs.org
EMAIL: cabla@onlineECS.org
YEAR FOUNDED: 2001
SPONSOR: Elkhart Unified School District 218
TYPE: Homeschool resource/online
SIZE: Small

In addition to individualized study, the real bonus of this program is that it provides students with a computer for completing the online assignments.

Hope Street Online Academy Charter School

1900 Southwest Hope Street
Topeka, KS 66604

PHONE: (785) 271-3650
FAX: (785) 271-3684
WEBSITE: www.hopestreetonline.org
EMAIL: HBagIII@aol.com
YEAR FOUNDED: 2001
SPONSOR: Topeka Unified School District #501
TYPE: Site-based/online
SIZE: Large

Hope Street has a rather unusual attendance policy: students attend school Monday through Thursday for twelve hours a day and eight hours on Fridays. The additional time provides for additional learning.

McPherson Alternative Center

1600 East Euclid Avenue
McPherson, KS 67460

PHONE: (316) 241-9507
FAX: (316) 241-9509

YEAR FOUNDED: 1998
SPONSOR: McPherson Unified School District #418
TYPE: Site-based
SIZE: Small

Enrollment is open to any resident of the district who has not earned a high school diploma.

REDI

1 East Ninth Avenue
Hutchinson, KS 67501

PHONE: (620) 367-4601
FAX: (620) 662-7340
WEBSITE: www.hutch-votech.com/redi/main_menu
YEAR FOUNDED: 2001
SPONSOR: Hutchinson Unified School District #308
TYPE: Site-based
SIZE: Small

REDI is open to high school juniors and seniors interested in learning how to operate their own business.

Louisiana

Lafayette Charter High School

516 East Pinhook Road
Lafayette, LA 70501

PHONE: (337) 261-8642
FAX: (337) 253-5178
YEAR FOUNDED: 1998
SPONSOR: State Board of Elementary and Secondary Education
TYPE: Site-based
SIZE: Small

Computer-assisted instruction in a site-based program. It provides an extended year and evening courses.

Louisiana High School for Agricultural Sciences

211 Tunica Drive West
Marksville, LA 71351

PHONE: (318) 253-8642
FAX: (318) 253-5178
YEAR FOUNDED: 2000
SPONSOR: State Board of Elementary and Secondary Education
TYPE: Site-based
SIZE: Small

Although the focus is obviously agricultural in nature, the school does offer three distinct tracks—remediation students; dropouts dropping back in; GED students—providing students with all sorts of options.

Milestone Academy of Learning

4334 Earhart Boulevard
New Orleans, LA 70125

PHONE: (504) 821-5442
FAX: (504) 821-5442
YEAR FOUNDED: 1999
SPONSOR: State Board of Elementary and Secondary Education
TYPE: Site-based
SIZE: Medium

One interesting feature of this program is that students are required to participate in the National Defense Cadet Corps for the first two years.

Massachusetts

City on a Hill Charter School

320 Huntington Avenue
Boston, MA 02115

PHONE: (617) 262-9838
FAX: (617) 262-9064
YEAR FOUNDED: 1995
SPONSOR: State Board of Education
TYPE: Site-based
SIZE: Medium

With a Great Books focus, City on a Hill provides a rigorous liberal arts curriculum that challenges students to do their best.

Lowell Middlesex Academy

33 Kearney Square
Lowell, MA 01852

PHONE: (978) 656-0170
FAX: (978) 459-0546
EMAIL: moorek@middlesex.cc.ma.us
YEAR FOUNDED: 1995
SPONSOR: State Board of Education
TYPE: Site-based
SIZE: Small

Serves an at-risk, highly challenged population of one hundred school dropouts, aged fifteen to twenty-one.

Pioneer Valley Performing Arts Charter High School

135 Russell Street
Hadley, MA 01035

PHONE: (413) 585-0003
FAX: (413) 585-8399
WEBSITE: www.pvpa.com
EMAIL: kentbrck@aol.com
YEAR FOUNDED: 1996
SPONSOR: State Board of Education
TYPE: Site-based
SIZE: Medium

The curriculum blends the performing arts with core academic subjects to create an exceptional learning opportunity.

SABIS International Charter School

160 Joan Street
Springfield, MA 01129

PHONE: (413) 783-2600
FAX: (413) 783-2555
WEBSITE: www.sabis.net
EMAIL: info@sabis.net
YEAR FOUNDED: 1995
SPONSOR: State Board of Education
TYPE: Site-based
SIZE: Very large

A truly inimitable school that emphasizes English, math, and languages.

Michigan

Academy for Business and Technology

26104 Eton Avenue
Dearborn Heights, MI 48125

PHONE: (313) 299-1550
FAX: (313) 299-1118
WEBSITE: www.leonagroup.com
EMAIL: info@leonagroup.com
YEAR FOUNDED: 1997
SPONSOR: Eastern Michigan University
TYPE: Site-based
SIZE: Large

This is a college-preparatory program that mixes business and technology with traditional academic subjects.

Academy of Inkster

28500 Avondale Avenue
Inkster, MI 48141

PHONE: (734) 641-1512
FAX: (734) 641-9439
YEAR FOUNDED: 1999
SPONSOR: Central Michigan University
TYPE: Site-based
SIZE: Large

The focus is on providing a bridge from school to future employment.

Advanced Technology Academy

21000 West Ten Mile Road
Southfield, MI 48075

PHONE: (248) 204-2400
FAX: (248) 204-2018
EMAIL: Taz_48238@yahoo.com
YEAR FOUNDED: 2000
SPONSOR: Lake Superior State University
TYPE: Site-based
SIZE: Medium

Provides students with the opportunity to finish college a year early. At completion of the program, students have accumulated a year of college credit (in addition to a high school diploma). Emphasis is on science and engineering.

Casman Alternative Academy

1710 West Merkey Road
Manistee, MI 49660

PHONE: (231) 723-4981
FAX: (231) 723-1555
YEAR FOUNDED: 1997
SPONSOR: Manistee Area Public Schools
TYPE: Site-based
SIZE: Small

The academy uses hands-on learning with students and offers block scheduling to apply academic skills through community service activities.

Cherry Hill School of Performing Arts

28500 Avondale Avenue
Inkster, MI 48141

PHONE: (734) 722-2811
FAX: (734) 641-9439
YEAR FOUNDED: 1999
SPONSOR: Central Michigan University
TYPE: Site-based
SIZE: Very large

A college-preparatory school with a particular emphasis on the performing arts.

Concord Academy Boyne

00401 Dietz Road
Boyne City, MI 49712

PHONE: (616) 582-0194
FAX: (616) 582-4214

WEBSITE: www.concordboyne.com
EMAIL: larrykubovchick@concordboyne.com
YEAR FOUNDED: 1995
SPONSOR: Central Michigan University
TYPE: Site-based
SIZE: Medium

Encourages critical thinking by infusing fine arts into the academic curriculum.

Concord Academy Petoskey

2230 East Mitchell Avenue
Petoskey, MI 49770

PHONE: (231) 347-1600
FAX: (231) 347-1676
YEAR FOUNDED: 2001
SPONSOR: Lake Superior State University
TYPE: Site-based
SIZE: Medium

Encourages critical thinking by infusing fine arts into the academic curriculum.

Detroit Community High School

9331 Grandville
Detroit, MI 48228

PHONE: (313) 835-3500
FAX: (313) 835-5177
YEAR FOUNDED: 1997
SPONSOR: Saginaw Valley State University
TYPE: Site-based
SIZE: Large

The curriculum is a fusion of the Coalition of Essential Schools program with the Waldorf Schools philosophy.

Detroit School of Industrial Arts

11406 Morang Street
Detroit, MI 48224

PHONE: (313) 839-1883
FAX: (313) 839-4194
YEAR FOUNDED: 1996
SPONSOR: Central Michigan University
TYPE: Site-based
SIZE: Large

The focus is on preparing students for careers in the industrial arts or for additional training in that field.

George Crockett Academy

4851 14th Street
Detroit, MI 48208

PHONE: (313) 896-6078
FAX: (313) 896-1363
WEBSITE: www.leonagroup.com
EMAIL: info@leonagroup.com
YEAR FOUNDED: 1998
SPONSOR: Ferris State University
TYPE: Site-based
SIZE: Large

Has as its central concept the seven Kwanzaa principles.

Health Careers Academy of St. Clair Academy

499 Range Road
Port Huron, MI 48061

PHONE: (810) 364-8990
FAX: (810) 364-8139
YEAR FOUNDED: 1999
SPONSOR: St. Clair Independent School District
TYPE: Site-based
SIZE: Small

Puts students on the right path toward a career in the health-care industry.

Henry Ford Academy of Manufacturing Arts

20900 Oakwood Boulevard
Dearborn, MI 48124

PHONE: (313) 982-6200
FAX: (313) 982-6195
WEBSITE: www.hfacademy.org
EMAIL: cchristmas@hfa.spfs.k12.mi.us
YEAR FOUNDED: 1997
SPONSOR: Wayne County Regional Educational Service Agency
TYPE: Site-based
SIZE: Large

Truly one of a kind, this school offers an unparalleled education for students interested in the manufacturing arts. It is a joint project of the Ford Motor Company and the Henry Ford Museum and Greenfield Village.

Honey Creek Community School

1735 South Wagner Road
Ann Arbor, MI 48106

PHONE: (734) 994-2636
FAX: (734) 994-2203

WEBSITE: http://hc.wash.k12.mi.us
EMAIL: lsfry@hc.wash.k12.mi.us
YEAR FOUNDED: 1995
SPONSOR: Washtenaw Independent School District
TYPE: Site-based
SIZE: Small

Particularly encourages parent and community involvement by having students draw on experiences in the world around them.

Information Technology Academy of St. Clair

499 Range Road
Port Huron, MI 48061

PHONE: (810) 364-8990
FAX: (810) 364-7474
YEAR FOUNDED: 2000
SPONSOR: St. Claire Independent School District
TYPE: Site-based
SIZE: Small

Particularly for students interested in careers in the computer industry.

Livingston Technical Academy

3700 Cleary Drive
Howell, MI 48843

PHONE: (517) 545-0828
FAX: (517) 545-7588
WEBSITE: www.livingstontech.com
EMAIL: lta@livingstontech.com
YEAR FOUNDED: 1995
SPONSOR: Central Michigan University
TYPE: Site-based
SIZE: Small

Provides training for a high-tech future.

Michigan Automotive Academy

28675 Northline Road
Romulus, MI 48174

PHONE: (734) 955-9755
FAX: (734) 955-9750
YEAR FOUNDED: 1995
SPONSOR: Central Michigan University
TYPE: Site-based
SIZE: Medium

Students are taught in an ASCE-certified facility about how to become a professional in the automotive industry.

Michigan Health Academy

15100 Northline Road
Southgate, MI 48195

PHONE: (734) 284-4569
FAX: (734) 284-4896
YEAR FOUNDED: 1996
SPONSOR: Saginaw Valley State University
TYPE: Site-based
SIZE: Small

Provides students with either the basic skills necessary to enter the health-care industry or to pursue additional training at a community college.

Michigan Institute for Construction Trades and Technology (MICTT)

PO Box 07472
Detroit, MI 48211

PHONE: (313) 963-7280
FAX: (313) 963-8211
YEAR FOUNDED: 1998
SPONSOR: Detroit Public Schools
TYPE: Site-based
SIZE: Medium

Like all employment, construction trades require very specific training. MICTT offers students the opportunity to learn these valuable skills from an early age.

Sankore Marine Immersion High School Academy

3100 East Jefferson
Detroit, MI 48207

PHONE: (313) 393-3062
FAX: (313) 393-3065
YEAR FOUNDED: 1998
SPONSOR: Wayne County Regional Educational Service Agency
TYPE: Site-based
SIZE: Medium

Special emphasis on marine science.

SER Casa Environmental and Technological Academy

3815 West Fort Street
Detroit, MI 48216

PHONE: (313) 843-5562
FAX: (313) 546-2247
YEAR FOUNDED: 1995

SPONSOR: Wayne County Regional Educational Service Agency
TYPE: Site-based
SIZE: Small

Uses a thematic approach to help students become better able to return to their home schools.

Timbuktu Academy of Science and Technology

9980 Gratiot Avenue
Detroit, MI 48213

PHONE: (313) 579-3250
FAX: (313) 579-3183
YEAR FOUNDED: 1997
SPONSOR: Detroit Public Schools
TYPE: Site-based
SIZE: Medium

The curriculum blends the study of science and technology with the other core areas.

West Michigan Academy for Hospitality Sciences

1625 Leonard Street, North East
Grand Rapids, MI 49503

PHONE: (616) 771-3150
FAX: (616) 771-3157
YEAR FOUNDED: 1995
SPONSOR: Grand Valley State University
TYPE: Site-based
SIZE: Small

The goal is a combination of basic education with training for the food service or hospitality industry

Minnesota

Agricultural and Food Sciences Academy

70 West County Road B2
Little Canada, MN 55117

PHONE: (651) 415-5370
FAX: (651) 415-5506
YEAR FOUNDED: 2001
SPONSOR: North East Metro Intermediate School District #916
TYPE: Site-based
SIZE: Small

Program is in partnership with the business community, community groups, and the Future Farmers of America.

Avalon School

1745 University Avenue
St. Paul, MN 55104

PHONE: (651) 649-5495
FAX: (651) 649-5462
YEAR FOUNDED: 2001
SPONSOR: Hamline University
TYPE: Site-based
SIZE: Medium

Curriculum revolves around student-generated projects and learning.

City Academy

958 Jessie Street
St. Paul, MN 55101

PHONE: (651) 298-4624
FAX: (651) 292-6511
WEBSITE: www.cityacademy.org
YEAR FOUNDED: 1992
SPONSOR: St. Paul District #625
TYPE: Site-based
SIZE: Small

City Academy's claim to fame is that it was the first charter school to open in the United States. Provides educational opportunities for the hardest-to-reach students.

Friendship Academy of Fine Arts Charter School

1500 Hall Curve
Minneapolis, MN 55411

PHONE: (612) 879-6703
FAX: (612) 879-6706
WEBSITE: www.friendshipacademy.org
EMAIL: school@friendshipacademy.org
YEAR FOUNDED: 2001
SPONSOR: Minneapolis Public Schools
TYPE: Site-based
SIZE: Small

The fine arts curriculum is spread throughout all of the core academic areas.

Harbor City International School

PO Box 3034
Duluth, MN 55803

PHONE: (218) 940-8335
WEBSITE: www.harborcityschool.org
EMAIL: info@harborcityschool.org
YEAR FOUNDED: 2002

SPONSOR: Volunteers for America
TYPE: Site-based
SIZE: Small

Uses a combination of approaches to alternative education including the standards of the International Baccalaureate Organization and the Tempe Preparatory Academy (in Arizona).

Heart of the Earth Center for American Indian Education

1209 Fourth Street, South East
Minneapolis, MN 55414

PHONE: (612) 331-8862
FAX: (612) 331-1747
YEAR FOUNDED: 1999
SPONSOR: Minneapolis Public Schools
TYPE: Site-based
SIZE: Medium

Primarily a program for Native Americans, it is infused with traditional values and culture.

High School for Recording Arts

550 Vandalia Street
St. Paul, MN 55114

PHONE: (651) 917-6960
FAX: (651) 917-6961
WEBSITE: www.hsra.org
EMAIL: admin@hsra.org
YEAR FOUNDED: 1998
SPONSOR: St. Paul School Board
TYPE: Site-based
SIZE: Small

What better way to entice students to do better in school (or even to come back to school) than music? The school operates in conjunction with a production studio.

Minnesota Academy of Software Technology

748 Goodrich Avenue
St. Paul, MN 55105

PHONE: (612) 369-0961
FAX: (612) 489-5565
YEAR FOUNDED: 2002
SPONSOR: St. Paul Technical College
TYPE: Site-based
SIZE: Medium

The goal is expertise with technology. The path to that goal is a combination of teamwork, technology, and local support.

Minnesota Technology High School

1745 University Avenue West
St. Paul, MN 55104

PHONE: (651) 649-5403
FAX: (651) 649-5490
WEBSITE: www.mthsonline.org
EMAIL: jholte@mthsonline.org
YEAR FOUNDED: 1998
SPONSOR: Inver Hills Community College
TYPE: Site-based
SIZE: Small

Provides a solid grounding in the liberal arts and in technology. It has an extended school year of 230 days.

Native Arts High School (NAHS)

3123 East Lake Street
Minneapolis, MN 55416

PHONE: (612) 721-6631, ext. 217
FAX: (612) 721-3936
YEAR FOUNDED: 2000
SPONSOR: Augsburg College
TYPE: Site-based
SIZE: Small

Requiring strong family participation, NAHS uses the arts to teach all of the core subjects.

Mississippi

Hayes Cooper Center for Math, Science, and Technology

500 North Martin Luther King, Jr.
Merigold, MS 38759

PHONE: (662) 748-2734
FAX: (662) 748-2735
EMAIL: bbhardy123@hotmail.com
YEAR FOUNDED: 1994
SPONSOR: Cleveland School District
TYPE: Site-based
SIZE: Large

The goal is a failure-free environment that creates the opportunity for all students to be successful. This is the only charter high school in the state.

Missouri

The Construction Careers Center

6301 Knox Industrial Drive
St. Louis, MO 63139

PHONE: (314) 644-1525
FAX: (314) 644-1536
YEAR FOUNDED: 2001
SPONSOR: St. Louis Public Schools
TYPE: Site-based
SIZE: Small

Provides initial training for the building trades.

The Don Bosco Education Center

531 Garfield Avenue
Kansas City, MO 64124

PHONE: (816) 691-2915
FAX: (816) 691-2958
YEAR FOUNDED: 1999
SPONSOR: Central Missouri State University
TYPE: Site-based
SIZE: Small

This was an alternative school that converted to a charter school. The focus is on dropout prevention.

Hogan Preparatory Academy

1221 East Meyer Boulevard
Kansas City, MO 64131

PHONE: (816) 444-3464
FAX: (816) 363-0473
YEAR FOUNDED: 1999
SPONSOR: Central Missouri State University
TYPE: Site-based
SIZE: Medium

Formerly Bishop Hogan High School, it provides a values-based college-preparatory program for at-risk youth.

Nevada

Andre Agassi College Preparatory Academy

1201 West Lake Mead Boulevard
Las Vegas, NV 89106

PHONE: (702) 948-6000
FAX: (702) 948-6002
WEBSITE: www.agassifoundation.org/charter_school.html
YEAR FOUNDED: 2001
SPONSOR: Clark County School District

TYPE: Site-based
SIZE: Medium

Perhaps its biggest claim to fame is the name. It is sponsored by the professional tennis player Andre Agassi and provides a mix of college preparatory and technology course work.

Odyssey Charter School of Nevada

6701 West Charleston Boulevard, Building A
Las Vegas, NV 89146

PHONE: (702) 257-0578
FAX: (702) 259-7793
WEBSITE: www.odysseycs.org
EMAIL: odyssey@odysseycs.org
YEAR FOUNDED: 1999
SPONSOR: Clark County School District
TYPE: Site-based
SIZE: Large

Advanced Learning System's popular A+ Computerized Curriculum composes the curriculum.

New Jersey

Charter Technical High School for Performing Arts

413 New Road
Somers Point, NJ 08244

PHONE: (609) 926-7694
FAX: (609) 926-8472
WEBSITE: www.chartertech.org
EMAIL: asmith@chartertech.org or jemdiver@aol.com
YEAR FOUNDED: 1999
SPONSOR: State Commissioner of Education
TYPE: Site-based
SIZE: Medium

Blends the arts with technology.

LEAP Academy University Charter School (Upper Campus)

639 Cooper Street
Camden, NJ 08102

PHONE: (856) 614-5600
FAX: (856) 614-5601
YEAR FOUNDED: 2001
SPONSOR: State Commissioner for Education
TYPE: Site-based
SIZE: Medium

In addition to superior academic standards, LEAP also focuses on partnering with the local community.

New Mexico

Academy for Technology and the Classics

47 Bataan Boulevard
Santa Fe, NM 87505

PHONE: (505) 474-1787
FAX: (505) 474-1789
EMAIL: jaime_michael@hotmail.com
YEAR FOUNDED: 2001
SPONSOR: Santa Fe Public School District
TYPE: Site-based
SIZE: Medium

Believes a serious study of the classics brings about the very best in students.

The Learning Community Charter School

PO Box 50693
Albuquerque, NM 87181

PHONE: (505) 332-3200
FAX: (505) 332-8780
YEAR FOUNDED: 2001
SPONSOR: Albuquerque Public School District
TYPE: Online
SIZE: Large

Students have access to computers for learning online. They can also use a home computer, if available.

Nuestros Valores Charter School

10609 Hackamore South West
Albuquerque, NM 87121

PHONE: (505) 352-3450
FAX: (505) 352-3486
WEBSITE: www.nvcharter.org
EMAIL: kirk.hartom.nvcs@att.net
YEAR FOUNDED: 2001
SPONSOR: Albuquerque Public School District
TYPE: Site-based
SIZE: Small

Serves at-risk youth.

Robert F. Kennedy Charter School

7121 Derickson North East
Albuquerque, NM 87109

PHONE: (505) 767-5827
FAX: (505) 767-5844
YEAR FOUNDED: 2001

SPONSOR: Albuquerque Public School District
TYPE: Site-based
SIZE: Small

Uses a community center model to serve at-risk youth and dropouts.

The Southwest Secondary Learning Center

4122 Constance Place, North East
Albuquerque, NM 87109

PHONE: (505) 296-7677
FAX: (505) 296-0510
WEBSITE: www.sslc-nm.com
EMAIL: djuarez@sslc-nm.com
YEAR FOUNDED: 2001
SPONSOR: Albuquerque Public School District
TYPE: Online
SIZE: Medium

Its goal is to improve, enhance, and change the educational delivery system through the integration of technology, service learning, and the development of personal and social responsibility.

New York

International High School: A Charter School at LaGuardia Community College

31-10 Thomson Avenue
Long Island City, NY 11101

PHONE: (718) 482-5455
FAX: (718) 392-6904
EMAIL: jmharnick@aol.com
YEAR FOUNDED: 1999
SPONSOR: State Board
TYPE: Site-based
SIZE: Medium

Serves immigrant populations. Students must have been in this country four years or less when entering school. Classrooms are on the LaGuardia Community College campus.

North Carolina

Cape Lookout Marine Science High School

1108 Bridges Street
Morehead City, NC 28557

PHONE: (252) 726-1601
FAX: (252) 726-5245

YEAR FOUNDED: 1998
SPONSOR: State Board of Education
TYPE: Site-based
SIZE: Medium

Formerly the North Carolina School of Maritime Studies, the school is now converted to charter status. Focus is on the study of marine science.

New Century Charter High School

1315-A New Hope Trace
Chapel Hill, NC 27516

PHONE: (919) 942-7722
FAX: (919) 942-8375
WEBSITE: www.newcenturyhs.com
EMAIL: janet@newcenturyhs.com
YEAR FOUNDED: 1998
SPONSOR: State Board of Education
TYPE: Site-based
SIZE: Medium

Fosters individual responsibility through personal growth, education, and community involvement.

Thomas Jefferson Classical Academy

2527 Highway 221A
Mooresboro, NC 28114

PHONE: (828) 657-9998
FAX: (828) 657-9012
WEBSITE: www.tjca.org
EMAIL: tjca@blueridge.net
YEAR FOUNDED: 1999
SPONSOR: State Board of Education
TYPE: Site-based
SIZE: Medium

Its goal is to develop thoughtful, articulate adults. Students are immersed in classical studies as preparation for university academics.

Ohio

Electronic Classroom of Tomorrow

3700 South High Street, Suite 95
Columbus, OH 43207

PHONE: (614) 492-8884 or (888) 326-8395
FAX: (614) 492-8894
WEBSITE: www.ecotohio.org
EMAIL: Info@ecotoh.org
YEAR FOUNDED: 2000

SPONSOR: Lucas County Educational Service Center
TYPE: Online
SIZE: Very large

A statewide, nonprofit, computer-enhanced charter school that provides home-based education for grades K–12.

Horizon Science Academy (Cleveland)

6000 South Marginal Road
Cleveland, OH 44103

PHONE: (216) 432-3660
FAX: (216) 432-3670
WEBSITE: www.hsas.org
EMAIL: info@hsas.org
YEAR FOUNDED: 1999
SPONSOR: State Board of Education
TYPE: Site-based
SIZE: Medium

Delivers a rigorous, innovative educational program integrating the following themes: curricular, attitudes, individual attention, and participation.

Life Skills Center of Cincinnati

2612 Gilbert Avenue
Cincinnati, OH 45206

PHONE: (513) 475-0220
FAX: (513) 475-0444
YEAR FOUNDED: 1999
SPONSOR: State Board of Education
TYPE: Site-based
SIZE: Medium

Offers students who traditionally might have earned the GED the chance to earn a regular high school diploma.

Life Skills Center of Cleveland

3222 Carnegie Avenue
Cleveland, OH 44115

PHONE: (513) 475-0220
FAX: (513) 475-0444
YEAR FOUNDED: 1999
SPONSOR: State Board of Education
TYPE: Site-based
SIZE: Large

Offers students who traditionally might have earned the GED the chance to earn a regular high school diploma.

Life Skills Center of Trumbull County

458 Franklin Street
Warren, OH 44483

PHONE: (330) 392-0231
FAX: (330) 392-0253
YEAR FOUNDED: 2000
SPONSOR: State Board of Education
TYPE: Site-based
SIZE: Medium

Offers students who traditionally might have earned the GED the chance to earn a regular high school diploma.

Life Skills Center of Youngstown

1555 Belmont Avenue
Youngstown, OH 44504

PHONE: (330) 743-6698
FAX: (330) 743-6702
YEAR FOUNDED: 1999
SPONSOR: State Board of Education
TYPE: Site-based
SIZE: Medium

Offers students who traditionally might have earned the GED the chance to earn a regular high school diploma.

Northwest Ohio Building Trades Academy

803 Lime City Road, Suite 300
Rossford, OH 43460

PHONE: (419) 666-0073
FAX: (419) 666-0336
YEAR FOUNDED: 1999
SPONSOR: Lucas County Education Service Center
TYPE: Site-based
SIZE: Small

Provides initial training for the building trades.

Performing Arts School of Metropolitan Toledo

630 South Reynolds Road
Toledo, OH 43615

PHONE: (419) 534-2228
FAX: (419) 531-8627
YEAR FOUNDED: 1999
SPONSOR: Lucas County Education Service Center
TYPE: Site-based
SIZE: Medium

In addition to the traditional subjects for performing arts schools—theater, dance, and music—it also requires students to participate in community service.

TRECA Digital Academy

2222 Marion-Mt. Gilead Road
Marion, OH 43302

PHONE: (740) 389-4798 or (888) 828-4798
FAX: (740) 389-4517
WEBSITE: www.tda.treca.org
YEAR FOUNDED: 2001
SPONSOR: State Board of Education
TYPE: Online
SIZE: Small

TRECA stands for Tri-Rivers Educational Computer Association. Courses are available for students aged five to twenty-one.

Oklahoma

Tulsa School of Arts and Sciences

5155 East 51st Street
Tulsa, OK 74135

PHONE: (918) 828-7727
FAX: (918) 828-7747
WEBSITE: www.tulsasas.org (but the site is mostly empty)
YEAR FOUNDED: 2001
SPONSOR: Tulsa School District
TYPE: Site-based
SIZE: Medium

In addition to a challenging curriculum, it offers an extended school day and a student-teacher ratio of sixteen to one.

Oregon

Armadillo Technical Academy

678 Normal Avenue
Ashland, OR 97520

PHONE: (541) 535-3487
FAX: (541) 535-3928
YEAR FOUNDED: 2000
SPONSOR: Phoenix-Talent School District
TYPE: Site-based
SIZE: Small

Provides technical training for at-risk youth.

Lincoln City Career Technical High School

PO Box 1110
Lincoln City, OR 97367

PHONE: (541) 996-5534
FAX: (541) 996-5534
YEAR FOUNDED: 2000
SPONSOR: Lincoln County School District
TYPE: Site-based
SIZE: Small

Initially an alternative school, it has followed the trend toward charter (and financial stability). The school Internet program is a simulated office.

Pioneer Youth Corps Military Academy

2855 Lincoln Street
Eugene, OR 97405

PHONE: (541) 988-0121
FAX: (541) 988-5814
YEAR FOUNDED: 2000
SPONSOR: Eugene School District
TYPE: Site-based
SIZE: Small

Provides an opportunity for high school students to learn in a highly structured environment.

Willamette Valley Community School

PO Box 866
Corvallis, OR 97339

PHONE: (541) 757-9880
FAX: (541) 757-8540
WEBSITE: www.wvcs.corvallis.or.us
EMAIL: wvcs@proaxis.com
YEAR FOUNDED: 2000
SPONSOR: Corvallis School District
TYPE: Site-based
SIZE: Small

Accredited by the Northwest Association of Schools and Colleges, the student-teacher ratio is five to one.

Pennsylvania

Charter High School for Architecture and Design (CHAD)

675 Sansom Street
Philadelphia, PA 19106

PHONE: (215) 351-2900
FAX: (215) 351-9458
WEBSITE: www.adchsop.org
EMAIL: contact@chadphila.org
YEAR FOUNDED: 2000
SPONSOR: School District of Philadelphia
TYPE: Site-based
SIZE: Large

Founded by the Philadelphia chapter of the American Institute of Architects. CHAD prepares students to assist in shaping the built, natural, and manufactured environment.

Center for Economics and Law Charter School

3020 Market Street
Philadelphia, PA 19151

PHONE: (215) 599-4956
FAX: (215) 599-4966
YEAR FOUNDED: 1998
SPONSOR: School District of Philadelphia
TYPE: Site-based
SIZE: Large

Primary focus is on economics and entrepreneurship.

Freire Charter School

1425 Arch Street
Philadelphia, PA 19102

PHONE: (215) 557- 8555
FAX: (215) 557-9051
EMAIL: j2129@aol.com
YEAR FOUNDED: 1999
SPONSOR: School District of Philadelphia
TYPE: Site-based
SIZE: Medium

Based on the teaching philosophies of the late Brazilian educator Paolo Freire, the goal is to relate education to the world around.

Multi-Cultural Academy Charter School

4666-68 North 15th Street
Philadelphia, PA 19140

PHONE: (215) 457-6666
FAX: (215) 457-1770
YEAR FOUNDED: 1998
SPONSOR: School District of Philadelphia
TYPE: Site-based
SIZE: Medium

The primary mission of the Multi-Cultural Academy is to educate the whole child. The school adheres to state academic standards.

PA Learners Online Regional Charter School

1400 Penn Avenue
Pittsburgh, PA 15222

PHONE: (412) 394-5796
FAX: (412) 394-5969
WEBSITE: www.palearnersonline.net
EMAIL: PALO@aiu3.net
YEAR FOUNDED: 2001
SPONSOR: School District of Pittsburgh
TYPE: Online
SIZE: Small

This school will only continue to grow as the rest of the state becomes more aware of its existence. It offers a challenging curriculum online.

Philadelphia Electrical and Technology Charter School

1701 Spring Garden Street
Philadelphia, PA 19130

PHONE: (215) 761-9260
FAX: (215) 761-9270
YEAR FOUNDED: 2002
SPONSOR: School District of Philadelphia
TYPE: Site-based
SIZE: Large

Founded by the International Brotherhood of Electrical Workers, it provides initial training for students interested in going into the electrical trade.

Spectrum Charter School

500-G Garden City Drive
Monroeville, PA 15146

PHONE: (412) 374-8130
FAX: (412) 374-9629
YEAR FOUNDED: 2000
SPONSOR: Gateway School District
TYPE: Site-based
SIZE: Small

Spectrum is a school-to-work program for students with autism as well as other challenges.

SusQ-Cyber Charter School

90 Lawton Lane
Milton, PA 17847

PHONE: (570) 523-1155
FAX: (570) 524-7104
WEBSITE: www.susqcyber.org
EMAIL: hbell@csiu.org
YEAR FOUNDED: 1998
SPONSORS: Berwick Area, Bloomsburg Area, and Milton Area School Districts, and the Central Susquehanna Intermediate Unit
TYPE: Online
SIZE: Small

Instruction is driven by personalized education plans to better meet students' needs and learning styles, which enables students to succeed.

Western Pennsylvania Cyber Charter School

173 Seventh Street
Midland, PA 15059

PHONE: (724) 643-1180
FAX: (724) 643-4887
YEAR FOUNDED: 2000
SPONSOR: Midland Borough School District
TYPE: Online
SIZE: Very large

Offers an online program that takes advantage of the vast amount of information available on the Internet.

Rhode Island

Textron/Chamber of Commerce Providence Public Charter School

130 Broadway
Providence, RI 02903

PHONE: (401) 456-1738
FAX: (401) 456 -741
WEBSITE: www.chamberschool.com/index1.htm
EMAIL: info@chamberschool.com
YEAR FOUNDED: 1997
SPONSOR: State Board of Regents
TYPE: Site-based
SIZE: Medium

An at-risk program, it has work placements available in partnership with the Rhode Island Chamber of Commerce.

South Carolina

Greenville Technical Charter High School

PO Box 5616
Greenville, SC 29606

PHONE: (864) 250-8844
FAX: (864) 250-8846
YEAR FOUNDED: 1999
SPONSOR: Greenville School District
TYPE: Site-based
SIZE: Medium

A combination of challenging academics, technology use, and career education is the hallmark of this program.

Tennessee

Memphis Academy of Science and Engineering

930 Madison Avenue, Suite 100
Memphis, TN 38103

PHONE: (901) 448-6273
FAX: (901) 448-8850
WEBSITE: www.MemphisScienceAcademy.org
EMAIL: thenderson@memphisbiotech.org
YEAR FOUNDED: 2003
SPONSOR: Memphis School District
TYPE: Site-based
SIZE: Medium

This was the first charter school to operate in Tennessee. With a focus on technology, science, and math education, it seeks to become a center of excellence for its students.

Upper Cumberland Learning Academy

600 Jeffrey Circle
Cookeville, TN 38501

PHONE: (931) 528-2543
EMAIL: sylvanck@usit.net
YEAR FOUNDED: 2002
SPONSOR: Cookeville School District
TYPE: Site-based
SIZE: Small

Currently in formation, the school is accepting students for the 2003–2004 school year.

Texas

Academy of Transitional Studies

2203 Baldwin Boulevard
Corpus Christi, TX 78405

PHONE: (361) 881-9988
FAX: (361) 881-9994
YEAR FOUNDED: 1996
SPONSOR: State Board of Education
TYPE: Site-based
SIZE: Medium

Offers both a high school diploma track and a GED track.

Blessed Sacrament Academy Charter High School

1135 Mission Road
San Antonio, TX 78210

PHONE: (210) 532-9161
FAX: (210) 533-5612
YEAR FOUNDED: 1996
SPONSOR: State Board of Education
TYPE: Site-based
SIZE: Medium

Becoming a charter provided economic stability for this school. To qualify, a student must be at least two years below grade level.

Dallas Can! Academy Charter School

325 West 12th Street, Suite 250
Dallas, TX 75208

PHONE: (214) 944-1955
FAX: (214) 944-1930
WEBSITE: www.dallascan.org

YEAR FOUNDED: 1996
SPONSOR: State Board of Education
TYPE: Site-based
SIZE: Very large

Offering both a high school diploma track and a GED track, this school serves students aged sixteen to twenty-one. With two daily schedules: 7:50 A.M. to 12:00 P.M. and 12:50 P.M. to 5:00 P.M.

Fort Worth Academy of Fine Arts

3901 S. Hulen Street
Fort Worth, TX 76109

PHONE: (817) 924-1483
FAX: (817) 926-9932
WEBSITE: www.fwafa.org/fwafa/index.htm
YEAR FOUNDED: 2001
SPONSOR: State Board of Education
TYPE: Site-based
SIZE: Small

Focus is on collaboration between traditional academics and the fine arts. It is also the home of the Texas Boys Choir.

Fort Worth Can! Academy

4301 Campus Drive, Suite D
Fort Worth, TX 76119

PHONE: (817) 431-4226
FAX: (817) 531-0443
WEBSITE: www.fortworthcan.org
EMAIL: keith@texanscan.org
YEAR FOUNDED: 2000
SPONSOR: State Board of Education
TYPE: Site-based
SIZE: Medium

Offering both a high school diploma track and a GED track, this school serves students aged sixteen to twenty-one.

Girls and Boys Preparatory Academy

8415 West Bellfort Avenue
Houston, TX 77071

PHONE: (713) 270-5994
FAX: (713) 270-1302
YEAR FOUNDED: 1996
SPONSOR: State Board of Education
TYPE: Site-based
SIZE: Large

Although boys and girls both attend this school, classes are separated by gender and students are required to wear uniforms. It offers a challenging core curriculum.

Katherine Anne Porter School

PO Box 2053, 515 FM 2325
Wimberley, TX 78676

PHONE: (512) 847-6867
FAX: (512) 847-0737
EMAIL: yanadevere@hotmail.com
YEAR FOUNDED: 1999
SPONSOR: State Board of Education
TYPE: Site-based
SIZE: Small

Provides an accelerated curriculum toward a high school diploma.

North Houston High School for Business

455 West Parker Road
Houston TX 77091

PHONE: (713) 691-3123
FAX: (713) 691-2511
EMAIL: twilliams@pdq.net
YEAR FOUNDED: 1999
SPONSOR: State Board of Education
TYPE: Site-based
SIZE: Small

Offers a focus on business, particularly management and economics.

Positive Solutions Charter School

302 South Flores
San Antonio, TX 78204

PHONE: (210) 299-1025
FAX: (210) 299-1052
YEAR FOUNDED: 1998
SPONSOR: State Board of Education
TYPE: Site-based
SIZE: Medium

Offers both a high school diploma track and a GED track for dropouts and parenting teens.

Sentry Technology Preparatory School

508 East Elizabeth Avenue
Brownsville, TX 78520

PHONE: (956) 542-3363
FAX: (956) 542-3139
EMAIL: aguiepena@hotmail.com
YEAR FOUNDED: 1998
SPONSOR: State Board of Education
TYPE: Independent study (print, computer-assisted, and videotapes)
SIZE: Medium

Primarily for students who have not been successful elsewhere, the school maintains student interest through the use of technology.

University Charter School

University of Texas High School Diploma Program
Box 7700
Austin, TX 78713

PHONE: (512) 232-7695
WEBSITE: www.utexas.edu/cee/dec/uths/diploma.shtml
EMAIL: kathy.uplinger@dec.utexas.edu
YEAR FOUNDED: 1998
SPONSOR: State Board of Education
TYPE: Online
SIZE: Medium

This program offers courses in both online and print formats. This unique opportunity to earn a high school diploma through the University of Texas is an exciting opportunity to learn online. It offers all of the traditional courses required for graduation.

Utah

Success School

4120 South 1785 West, Suite 2B
Taylorsville, UT 84119

PHONE: (801) 964-4258
FAX: (801) 964-4259
YEAR FOUNDED: 1999
SPONSOR: State Board of Education
TYPE: Site-based
SIZE: Small

Offers three tracks: traditional, vocational, and GED preparation.

Tuacahn High School for the Performing Arts

1100 Tuacahn Drive
Ivins, UT 84738

PHONE: (435) 652-3201
FAX: (435) 722-2331
WEBSITE: www.tuacahn.com/hs
EMAIL: tca@infowest.com
YEAR FOUNDED: 2000
SPONSOR: State Board of Education
TYPE: Site-based
SIZE: Small

Intensive instruction in the performing arts of music, dance, and drama. If location is important, you couldn't ask for more beautiful surroundings.

Uintah River High School

PO Box 1990
Ft. Duchesne, UT 84026

PHONE: (435) 722-2331
FAX: (435) 722-0511
EMAIL: kathyc@ubtanet.com
YEAR FOUNDED: 2000
SPONSOR: State Board of Education
TYPE: Site-based
SIZE: Small

Particularly designed to serve Ute Indian Tribe members as well as others who are economically disadvantaged.

Virginia

Blue Ridge Technical Academy

Roanoke Higher Education Center, Suite 122
108 North Jeff Street
Roanoke, VA 24016

PHONE: (540) 767-6060
FAX: (540) 767-6066
EMAIL: rkelley1@roanoke.infi.net
YEAR FOUNDED: 2001
SPONSOR: Roanoke City Local Education Agency
TYPE: Site-based
SIZE: Small

Its mission is to serve at-risk youth in danger of failing the State Standards of Learning tests with the entry-level technical skills required by employers.

Hampton University Charter School for Mathematics, Science, and Technology

Department of Education
Hampton University
PO Box 6195
Hampton, VA 23668

PHONE: (757) 727-5793
FAX: (757) 727-5084
WEBSITE: www.hamptonu.edu/charterschool/Home.htm
EMAIL: hucharterschool@hamptonu.edu
YEAR FOUNDED: 2002
SPONSOR: Hampton City Local Education Agency
TYPE: Site-based
SIZE: Medium

This new charter school was founded by the Education Department at Hampton University. It offers a ten-point model for school instruction that includes high academic expectations, character building, civic skill development, leadership development, technological proficiency, a safe environment, individualized instruction, dedicated and committed staff, a nurturing and caring school family, and a disciplined environment.

Murray High School

1200 Forest Street
Charlottesville, VA 22901

PHONE: (434) 296-3090
FAX: (434) 979-6479
WEBSITE: http://k12.albemarle.org/murrayhs
EMAIL: vcrews@albemarle.org
YEAR FOUNDED: 2001
SPONSOR: Albemarle Local Education Agency
TYPE: Site-based
SIZE: Small

Operates on the belief that students will blossom and prosper in an active learning environment. It provides an experiential learning program that takes into account the interests of the students.

Wisconsin

Academic Center High School

601 University Avenue
Colfax, WI 54730

PHONE: (715) 962-3155
FAX: (715) 962-4024
YEAR FOUNDED: 1998
SPONSOR: Colfax School District
TYPE: Site-based
SIZE: Small

The goal is to discover how each student learns best.

Comprehensive Learning Center

1350 Peebles Drive
Richland Center, WI 53581

PHONE: (608) 647-9177
FAX: (608) 647-2033
YEAR FOUNDED: 2000
SPONSOR: Richland School District
TYPE: Site-based
SIZE: Small

This program specifically targets those students who have the most difficulty existing within the traditional school environment.

Crandon Alternative Resource School

PO Box 3310
Crandon, WI 54520

PHONE: (715) 478-3713
FAX: (715) 478-5570
YEAR FOUNDED: 2000
SPONSOR: School District of Crandon
TYPE: Site-based
SIZE: Small

Offers a two-track program toward completion of either a high school diploma or the GED.

Jefferson County Alternative School

131 Hall Street
Watertown, WI 53549

PHONE: (920) 262-1480
FAX: (920) 262-1468
YEAR FOUNDED: 1999
SPONSOR: School District of Jefferson
TYPE: Online
SIZE: Small

Provides an opportunity to earn a high school diploma online.

Laurel High School

WWTC Campus
220 South Main Street
Viroqua, WI 54665

PHONE: (608) 637-8486
FAX: (608) 789-6268
YEAR FOUNDED: 1999
SPONSOR: Viroqua Area School District
TYPE: Site-based
SIZE: Small

Seeks to impart the necessary skills to succeed in employment, at a technical college, or in the university setting.

Milwaukee Leadership Training Center

South 27th Street
Milwaukee, WI 53215

PHONE: (414) 672-3487
YEAR FOUNDED: 2000
SPONSOR: Milwaukee Public Schools
TYPE: Site-based
SIZE: Small

Located on the campus of the School Sisters of Saint Francis (along with many other nonprofit organizations). It provides a structured and disciplined learning environment for at-risk youth.

Renaissance School for the Arts

610 North Badger Avenue
Appleton, WI 54915

PHONE: (920) 832-4104
FAX: (920) 832-4198
WEBSITE: www.aasd.k12.wi.us/west/rsa/rsa%20p2%20we%20are.htm
YEAR FOUNDED: 2000
SPONSOR: Appleton Area School District
TYPE: Site-based
SIZE: Medium

All students are immersed in the arts. It is a half-day program and draws from all three of the local high schools. Students earn their diploma through their home campus.

Technology Charter School

500 Main Street
Eau Claire, WI 54701

PHONE: (715) 833-3403
FAX: (715) 833-3481
YEAR FOUNDED: 2000
SPONSOR: Eau Claire Area School District
TYPE: Site-based
SIZE: Small

The goal is for students to develop their abilities in emerging technologies.

Internet Resources

Do you want to learn everything there is to know about charter schools? There is only one site that gives you everything (and more): CharterSchooLaw.com is the complete guide to charter school resources on the Web.

One of the many resources provided is a list of Top Ten Charter School Resources on the Web. Since CharterSchooLaw is the expert, its list is included below with my notes for each site. (Note that its top ten list only has nine entries. Conveniently, from my perspective, the tenth should be its own website.)

1. U.S. Charter Schools Website

www.uscharterschools.org

> Provides information on charter schools across the country. It is quite easy to look up your local charter school and get more information than from any other source.

2. Center for Education Reform's Charter School Page

www.edreform.com/charter_schools

> The Center for Education Reform (CER), besides being one of the most important sources of information on charter schools, also publishes the *Charter School Directory*, the single best source, online or in print, for charter school contact and program information.

3. Charter Friends National Network

www.charterfriends.org

> A national organization that promotes quality charter schools through networking.

4. DMOZ's Charter School Page

http://dmoz.org/Reference/Education/Methods_and_Theories/ Learning_Theories/Charter_Schools

> Links, links, and more links, all on charter schools. This is a good starting place for doing your own research.

5. The Heritage Foundation's School Choice and Charter Schools Page

www.heritage.org

> The Heritage Foundation offers a great deal of research on charter schools. It is of particular value if you come at the issue with a conservative framework (because the Heritage Foundation is unabashedly conservative).

6. U.S. Department of Education's Charter School Roadmap

www.ed.gov/pubs/Roadmap

> Everything that you could ever possibly want to know on charter schools and how to make one from the perspective of the United States government is available here.

7. U.S. Department of Education-2000 Charter School Report

www.ed.gov/pubs/charter4thyear

The federal government's take on charter schools and their efficacy.

8. Education Week's Charter School Page

www.edweek.org/context/topics/issuespage.cfm?id=42

The preeminent education magazine offers information of a general nature on the topic.

9. State-by-State Charter School Law Rankings

http://edreform.com/press/2003/charterlaws.htm

As discussed at the beginning of this chapter, the Center for Education Reform ranks each state according to the ease or difficulty involved in its charter school laws. This website includes the complete statistics for each ranking.

If your favorite charter school is not listed in this chapter and you would like it to be considered for subsequent editions, please send a note to me at hsd@degree.net providing all relevant information. Likewise, if you are listed here, but would like your information updated in potential future editions, also send a note.

CHAPTER 7

University-Based High Schools

"A university should be a place of light, of liberty, and of learning."

—*Benjamin Disraeli*

While many universities offer high school–level correspondence courses, few award high school diplomas through their correspondence study. Most universities assume that you will be transferring the credits to a traditional high school. There are, however, a few universities that do offer diplomas.

It is important to note that university-based high schools tend to provide a rigorous academic curriculum. While almost all are site-based, they can be excellent choices for students who are looking for something different and more challenging than the traditional high school. Although there are some remedial courses available at a few of these schools, the general assumption is that the student is ready for a higher level of thinking and learning.

What to Look For

As a group, university-based high school programs all tend to have a strong, academically challenging curriculum. They offer extracurricular activities designed to enhance the learning experience. They also tend to offer exceptional student support.

Often, in choosing a school, location is the deciding factor. Most students (and their parents) are not willing to relocate for a high school program. If you feel like a particular program is exceptional or you live in a place without similar options, you might want to consider relocating. Yes, some of the programs really are that good.

Frequently Asked Questions

Most of these universities offer diploma programs. Will that high school diploma be accepted for college admissions?
Yes. In fact, most universities will likely view such attendance in a very favorable light. It's quite possible that, in addition to the regular high school curriculum, you will also have taken (and proved that you can do well in) university classes.

If your goal is to attend a top-notch university, you may want to consider a high school program that is located at a top-notch university. For example, those students who go to Yeshiva University high schools are accepted into that university at a greater percentage than students from other high schools. This is not coincidental. Even if your goal is to attend another university than the one associated with the high school program, it can certainly increase your likelihood of success to have gone to a university high school and to have taken classes through a university.

Will I only take high school courses? What are the possibilities for taking college classes?
While each university has its own rules, almost all of the programs listed below offer the possibility of taking courses from the university, and some require it as part of their curriculum. For example, University High School at California State University-

Fresno provides students with a year of university education as part of their curriculum. When you graduate, you get a year's worth of college credit.

What you may discover in your quest for more challenging courses is that they are already offered within the high school program. In contrast to what you may have experienced in your middle school or junior high, most of these programs start with the supposition that you are ready for challenging course work.

I don't live where any of these programs are located. Is it possible to live in the dorms?

Yeshiva University is the only school that offers a small number of dorm rooms and they are only for male students. However, it might be possible to find a place in a private home or with a relative. Your parents might even consider moving closer to one of these programs, given how good the programs are.

Are there scholarships available for any of these schools?

Many of these schools do offer financial aid, but it is almost all based on need. Contact the admissions office of your school of choice and the administrator will be able to provide more complete information.

Most of these schools are private, so they do charge fees for attendance. The exceptions are University High School at California State University-Fresno, University Schools at the University of Northern Colorado, Hampton University Charter School, and Florida State University School. They are all charter schools, so they are paid for with public funding.

Programs

Ball State University, Burris Laboratory School

Teachers College 1003B
Muncie, IN 47306

PHONE: (765) 285-5251
FAX: (765) 285-5455
WEBSITE: www.bsu.edu/teachers/charter
EMAIL: askus@bsu.edu
YEAR FOUNDED: 2002

The Burris Laboratory School provides opportunities to teaching majors for classroom experience. Admissions criteria closely match those for other public schools.

Ball State University, Indiana Academy for Science, Mathematics, and Humanities

Teachers College 1003B
Muncie, IN 47306

PHONE: (765) 285-5251
FAX: (765) 285-5455
WEBSITE: www.bsu.edu/teachers/charter
EMAIL: askus@bsu.edu
YEAR FOUNDED: 2002

The Indiana Academy is the only public residential high school in Indiana. Admissions selection is based on academic ability.

Bard College, Bard High School Early College

525 East Houston Street
New York, NY 10002

PHONE: (212) 982-5024
WEBSITE: www.bard.edu/bhsec
EMAIL: bhsec@bard.edu
YEAR FOUNDED: 2001

This program is run collaboratively by the New York City Board of Education and Bard College. Highly motivated students are given the opportunity to move from the beginning of their freshman year of high school to the end of their second year of college in only four years. This program is not for the faint of heart; you will work and you will work hard. At the end of four years, students earn an Associate of Arts degree. You must be a resident of New York City (and the program would be worth moving there for the right student). Students with at least a 3.0 grade point average automatically earn admission into the Bachelor of Arts programs at Simon's Rock College of Bard in Great Barrington, Massachusetts.

Boston College High School

150 Morrissey Boulevard
Boston, MA 02125

PHONE: (617) 436-3900
FAX: (617) 474-5015
WEBSITE: www.bchigh.edu
EMAIL: o'horo@bchigh.edu
YEAR FOUNDED: 1863

Boston College High School has a long history of providing a solid, Jesuit education to young men, regardless of religion. It offers both Advanced Placement and honors courses; a test at entrance is required. This is quite a demanding academic program, and only those who can succeed in such an environment are admitted.

Brigham Young University, High School Programs

PO Box 21514
Provo, UT 84602-1514

PHONE: (801) 378-5078
WEBSITE: http://ce.byu.edu/is/site/catalog/trans.dhtm
EMAIL: indstudy@byu.edu
YEAR FOUNDED: 1982

With an extensive catalog of online and correspondence high school courses, Brigham Young University has a program where adult students who are nineteen or older can earn a high school diploma through cooperating school districts. In addition to offering this adult diploma program, it has programs for college preparation, vocational-technical preparation, and GED preparation.

California State University—Fresno, University High School

2355 East Keats Avenue, M/S UH134
Fresno, CA 93740

PHONE: (559) 278-8263
FAX: (559) 278-0447
WEBSITE: www.csufresno.edu/univhigh
EMAIL: uhs@listserv.csufresno.edu
YEAR FOUNDED: 2000
CHARTER SPONSOR: Sierra Unified School District

University High School is a relatively new college-preparatory program. It is a charter school and is free for students. There is a strong emphasis on music. By the end of the four-year program, in addition to having earned a high school diploma, students earn one year of college credit. Students are chosen by lottery from an applicant pool. To enter the applicant pool, you must have already completed Algebra 1 with a grade of C or better and be able to read music and play an instrument at the intermediate level.

Columbia University High School Programs

303 Lewisohn Avenue
(116th and Broadway)
New York, NY 10027

PHONE: (212) 854-9699
WEBSITE: www.ce.columbia.edu/hs
EMAIL: sp-info@columbia.edu
YEAR FOUNDED: 1986

Columbia University does not offer a diploma program, but it does provide an opportunity to take what might be a typical high school education and make it more demanding. It offers noncredit courses during both the summer and the academic year, primarily on Saturdays, which can strengthen not only academic knowledge but also college admissions applications.

Florida State University School

Florida High
3000 School House Road
Tallahassee, FL 32311

PHONE: (850) 245-3700
FAX: (850) 245-3737
WEBSITE: www.fsus.fsu.edu/index.asp
EMAIL: clane@mailer.fsu.edu
YEAR FOUNDED: 1922

Every graduate is guaranteed to receive a career certificate and be college-ready or the school will pay for the first required college remediation course in mathematics, reading, and writing.

Hampton University Charter School for Mathematics, Science, and Technology

Department of Education
PO Box 6195
Hampton, VA 23668

PHONE: (757) 727-5793
FAX: (757) 727-5084
WEBSITE: www.hamptonu.edu/charterschool/Home.htm
EMAIL: hucharterschool@hamptonu.edu
YEAR FOUNDED: 2002

This new charter school was founded by the Education Department at Hampton University and is sponsored by the Hampton City Local Education Agency. It offers a ten-point model for school instruction that includes high academic expectations, character building, civic skill development, leadership development, technological proficiency, safe environment, individualized instruction, dedicated and committed staff, nurturing and caring school family, and disciplined environment.

Indiana University High School

Owen Hall 001
790 East Kirkwood Avenue
Bloomington, IN 47405-7101

PHONE: (800) 334-1011
WEBSITE: http://scs.indiana.edu
EMAIL: scs@indiana.edu
YEAR FOUNDED: 1999

Indiana University's School of Continuing Studies, provider of the university's distance-learning degrees, also offers a high school diploma program. Courses, which are developed and taught by certified high school teachers, are mostly print based, though some employ the Internet, CD-ROMs, or other technologies. It is possible to either complete an entire diploma program or finish a diploma program already in progress. The program is accredited by the North Central Association Commission on Accreditation and School Improvement.

Marquette University High School (MUHS)

3401 West Wisconsin Avenue
Milwaukee, WI 53208

PHONE: (414) 933-7220
WEBSITE: www.muhs.edu
EMAIL: Klestinski@muhs.edu
YEAR FOUNDED: 1857

MUHS provides a rigorous academic education within the Jesuit tradition. The school has recently seen unparalleled growth in the student body and now has more than a thousand students. MUHS only admits male students. As a Catholic school, it welcomes all students regardless of religion.

Riverside University High School

1615 East Locust Street
Milwaukee, WI 53211

PHONE: (414) 906-4900
FAX: (414) 906-4915
WEBSITE: www.ruhs.uwm.edu/index.htm
EMAIL: benishr@mail.milwaukee.k12.wi.us
YEAR FOUNDED: 1868

While not onsite at the University of Wisconsin-Madison, this program has a special relationship with the university that allows students to get a jump on college by taking university courses. It also offers Advanced Placement courses for those students who qualify. A combination of the two could easily result in fewer years in college.

St. Louis University High School

4970 Oakland Avenue
St. Louis, MO 63110

PHONE: (314) 531-0330 ext. 128
FAX: (314) 531-3441
WEBSITE: www.sluh.org
EMAIL: admission@sluh.org
YEAR FOUNDED: 1818

The oldest school in the chapter, it was founded in 1818. Girls need not apply; this Jesuit school is for boys only. It provides a challenging and exciting humanistic education rooted in the Catholic faith.

Texas Tech University High School

PO Box 42191
Lubbock, TX 79409

PHONE: (806) 742-2352 or (800) 692-6877, ext. 244
WEBSITE: www.dce.ttu.edu/ttuisd/ttuhs.cfm
EMAIL: distlearn@ttu.edu
YEAR FOUNDED: 1993

Texas Tech University High School is accredited by the Texas Education Agency, but it is open to all students. Bear in mind that you will be receiving a State of Texas accredited curriculum. There is an interesting twist to this program. Regardless of age or location, you are required to take the Texas Assessment of Academic Skills (TAAS) before you can graduate. It is possible to arrange to take the test in your home state (but it is unlikely that an overseas student would be able to arrange this accommodation).

University of Chicago Laboratory School

1362 East 59th Street
Chicago, IL 60637

PHONE: (773) 702-9450
FAX: (773) 702-7455
WEBSITE: www.ucls.chicago.edu
EMAIL: lab@ucls.chicago.edu
YEAR FOUNDED: 1896

Started by John Dewey, the school is thriving. Ninety-nine percent of graduating students go on to college. The standard for achievement is quite rigorous. The focus is on analyzing and solving problems. Students are allowed to take classes in the university.

University of Illinois, University Laboratory High School

1212 West Springfield Avenue
Urbana, IL 61801

PHONE: (217) 333-2870
WEBSITE: www.uni.uiuc.edu
EMAIL: uniweb@uni.uiuc.edu
YEAR FOUNDED: 1921

Thirty-seven percent (22 of 60 students) of the class of 2002 were named National Merit Scholarship semifinalists. This is a program for students who excel in school. Although only offering Spanish since 1995, it has offered Russian since 1963. Among its graduates are three Nobel Prize laureates.

University of Missouri—Columbia High School

Center for Distance and Independent Study
136 Clark Hall
Columbia, MO 65211-4200

PHONE: (573) 882-2491 or (800) 692-6877
FAX: (573) 882-6808
WEBSITE: cdis.missouri.edu/MUHighSChool/HShome.htm
EMAIL: cdis@missouri.edu
YEAR FOUNDED: 1999

This program, accredited by the North Central Association of Colleges and Schools, provides a diploma program with more than 150 courses. The diploma program is open to adults and high school age students. This is not a site-based program, but a program that provides access to a high school diploma for homeschooled students or students seeking a more challenging educational environment.

University of Northern Colorado, University Schools

6525 West 18th Street
Greeley, CO 80634

PHONE: (970) 330-2221
FAX: (970) 506-7070
WEBSITE: www.universityschools.com
EMAIL: gpierson@universityschools.com
YEAR FOUNDED: 1999

Although it is now a charter school, this school has been on the University of Northern Colorado's campus for over a hundred years. It is accredited by the North Central Association of Schools and Colleges and sponsored by the Weld County School Board.

University of Southern Colorado, Pueblo School for the Arts and Sciences

1745 Acero Avenue
Pueblo, CO 81004

PHONE: (719) 549-2737
FAX: (719) 549-2725
WEBSITE: www.uscolo.edu
EMAIL: romanh@uscolo.edu
YEAR FOUNDED: 1994

The University of Southern Colorado operates this high-achieving school that focuses on the arts and sciences. It is sponsored by the Pueblo 60 School District.

University of Texas—Austin, UT High School Diploma Program

PO Box 7700
Austin, TX 78713-7700

PHONE: (512) 232-7695
WEBSITE: www.utexas.edu/cee/dec/uths/diploma.shtml
EMAIL: kathy.uplinger@dec.utexas.edu
YEAR FOUNDED: 1998

This program offers courses both online and in print format. This is a unique opportunity to earn a high school diploma, online, through the University of Texas. It offers all of the traditional courses required for graduation. Sponsored by the state board of education.

Yeshiva University, Marsha Stern Talmudical Academy/Yeshiva University High School for Boys

500 West 185th Street
New York, NY 10033

PHONE: (212) 960-5337
WEBSITE: www.yuhsb.org
EMAIL: tmsta@ymail.yu.edu
YEAR FOUNDED: Unknown

This school provides a unique relationship to one of the top fifty research universities in the country. Graduates have an unparalleled admissions rate into Yeshiva University. Dormitory facilities are available for some students. The school is dedicated to preparing young men for their adult lives both as knowledgeable and committed Jews and as broadly educated, intellectually curious, and caring members of the general society. The school offers both Judaic studies and general studies, and students take courses from both departments.

Yeshiva University, The Samuel H. Wang Yeshiva University High School for Girls

86-86 Palo Alto Street
Holliswood, NY 11423

PHONE: (718) 479-8550
FAX: (718) 479-8686
WEBSITE: www.yu.edu/yuhsg/index.html
EMAIL: inquiries@yuhsg.org
YEAR FOUNDED: Unknown

A truly matchless educational opportunity for high school aged girls. Only Jewish girls need apply, but what an incredible opportunity for those who do qualify. The program offers a demanding dual curriculum of Judaic and college-preparatory courses. Unlike the boys school, no dormitory facilities are available. Students that do well at this school are likely to do well at any university in the country.

Part III: Diplomas through Assessment

CHAPTER 8

The GED

"More than 95 percent of employers in the United States consider GED graduates the same as traditional high school graduates in regard to hiring, salary, and opportunity."

—*American Council on Education*

For the vast, vast majority of employers, there is little difference between people who have a high school diploma and those who have successfully taken and passed the GED test. Worldwide, 860,000 people take the GED test each and every year. Some quite famous people, including Bill Cosby, U.S. Senator Ben Nighthorse Campbell, and the late Dave Thomas (of the Wendy's restaurant chain) all took and passed the examination. Who else? How about Mary Lou Retton and Waylon Jennings? Or Wally "Famous" Amos and Michael J. Fox?

The American Council on Education (ACE), producers of the GED, performs an interesting experiment every spring. It goes out and finds some high school seniors preparing to graduate and gives them the GED test. Now, bear in mind that these are students who will be graduating—diplomas are almost in hand. Thirty percent of these soon-to-be high school graduates fail the test.

In far too many schools, all that it takes to earn a high school diploma is minimum effort and seat time. Many states are either beginning to or now require students to prove that they have actually learned something in high school. To do this, they must pass a test. Most of these tests do not cover the range of subjects that the GED focuses on; they include only reading, writing, and math. The GED tests in science and social studies as well.

Basic Structure of the Test

In 2002, the American Council on Education came out with an improved GED test that more accurately portrays a typical high school education. The test is now more rigorous than it was previously. Although the subjects tested are similar, the depth of knowledge required has increased. It has become more important to take a preparation course. Many organizations are now changing their GED preparation courses to reflect what is on the test.

For a test that is given internationally, the GED has some interesting quirks. It is decided locally whether you can take all of the tests in the same day or whether there is a limit to the number. The minimum age requirement (as noted below) is also decided locally. In addition, the passing score changes from year to year.

Test	Number of Questions	Time
Language Arts, Writing (Part 1)	50	75 minutes
Language Arts, Writing (Part 2)	1 essay	45 minutes
Language Arts, Reading	40	65 minutes
Social Studies	50	70 minutes
Science	50	80 minutes
Mathematics	50	90 minutes

What Does It Take to Pass?

The passing score is based on a test given in the spring of each year to a group of graduating seniors. You must pass all the parts of the test, doing as well as or better than 60 percent of those test takers.

Most students will find that they need to study for the GED. This is particularly true for younger students and less true for older students. Life experience really does help in completing the GED with a satisfactory score.

If you're not sure whether or not you could pass the GED without studying, go out and buy one of the many test preparation books on the market. It doesn't really matter which one, but make sure that you purchase a book that has all of the parts of the test.

It is important to understand that the GED presupposes a ninth grade reading level. If your reading level is lower than that, it will make passing the test without further study more difficult.

If you can pass a practice test and have a few points to spare, you may want to go ahead and take the real test. If you don't pass or if you barely pass, it would be a good idea to get some additional education. Most adult schools, many community colleges, and some high schools offer courses that will help you to pass the GED. While the cost of these courses varies, none are particularly expensive.

Disability Accommodation

If you have some form of disability and can provide proof, the American Council on Education allows for the following GED accommodations:

- Audiocassette edition (with large-print reference copy)
- Braille edition
- Extended time
- Large-print edition
- One-on-one testing at a health facility or in a private home
- Sign language interpreter
- Supervised frequent breaks
- Use of a private room
- Use of a scribe
- Use of a talking calculator or abacus
- Use of video equipment
- Vision-enhancing technologies
- Other accommodations in accordance with the particular disability

Wanting more time on the test is not an acceptable reason for requesting accommodation. Typically, your disability documentation must be from a doctor, education professional, or the equivalent. After getting the required documentation, you should contact your local GED testing center and request an accommodation form.

Minimum Age

Following is a list of the minimum age requirement that each state has for taking the GED. Most states also have loopholes. If you are a legally emancipated minor, it may be possible to take the test at a younger age. Incarcerated youths who are under court order to take the test may also be able to take the test earlier. While each jurisdiction (state, territory, what have you) decides the minimum age, note that it can be no lower than sixteen.

States

State	Age	State	Age
Alabama	18	North Carolina	18
Alaska	18	North Dakota	18
Arizona	18	Ohio	19
Arkansas	16	Oklahoma	18
California	18	Oregon	18
Colorado	17	Pennsylvania	18
Connecticut	17	Rhode Island	18
Delaware	18	South Carolina	17
District of Columbia	18	South Dakota	18
Florida	18	Tennessee	18
Georgia	18	Texas	18
Hawaii	17	Utah	18
Idaho	18	Vermont	18
Illinois	18	Virginia	18
Indiana	17	Washington	19
Iowa	17	West Virginia	18
Kansas	18	Wisconsin	18.5
Kentucky	19	Wyoming	18
Louisiana	17		
Maine	18		
Maryland	16		
Massachusetts	18		
Michigan	18		
Minnesota	19		
Mississippi	18		
Missouri	18		
Montana	17		
Nebraska	18		
Nevada	18		
New Hampshire	18		
New Jersey	16		
New Mexico	17		
New York	19		

U.S. Territories

Territory	Age
American Samoa	17
Federated States of Micronesia	17
Guam	18
Northern Mariana Islands	18
Puerto Rico	18
Republic of the Marshall Islands	17
Republic of Palau	17
U.S. Virgin Islands	17

Canada

Region	Age
Alberta	18
Northwest Territories	18
Rest of Canada	19

GED Contacts in the United States

Each state has its own contact person for all information concerning the GED. In addition, information and application forms can be found at all adult schools and most community colleges. The advantage of contacting your local administrator is that he or she can likely provide everything that you will need in order to register for the exam.

Alabama GED Administrator

GED Testing Program
State Department of Education
5343 Gordon Persons Building
PO Box 302101
Montgomery, AL 36130-2101
PHONE: (334) 242-8181

Alaska ABE/GED State Director

Alaska Department of Education
GED Testing Program
DOLWD-ES Division
1111 West Eighth Street
PO Box 25509
Juneau, AK 99802-5509
PHONE: (907) 465-8714

Arizona State Department of Education

State Director, Adult Education
1535 West Jefferson
Phoenix, AZ 85007
PHONE: (602) 254-0265

Arkansas Department of Workforce Education

GED Test Administrator
Luther S. Hardin Building
Three Capitol Mall, Room 304
Little Rock, AR 72201-2729
PHONE: (501) 682-1970

California State GED Office

GED Administrator
California Department of Education
721 Capitol Mall, Sixth Floor
PO Box 710273
Sacramento, CA 94244-0273
PHONE: (916) 651-6623 or (800) 331-6316

Colorado Department of Education

GED Administrator
201 East Colfax Avenue, Room 100
Denver, CO 80203
PHONE: (303) 866-6611

Connecticut Bureau of Adult Education and Training

GED Administrator
State Department of Education
25 Industrial Park Road
Middletown, CT 06457
PHONE: (860) 807-2110

Delaware Department of Public Instruction

State Supervisor
Adult and Community Education
J.G. Townsend Building
PO Box 1402
Dover, DE 19903
PHONE: (302) 739-3743

District of Columbia GED Office

GED Administrator
4200 Connecticut Avenue NW
Washington, DC 20008
PHONE: (202) 274-7173

Florida Bureau of Program Planning and Development

GED Administrator
325 West Gaines Street
Turlington Building, Room 714
Tallahassee, FL 32399-0400
PHONE: (850) 488-7153

Georgia Department of Technical and Adult Education

Director, Assessment, Evaluation, and GED Administrator
1800 Century Place NE, Suite 555
Atlanta, GA 30345-4304
PHONE: (404) 679-1621

Hawaii Department of Education

GED Administrator
School Improvement/Community Leadership Branch
634 Pensacola Street, Room 222
Honolulu, HI 96814
PHONE: (808) 594-0170

Idaho Department of Education

Adult Education Coordinator and GED Administrator
PO Box 83720
Boise, ID 83720-0027
PHONE: (208) 332-6933

Illinois State Board of Education

State GED Administrator
Community and Family Partnerships Division
100 North First Street C-418
Springfield, IL 62777
PHONE: (217) 782-3370

Indiana Department of Education

GED Administrator
Division of Adult Education
State House, Room 229
Indianapolis, IN 46204
PHONE: (317) 232-0522

Iowa Department of Education

GED Administrator
Division of Community Colleges
Grimes State Office Building
Des Moines, IA 50319-0146
PHONE: (515) 281-3636

Kansas Board of Regents

Associate Director, Academic Affairs
1000 SW Jackson Street, Suite 520
Topeka, KS 66612-1368
PHONE: (785) 296-4917

Kentucky Department for Adult Education and Literacy

GED Administrator
Capitol Plaza Tower
500 Mero Street, Third Floor
Frankfort, KY 40601
PHONE: (502) 564-5117

Louisiana Department of Education

Director, Adult Education and Training
626 North Fourth Street
Baton Rouge, LA 70802
PHONE: (225) 342-0444

Maine State Department of Education

GED Administrator
#23 State House Station
Augusta, ME 04333-0023
PHONE: (207) 624-6754

Maryland State Department of Education

GED Administrator
200 West Baltimore Street
Baltimore, MD 21201
PHONE: (410) 767-0538

Massachusetts Department of Education

GED Administrator
Office of Certification
350 Main Street
PO Box 9120
Malden, MA 02148-9120
PHONE: (781) 388-3300, ext. 651

Michigan Department of Career Development

State GED Administrator
Adult Education Office
201 North Washington Square
PO Box 30714
Lansing, MI 48909
PHONE: (517) 373-1692

Minnesota Department of Children, Families, and Learning

GED Administrator
1500 Highway 36 West
Roseville, MN 55113-4266
PHONE: (651) 582-8437
FAX: (651) 634-8458

Mississippi State Board for Community and Junior Colleges

GED Administrator
3825 Ridgewood Road
Jackson, MS 39211
PHONE: (601) 432-6481

Missouri State Department of Elementary and Secondary Education

GED Administrator
402 Dix Road, PO Box 480
Jefferson City, MO 65102
PHONE: (573) 751-3504

Montana Office of Public Instruction

GED Administrator
1300 11th Avenue
Box 202501
Helena, MT 59620-2501
PHONE: (406) 444-4438

Nebraska Department of Education

Director, Adult Education
301 Centennial Mall South
PO Box 94987
Lincoln, NE 68509-4987
PHONE: (402) 471-4807

Nevada Department of Education

GED Administrator
Workforce Education
700 East Fifth Street
Carson City, NV 89701-5096
PHONE: (775) 687-9167

New Hampshire State Department of Education

GED Administrator
State Office Park South
101 Pleasant Street
Concord, NH 03301
PHONE: (603) 271-6698

New Jersey Office of School-to-Career College Initiatives

GED Administrator
100 River View Plaza
PO Box 500
Trenton, NJ 08625-0500
PHONE: (609) 633-0665

New Mexico State Department of Education

State Director, Assessment and Evaluation
Education Building
300 Don Gaspar
Santa Fe, NM 87501-2786
PHONE: (505) 827-6631

New York State Education Department

State GED Chief Examiner
PO Box 7348
Albany, NY 12224-0348
PHONE: (518) 486-5746
HOTLINE: (518) 474-5906

North Carolina Community College System

Coordinator of Adult High School Programs
5024 Mail Service Center
Raleigh, NC 27699-5024
PHONE: (919) 733-7051, ext. 720

North Dakota Department of Public Instruction

Assistant Superintendent
Adult Education and Literacy
600 East Boulevard Avenue
State Capitol Building
Bismarck, ND 58505-0440
PHONE: (701) 328-2393

Ohio State Department of Education

GED Administrator
25 South Front Street
Room 106, First Floor
Columbus, OH 43215
PHONE: (614) 466-1577

Oklahoma State Department of Education

GED Director
2500 North Lincoln Boulevard
Oklahoma City, OK 73105-4599
PHONE: (405) 521-3321 or (800) 405-0355

Oregon Department of Community Colleges and Workforce Development

Unit Leader, Adult Basic Skills and Family Literacy Unit
255 Capitol Street NE
Salem, OR 97310-1341
PHONE: (503) 378-8648, ext. 368

Pennsylvania State Department of Education

GED Administrator
333 Market Street, 12th Floor
Harrisburg, PA 17126-0333
PHONE: (717) 787-6747

Rhode Island Department of Elementary and Secondary Education

GED Administrator
Office of Career and Technical Education
Shepard Building
255 Westminster Street
Providence, RI 02903-3414
PHONE: (401) 222-4600, ext. 2180

South Carolina State Department of Education

GED Administrator
402 Rutledge Building
1429 Senate Street
Columbia, SC 29201
PHONE: (803) 734-8347

South Dakota Department of Labor

GED Administrator
Adult Education and Literacy/GED Literacy
700 Governor's Drive
Pierre, SD 57501-2291
PHONE: (605) 773-3101

Tennessee Department of Labor and Workforce Development

GED Administrator
11th Floor, Davy Crockett Tower
500 James Robertson Parkway
Nashville, TN 37245
PHONE: (615) 741-7054 or (800) 531-1515

Texas Education Agency

Manager III for Continuing Education
William B. Travis Building
1701 North Congress Avenue
Austin, TX 78701
PHONE: (512) 463-9292
FAX: (512) 305-9493

Utah State Office of Education

GED Administrator
Adult Education Services
250 East 500 South
PO Box 144200
Salt Lake City, UT 84114-4200
PHONE: (801) 538-7870

Vermont State Department of Education

GED Administrator
Career and Workforce Development
120 State Street
Montpelier, VT 05620
PHONE: (802) 828-3132

Virginia Department of Education

GED Administrator
Virginia Office of Adult Education
PO Box 2120
Richmond, VA 23218-2120
PHONE: (804) 225-2075

Washington State Board for Community and Technical Colleges

GED Administrator
319 Seventh Avenue
PO Box 42495
Olympia, WA 98504-2495
PHONE: (360) 664-0288
FAX: (360) 664-8808

West Virginia Department of Education

GED Administrator
1900 Kanawha Boulevard East
Building 6, Room 250
Charleston, WV 25305-0330
PHONE: (304) 558-6315 or (800) 642-2670

Wisconsin Department of Public Instruction

State GED Administrator
Wisconsin High School Equivalency Program
PO Box 7841
125 South Webster Street
Madison, WI 53707-7841
PHONE: (608) 267-2402 or (800) 441-4563

Wyoming Community College Commission

GED Administrator
2020 Carey Avenue, Eighth Floor
Cheyenne, WY 82002
PHONE: (307) 777-3545

Corrections

Federal Bureau of Prisons

Education Specialist
Department of Justice
320 First Street NW, Room 7026
Washington, DC 20534
PHONE: (202) 305-3810

Michigan Department of Corrections

Education Director
Grand View Plaza
PO Box 30003
Lansing, MI 48909
PHONE: (517) 373-3642

U.S. Military

Defense Activity for Non-Traditional Education Support

DANTES Administrator
Attn: Code 20B
6490 Saufley Field Road
Pensacola, FL 32509-5243
PHONE: (850) 452-1089

U.S. Territories

American Samoa

GED Administrator
Government of American Samoa
Pago Pago, AS 96799
PHONE: 011 (684) 633-5237

Guam

GED Administrator
Guam Community College
PO Box 23069
Main Postal Facility
Guam, GU 96921
PHONE: 011 (671) 735-6511

Marshall Islands

President and GED Administrator
College of the Marshall Islands
PO Box 1258
Republic of Marshall Islands
Majuro, MH 96960
PHONE: 011 (692) 625-3394

Micronesia

GED Administrator
Federated States of Micronesia
National Government
Palikir, Pohnpei, FM 96941
PHONE: 011 (691) 320-2647

Northern Mariana Islands

GED Administrator
Northern Marianas College
Adult Basic Education Program
PO Box 501250
Saipan, MP 96950
PHONE: 011 (670) 234-5498

Palau

GED Administrator
Ministry of Education
Bureau of Curriculum and Instruction
PO Box 189
Koror, Republic of Palau, PW 96940
PHONE: 011 (680) 488-5452

Puerto Rico

GED Administrator
Administration Adult Education Services
Department of Education
PO Box 190759
San Juan, PR 00919-0759
PHONE: (787) 759-2000, ext. 4567

Virgin Islands

Director and GED Administrator
Division of Adult Education
Department of Education
44-46 Kongens Gade
Charlotte Amalie
St. Thomas, VI 00802
PHONE: (340) 776-3484

International Testing Sites (Regional Registration Centers)

Many people need access to the GED test around the world. In addition to foreign nationals who see some value in earning this credential, there are also many Americans living abroad who may have been homeschooled or participated in some other alternative education. Needing to now prove knowledge in a way acceptable to some colleges and universities, they take the GED. There are, indeed, test sites all over the world.

Australia/New Zealand RRC

Mail Address:
    Prometric
    PO Box 5343
    Chatswood, NSW 2057
    Australia

Courier Address:
    Prometric
    Attn: Regional Registration Center
    Level 2, 10 Help Street
    Chatswood, NSW 2067
    Australia
    PHONE: +61-2-9903-9797 (8:00 A.M. to 5:30 P.M.)
    FAX: +61-2-9415-3105

Countries served by the Australia/New Zealand RRC:
    Australia
    Fiji
    French Polynesia
    New Zealand

Europe/NIS RRC

Mail Address:
    Prometric
    PO Box 1109
    6801 BC Arnhem
    The Netherlands
Courier Address:
    CITO
    Attn: Prometric Regional Registration Center
    Nieuwe Oeverstraat 50
    6811 JB Arnhem
    The Netherlands
    PHONE: +31-26-352-1577 (9:00 A.M. to 6:00 P.M.)
    FAX: +31-26-352-1278
    EMAIL: registration@cito.nl

Countries served by the Europe/NIS RRC:

Armenia	Bulgaria
Austria	Croatia
Azerbaijan	Cyprus
Belarus	Czech Republic
Belgium	Denmark
Estonia	Netherlands
Finland	North Cyprus
France	Norway
Germany	Poland
Greece	Portugal
Hungary	Romania
Iceland	Russian Federation
Ireland	Slovakia
Israel	Spain
Italy	Sweden
Kazakhstan	Switzerland
Kyrgyzstan	Tajikistan
Latvia	Turkey
Lithuania	Turkmenistan
Luxembourg	Ukraine
Macedonia	United Kingdom
Malta	Uzbekistan
Moldova	

India RRC

Mail/Courier Address:
    Prometric
    Senior Plaza
    160-A, Gautam Nagar
    Yusuf Sarai
    Behind Indian Oil Building
    New Delhi 110-049
    India
    PHONE: +91-11-651-1649 or 699-0637
    FAX: +91-11-699-7103 or 652-9741

Indonesia RRC

Mail/Courier Address:
    The International Educational Foundation/Prometric
    Menara Imperium
    28th Floor, Suite B
    Jalan H.R. Rasuna Said
    Metropolitan Kuningan, Super Blok Kav No. 1
    12980 Jakarta
    Indonesia
    PHONE: +62-21-831-7304
    FAX: +62-21-831-7306

Japan RRC

Mail/Courier Address:
   R-Prometric K.K.
   Kayabacho Tower Bldg., 15th Floor
   1-21-2 Shinkawa
   Chuo-ku
   Tokyo 104-0033
   Japan
   PHONE: +81-3-5541-4800
   FAX: +81-3-5541-4810

Korea RRC

Mail/Courier Address:
   Korean-American Educational Commission
   (KAEC)/Prometric
   Mapo-gu Yeon Li Dong
   168-15
   Seoul 121-090
   Republic of Korea
   PHONE: +82-2-321-11233
   FAX: +82-2-327-54029

Latin America/Caribbean RRC

Mail/Courier Address:
   Prometric
   Attn: Latin America/Caribbean Registration
   3110 Timanus Lane, Suite 200
   Woodlawn, MD 21244
   PHONE: +1-443-923-8160 (9:00 A.M. to 5:00 P.M.)
   FAX: +1-443-923-8569

Countries served by the Latin America/Caribbean RRC:

Antigua and Barbuda	Guyana
Argentina	Haiti
Aruba	Honduras
Bahamas	Jamaica
Barbados	Mexico
Belize	Netherlands Antilles
Bermuda	Nicaragua
Bolivia	Panama
Brazil	Paraguay
Chile	Peru
Colombia	Saint Lucia
Costa Rica	Suriname
Dominican Republic	Trinidad and Tobago
Ecuador	Uruguay
El Salvador	Venezuela
Guatemala	

Middle East/North Africa RRC

Mail Address:
   AMIDEAST-Prometric
   PO Box 96
   Magles El Shaab
   Cairo
   Egypt
Courier Address:
   AMIDEAST
   Attn: Prometric Regional Registration Center
   23 Mossedak Street
   Dokki-Cairo
   Egypt
   PHONE: +20-2-337-8973 (9:00 A.M. to 6:00 P.M.)
   FAX: +20-2-354-0896

Countries served by the Middle East/North Africa RRC:

Bahrain	Oman
Egypt	Qatar
Israel	Saudi Arabia
Jordan	Syria
Kuwait	Tunisia
Lebanon	United Arab Emirates
Morocco	Yemen

People's Republic of China RRC

Mail Address:
   PO Box 8717
   Beijing 100080
   People's Republic of China
   PHONE: +86-10-6251-0901
   FAX: +86-10-6251-5002
   WEBSITE: www.51test.com

South East Asia RRC

Mail Address:
   Prometric
   PO Box 12964
   50794 Kuala Lumpur
   Malaysia
Courier Address:
   Prometric
   Attn: Regional Registration Center
   21A-15-1 Faber Imperial Court
   Jalan Sultan Ismail
   50250 Kuala Lumpur
   Malaysia
   PHONE: +60-3-467-8610 (8:00 A.M. to 5:00 P.M.)
   FAX: +60-3-467-8606

Countries served by the South East Asia RRC:

Bangladesh	Nepal
Brunei Darussalam	Pakistan
Hong Kong	Philippines
Malaysia	Singapore
Mongolia	Sri Lanka

Sub-Saharan Africa RRC

Mail Address:
Prometric
PO Box 218
Auckland Park 2006
South Africa
Courier Address:
Prometric
Attn: Regional Registration Center
Block C, Empire Park
55 Empire Road
Parktown 2001
South Africa
PHONE: +27-11-713-0600
FAX: +27-11-482-4062

Countries served by the Sub-Saharan Africa RRC:

Benin	Guinea
Botswana	Guinea Bissau
Burkina Faso	Kenya
Cameroon	Lesotho
Chad	Madagascar
Comoros	Malawi
Congo	Mali
Côte d'Ivoire	Mauritius
Eritrea	Mozambique
Ethiopia	Namibia
Gabon	Nigeria
Gambia	Reunion
Ghana	Rwanda

Senegal	Togo
Sierra Leone	Uganda
South Africa	Zaire
Swaziland	Zambia
Tanzania	Zimbabwe

Taiwan RRC

Mail Address:
The Language Training and Testing Center/Prometric
PO Box 23–41
Taipei
Taiwan, R.O.C.
Courier Address:
The Language Training and Testing Center/Sylvan Prometric
Attn: Regional Registration Center
170 Hsin-hai Road, Sec. 2
Taipei 106
Taiwan, R.O.C.
PHONE: +886-2-2369-1154 (8:00 A.M. to 5:00 P.M.)
FAX: +886-2-2363-8840

Thailand RRC

Mail Address:
Institute of International Education/Prometric
GPO Box 2050
Bangkok 10501
Thailand
Courier Address:
Institute of International Education/Prometric
Attn: Regional Registration Center
Ninth Floor, Citibank Tower
82 North Sathorn Road
Bangrak, Bangkok 10501
Thailand
PHONE: +66-2-639-2703 (8:30 A.M. to 4:30 P.M.)
FAX: +66-2-639-2706

Books

Make sure that any GED book you purchase conforms to the 2002 test. Any previous editions are worthless because of the drastic nature of the changes involved. In addition to a book that covers the entire test, it's also a good idea to purchase books on any specific subject areas you particularly need concentration on. While retail prices are provided below, check out Half.com or Amazon.com for better pricing.

General Reference

Arco Master the GED 2002: Teacher-Tested Strategies and Techniques for Scoring High by Ronald Kaprov, et al (Arco, 2001). 732 pages, $16.95.

Arco 30 Days to the New GED 2003 by Nathan Barber (Arco, 2002). 300 pages, $12.95.

Barron's How to Prepare for the GED with CD-ROM by Murray Rockowitz, et al. (Barron's, 2002). 800 pages, $24.95.

Cracking the GED: 2002 Edition by Geoff Martz (The Princeton Review, 2002). 596 pages, $18.

Kaplan GED by Caren Van Slyke (Kaplan, 2001). 704 pages, $23.00.

McGraw-Hill's GED: The Most Complete and Reliable Study Program for the GED Tests by Patricia Mulcrone, ed. (McGraw-Hill, 2001). 464 pages, $16.95.

Spanish Versions

Arco Master the GED en Español 2002: estrategias hechas y probadas por maestros para obtener notas altas by Antonio Ginés Serrán-Pagán (Arco, 2001). 736 pages, $16.95.

El GED esencial by Contemporary Books, ed. (Contemporary Books, 1999). $18.15.

Math Section

Arco GED Math Workbook, 5th ed., by David Alan Herzon and Mary Jane Sterling (Arco, 2000). 230 pages, $11.95.

Barron's Math Workbook for the GED by Johanna Holm (Barron's, 1997). 240 pages, $13.95.

Steck-Vaughn GED: Mathematics by Liz Anderson, et al. (Raintree/Steck-Vaughn, 2001). 474 pages, $14.07.

Language Arts/Writing Sections

Essential Words for the GED by Sydney L. Langosch (Barron's, 1999). 256 pages, $8.95.

GED: The Essay by Steck-Vaughn Staff, ed. (Raintree/Steck-Vaughn, 2002). $14.07.

GED Language Arts Reading: Review for the Language Arts Reading Section of the GED Test by Deanna Corona (Comex Systems, 2002). 126 pages, $16.95.

GED Language Arts Writing: Review for the Language Arts Writing Section of the GED Test by Michelle Vernamonti and Rosemary Lewis (Comex Systems, 2002). 176 pages, $16.95.

Steck-Vaughn GED: Language Arts, Reading by Steck-Vaughn Staff, ed. (Raintree/Steck-Vaughn, 2001). $14.07.

Science Section

Contemporary's GED Science: Preparation for the High School Equivalency Examination by Robert Mitchell (McGraw-Hill, 2002). 477 pages, $18.75.

Steck-Vaughn GED Science by Steck-Vaughn Staff, ed. (Raintree/Steck-Vaughn, 2001). $14.07.

Social Studies Section

Contemporary's GED Test 2: Social Studies by Cathy Niemet (NTC/Contemporary Publishing, 1993). 327 pages, $12.

Master the GED Social Studies 2002: Updated for the All-New GED by Arco, ed. (Arco, 2001). 256 pages, $12.95.

Internet Resources

American Council on Education—the Official GED Website

www.acenet.edu/calec/ged
ACE is the maker and distributor of the GED exam. This website offers authoritative information on how, where, and when to take the examination.

GEDonline.com

www.gedonline.com
For a fee, this site provides online tests and practice help for the GED.

PBS Literacy Link: GED Connection

www.pbs.org/literacy/ged/gedhome.html
This resource is provided by the Public Broadcasting System, which has a "GED on TV" program that teaches the necessary information to pass the test.

Rio Salado College Online GED Preparation Program

www.rio.maricopa.edu/ci/programs/ged/start_ged.shtml
Provides information and instruction online for GED students. The cost is $50 for the program, plus the cost of materials.

Virginia Adult Learning Resource Center GED Resources

www.aelweb.vcu.edu/favoritelinks_GED.htm
This page is a compilation of all of the best GED links. It includes dropout rate information, practice tests, and links for all of the subject areas.

CHAPTER 9

High School Proficiency Examinations

Learning without thinking is labor lost; thinking without learning is dangerous.

—*Chinese proverb*

A few states now offer an examination that results in a diploma (or certificate) that is equivalent to a high school diploma. The rules tend to be quite specific and the tests are no cakewalk, but these high school proficiency exams can be a good alternative to the GED for certain students.

For one thing, the high school proficiency exam usually can be taken at a younger age. In California, for example, you can take the proficiency examination at sixteen, but you have to wait until you're eighteen to take the GED. Depending upon your state, the proficiency exam may also be easier to pass than the GED.

As you research your state's specific requirements for its high school proficiency exam, note that two completely different tests can go by this name. You are looking for the test that will allow you to leave high school early. (The other type of test is a high school graduation requirement test, which students take at the end of four years.)

A certificate of proficiency from one of these tests has a number of uses. In California and some other states, it will qualify you to enroll in a community college. Some colleges and universities will accept you as a student as well. The United States military also accepts a certificate of proficiency in lieu of a traditional high school diploma for enlistment purposes.

Although the test varies state by state, most of them contain three parts: reading, math, and writing. The reading typically consists of multiple-choice questions about reading passages. The math portion offers a wide array of math topics up to and including some algebra and geometry. The writing portion involves writing an essay.

Frequently Asked Questions

Is a high school proficiency exam only for people of high school age?
Not at all. In some states, the largest group taking this test are people over the age of twenty-five. One example is the state of Wisconsin, where about 40 percent of the adults over the age of twenty-five—about 800,000—do not have a high school diploma. Many of them will take the proficiency exam.

If your state doesn't offer the proficiency exam, can you take the test in another state?
Quite a few residents of states like Oregon and Nevada hop across the border and take the California High School Proficiency Examination (CHSPE). Wisconsin laws allow you to earn that state's High School Equivalency Diploma (HSED) after "living" in the state for only ten days. Because of the full faith and credit clause in the Constitution, other states must recognize you as a high school graduate if you have completed any state's necessary requirements to become one. Quite a few of Wisconsin's test takers come from other states that do not offer the test as an option.

California

California Proficiency Testing

PO Box 1478
Rancho Cordova, CA 95741-1478

PHONE: (916) 319-0791
WEBSITE: www.cde.ca.gov/statetests/chspe
EMAIL: chspe@citlink.net
RULES: Students must be sixteen years old to take the test or be turning sixteen within the semester the test is given. No parental permission is required to take the test. Passing the test provides the student with a certificate of proficiency that is legally equivalent to a high school diploma.

Who accepts the CHSPE as a valid diploma? In California, everyone by state law is supposed to accept the certificate as a valid diploma, including the prestigious University of California. The university will accept the CHSPE in lieu of a traditional high school diploma, but you must be able to adequately satisfy all of the remaining admissions requirements.

New York

Office of New York City School and Community Services

New York State Education Department
Education Building-375 EBA
Albany, NY 12234

PHONE: (518) 474-4715
FAX: (518) 474-7948
WEBSITE: www.emsc.nysed.gov/part100/pages/1007.html
RULES: New York's High School Equivalency Diploma is targeted at young adults between the ages of eighteen and twenty-one. You must have lived in the state for at least one month. It is possible to earn the diploma at age seventeen if you meet one of the following criteria:

1. You can't have attended high school at any time during the last twelve months.

2. You are a member of a high school class that already graduated (but you are younger than average).

3. You are living in a narcotic addiction control center or are an adjudicated youth (which means that you have been found guilty of something by the court system).

Texas

High School Equivalency Program

Texas Education Agency
(In School GED Program)
1701 N. Congress Avenue
Austin, TX 78701

PHONE: (512) 475-2160
FAX: (512) 463-6782
WEBSITE: www.tea.state.tx.us/hsep
EMAIL: eddevprj@tea.state.tx.us
RULES: Ordinarily, a student must wait until the age of eighteen to take the test. However, if you can meet *all* of the following conditions, you can take the test at sixteen:

1. You are at least sixteen years old at the beginning of the school year or semester.

2. You are in danger of dropping out of school.

3. You and your parents, or guardian, agree in writing to your taking the test.

4. At least two school years have elapsed since you first enrolled in ninth grade and you have completed less than one year's worth of the credits required to graduate.

5. Any other rules the commissioner of education elects to apply to you. (The enforcement of the rule is quite rare.)

Texas offers an in-school program to prepare students to take and pass the GED. In other states, in order to receive GED instruction, you must no longer be a high school student. Texas allows students to stay in school and prepare for the GED.

Wisconsin

High School Equivalency Diploma Program

Wisconsin Department of Public Instruction
125 South Webster Street
PO Box 7841
Madison, WI 53707

PHONE: (800) 441-4563
WEBSITE: www.dpi.state.wi.us/dpi/dlsis/let/gedhsed.html
EMAIL: lawrence.allen@dpi.state.wi.us
RULES: You must have lived in the state for at least ten days. You must be at least eighteen and a half years old or the class with which you entered high school must have graduated. Wisconsin offers five different ways to earn the High School Equivalency Diploma:

1. Pass the GED; complete the health, citizenship, and employability skills requirement; and receive career-awareness counseling.

2. Earn any missing high school credits at a local high school or technical college.

3. Finish twenty-four semester credits or thirty-two quarter credits at a university or technical college, including instruction in any area of study you didn't cover in high school.

4. Complete a foreign degree or diploma program.

5. Complete a program offered by a technical college or community-based group that has been approved by the state superintendent of public instruction as a high school program.

Note

I am particularly interested in adding to this brief list. If you have knowledge of other high school proficiency or equivalency examinations offered by states, please let me know by sending a note to hsd@degree.net. Thank you for your support.

Rich Douglas has had a long career in the military and the private sector, and is still quite young. He is completing a doctorate at the Union Institute and University, a school well known for its nontraditional offerings.

Bears' Guide: Please briefly describe your background prior to taking the California High School Proficiency Exam.

Rich Douglas: I grew up in San Diego, California. I attended public schools, getting decent grades, but family life had challenges. As a result, I was working part-time by age fifteen, and looking to get on with earning a living. I faced the serious possibility of dropping out of school to work full-time. Still, I had an eye on completing college someday.

BG: Why did you decide to pursue an alternative route for your high school education?

RD: Working about thirty hours per week during my sophomore year (in 1976), I was faltering in school. I'd transferred to a self-paced alternative school and was just four classes shy of graduation (while still a sophomore). But I was also on the verge of dropping out completely.

BG: How did you receive your high school diploma?

RD: In May, 1976, I took what was then the second administration of the California High School Proficiency Examination (CHSPE), which resulted in a state-issued high school diploma. I "dropped out" immediately after the examination, anticipating receiving my diploma a couple of months later, which I did.

BG: Do you feel you missed out on anything by not participating in a traditional high school?

RD: Absolutely. My peers went on to some of the better colleges and universities in the country. I went to work. I also missed out on a lot of the socialization that occurs in high school, the "soft skills" that are not easily acquired in the classroom or by studying on one's own.

BG: What did you gain by not participating in a traditional high school?

RD: I graduated two years ahead of my peers. This allowed me to work and make a desperately needed income. Also, it helped me sort out my goals and the means by which I might attain them. I mean, by working and missing out on school activities, I grew to know what I *didn't* want in life!

BG: What has your life been like since earning the diploma?

RD: Knowing I wanted to break out of my situation, I enlisted in the U.S. Air Force right after my eighteenth birthday. Ironically, they made me an education specialist, counseling thousands of others regarding their education benefits and goals. I began taking college-level examinations for credit and enrolled in what was then the University of the State of New York's Regents External Degree program (now Excelsior College), earning an associate's and two bachelor's degrees in less than two years. Transferring to the Air Force Reserve, I attended graduate school and earned a commission returning to active duty and completing a career as an officer. I took an MBA from National University, and retired from active duty in 1996. Since that time, I've been a corporate trainer. I'm currently a doctoral candidate, expecting to graduate in 2003.

BG: If you had to do it all over again, would you make the same choices? What would you do differently?

RD: Well, I wouldn't recommend it for everyone, but faced with the same circumstances, I'd make the same choices. I'm grateful for the opportunity to have earned my diploma with the CHSPE, which opened the door to serving in the Air Force, which provided me the opportunity to build both a career and an education. Without the CHSPE, I would have continued in my dead-end job, trying to go to night school to finish my diploma or GED. Who knows when I would have been eligible to enter the Air Force, which opened the world to me?

BG: Do you have any wisdom to offer?

RD: Life is full of hurdles. Some we leap over. But others require we work around them. Sometimes, given the obstacles we face, we're left with finding an alternate path around the obstacle. It may not be the optimal route. But sometimes it is the only one available.

Part IV: Other Options and Information

CHAPTER 10

Skipping High School

"Freedom is always and exclusively freedom for the one who thinks differently."

—*Rosa Luxemburg, German revolutionary*

Here's advice that your parents never gave you: drop out! If school just isn't working for you, then go find something else to do. There are a number of exciting possibilities available.

However, before you make this radical change, consider the following pieces of information:

1. People who don't graduate from high school make significantly less money in the short- and long-term.

2. Not having a high school diploma makes finding rewarding and fulfilling employment much more difficult.

3. You will have problems with your parents. Practically guaranteed. The more so if they also didn't graduate from high school.

If you're convinced that high school is not for you, sometimes the best option is to skip it and go on to college. While most traditional colleges and universities will not accept you, there are many community colleges that will gladly let you enroll. If you're under eighteen, you may have to get your parents' permission. Or instead of going to college, you may want to explore a year overseas or devote some time to volunteering.

Community College

Why not start college? Your local community college may let you enroll under certain circumstances. Based on state law, some community colleges require that you pass the GED or your state's high school equivalency test. For example, in California, if you pass the California High School Proficiency Examination, community colleges can admit you. It's also possible that some four-year colleges and universities would admit you.

The easiest way to find out the rules in your state is to visit the admissions department of your local community college. If you have no community college in your area, I would suggest checking out this community college in Oregon:

Chemeketa Online

Chemeketa Community College
4000 Lancaster Drive NE
PO Box 14007
Salem, OR 97309

PHONE: (503) 399-7873
FAX: (503) 589-7628
WEBSITE: www.bbs.chemeketa.edu
EMAIL: col@chemeketa.edu

Why do I offer only this one suggestion? The fact is, if a local college is available, you will probably choose it. If not, Chemeketa is a good choice for out-of-state residents because it offers online courses at in-state tuition rates. This can mean a sizable savings. While Chemeketa is not the least expensive community college, it is among them. The only way to do better is if you live in California (land of many, many community colleges and eleven dollars per unit tuition!). Also, Chemeketa Community College allows sixteen-year-olds to register for classes. You do have to fill out a special form, but otherwise you're in!

High School Exchange Programs

If money isn't an issue, you might consider taking a year off and living in a foreign country. There are a number of programs devoted to foreign exchange, which may or may not require you to be a high school student overseas. Even if you do have to go to high school, you might find it more interesting to spend a year at a high school in Addis Ababa, Ethiopia, than in Fresno, California. Having been to both places and having been sixteen once, I think the first option would look rather good to a sixteen-year-old. Below I have included contact information for the largest exchange organizations.

American Field Service (AFS)

71 West 23rd Street, 17th Floor
New York, NY 10010

PHONE: (212) 807-8686
FAX: (212) 807-1001
WEBSITE: www.afs.org
EMAIL: afsinfo@afs.org

American Institute for Foreign Study, Inc.

River Plaza
9 West Broad Street
Stamford, CT 06902

PHONE: (203) 399-5000
FAX: (203) 399-5590
WEBSITE: www.aifs.com
EMAIL: info@aifs.com

American Intercultural Student Exchange

7720 Herschel Avenue
La Jolla, CA 92037

PHONE: (858) 459-9761
FAX: (858) 459-5301
WEBSITE: www.aise.com
EMAIL: info.request@aise.com

AYUSA Global Youth Exchange

2226 Bush Street
San Francisco, CA 94115

PHONE: (800) 727-4540, ext. 543
WEBSITE: www.ayusa.org
EMAIL: info@ayusa.org

Cultural Homestay International

104 Butterfield Road
San Anselmo, CA 94960

PHONE: (415) 459-5397 or (800) 395-2726
FAX: (415) 459-2182
WEBSITE: www.chinet.org
EMAIL: chimain@msn.com

Rotary International Youth Exchange

One Rotary Center
1560 Sherman Avenue
Evanston, IL 60201

WEBSITE: www.rotary.org/programs/youth_ex/index.html
EMAIL: leighm@rotaryintl.org

With this particular program, your odds increase if you contact the local Rotary Club. Check the yellow pages of your phone book for the number.

Youth for Understanding USA

YFU International Center
3501 Newark Street NW
Washington, DC 20016

PHONE: (202) 966-6800
FAX: (202) 895-1104
WEBSITE: www.youthforunderstanding.org
EMAIL: info@yfu.org

Volunteer Opportunities

If you decide to leave school and want to volunteer, you will probably have to create most of the volunteer opportunities yourself. The reason is simple—most reputable programs want college graduates. Sure the Peace Corps doesn't say you have to have a degree, but the number of folks accepted without one is tiny—unless, and this is a big unless, you have a skill that they have a lot of difficulty in finding.

While there are many places that you might approach about a one-year volunteer position, here are some ideas:

- Your church.

- The local zoo.

- Social service organizations (United Cerebral Palsy, Muscular Dystrophy Association, Association of Retarded Citizens, and so on).

- The local seniors center.
- Convalescent hospitals.
- Hospitals.

The best book on the topic is by Rebecca Greene and is called *The Teenagers' Guide to School Outside the Box.* It is available on Amazon.com and from Free Spirit Publishing. It includes incredible detail on internships, mentorships, apprenticeships, volunteering, and so on.

Don't forget that your parents likely have contacts around the city. Get them thinking about this as well.

Note

If you are planning on leaving school, please check out the GED or other high school equivalency programs available to you. Passing one of these could enable you to go to college later or to get employment now. Either way, it is much easier to take one of these tests at seventeen than at twenty-seven.

CHAPTER 11

World War II Veterans and Operation Recognition

"I finally did it. I finally graduated high school. And it didn't take me but sixty-one years."

—Harvey Lee, World War II Veteran

Given what we owe to our World War II veterans, providing them with a high school diploma seems little enough. Tom Brokaw (and many others) calls this generation "the greatest generation." Many of our veterans from World War II had to leave school to fight in the war. When they returned, many went to work, got married, had children, and never got back to high school.

Operation Recognition is the brainchild of Robert McKean, the Massachusetts director of State Veterans' Memorial Cemeteries. It began in 1999 as a way to honor veterans who were not able to complete their high school education. In Massachusetts alone, more than eight thousand diplomas have been issued since 1999. One interesting aspect of the program is that the participating states have each taken the initiative upon themselves to start—there is no federal mandate or cooperation in the program.

Some states have adopted their own policies. In California, for example, the county offices of education run Operation Recognition, and California has expanded eligibility for the program to include Japanese Americans. Since many Japanese Americans were interned in relocation camps during the war, some also missed out on the opportunity to earn a high school diploma; they are eligible now to receive one under Operation Recognition.

The Rules

While each state is free to choose its own parameters, McKean gives some recommendations (they were adopted by Massachusetts):

1. You must be an honorably discharged veteran who served in the military between September 16, 1940 and December 31, 1946.

2. You must have been a high school student who would have graduated between the years 1937 and 1946.

3. You are eligible for the high school diploma even if you have already obtained a GED.

4. If families are interested, diplomas may be awarded posthumously.

In order to prove that you are qualified for this award, you must be able to provide a copy of your honorable discharge papers as well as a completed application form to whichever entity is providing the diplomas.

Participation

At present, the states listed below are participating in this program. While programs are available in all of these states, not all of the programs are state-run programs; county offices of education or school districts coordinate some of them. Your best bet in locating a program is to talk to your local Veteran's Administration office, American Legion, or Veterans of Foreign Wars organization.

Arizona	Kentucky	Ohio
Arkansas	Louisiana	Oklahoma
California	Maine	Rhode Island
Colorado	Michigan	South Carolina
Connecticut	Minnesota	Texas
Delaware	Mississippi	Virginia
Florida	Nebraska	Washington
Idaho	New Hampshire	West Virginia
Illinois	New Jersey	Wisconsin
Indiana	New York	
Kansas	North Carolina	

Reprinted with permission from the December 28, 2001, column by Rick Smith in the San Angelo Standard Times.)

Barely sixteen years old and in need of spending money, Harvey Lee joined the National Guard while a senior at Ballinger High School.

"We made a dollar a week for drilling," said the Harvey County rancher. "And it was Depression times."

It was also the summer of 1941.

Months later the country entered World War II, the National Guard mobilized and Harvey and many, many young Texas men put away schoolbooks, picked up rifles and headed toward some of the bloodiest fighting of World War II as part of the Army's 36th Infantry Division.

"I nearly had all my school credits, but I just had to go help my country out," Harvey said. "I was awfully patriotic then, but, to tell you the truth, I didn't know what I was getting into."

Harvey wouldn't return home for six and a half years.

While his classmates back in Ballinger walked across the stage to receive their diplomas, Harvey was fighting his way across North Africa with the 36th.

While some members of the Class of '42 were starting careers or college, Harvey was sustaining serious injuries during the invasion of Italy.

While many of his classmates were beginning families after the war, Harvey was spending one and a half years in a Temple hospital, recuperating from war wounds.

Harvey said he never regretted the time he spent serving his country, but he worried about not graduating from high school.

"Later on, I'd go to class reunions and it would bother me that I didn't have my diploma," the eighty-year-old said.

Early on, the lack of a degree also hurt his job prospects.

"One old boy called me after he read my job application and said, "If I ever need a professional killer, I'll call you in a minute, but . . .""

That's when he started thinking about getting the diploma.

"The high school principal told me to come up and take an exam and he'd put it through. I kept putting it off and putting it off. But I never stopped thinking about it."

"He never talked about it much," said Harvey's wife, Billie, "but it always bothered him that he missed out and never got to graduate."

Several months ago Harvey's old school friend Doug Cox told him about a recent Texas law allowing school districts to award diplomas to WW II veterans who didn't finish school.

With Harvey's blessing, Doug, a former Ballinger superintendent, went to work. Doug worked with current superintendent Rodney Flanagan and the Ballinger School Board to push through the paperwork and get Harvey's diploma.

They planned to present it to him at a school board meeting in mid-December, but Harvey fell ill.

Doug accepted the diploma for Harvey, then took it to him at the hospital. Harvey's home now and feeling fine. When I called him Wednesday he said the new still hasn't worn off the diploma.

"I'm sitting here looking at it right now," he said. "I think I'm going to drive a nail in the wall and hang it next to my Army discharge papers."

At eighty years of age, Harvey said the diploma probably won't help him land a job.

"But I'm sure proud to have it," he said.

"I finally did it. I finally graduated high school. And it didn't take me but sixty-one years."

For additional information on this program, you can contact

Robert McKean, Director of State Veterans' Memorial Cemeteries
c/o Massachusetts Veterans' Memorial Cemetery
1390 Main Street
Agawam, MA 01001
PHONE: (413) 821-9500
FAX: (413) 821-9839
EMAIL: Robert.McKean@state.ma.us

CHAPTER 12

Portfolio Assessment and Transcripts

"A tangible portfolio may be what you're after—you have meetings with the principal, a college admissions, interview, etc.—but the portfolio process, the creation of a physical portfolio, brings valuable memories to the surface."

—Loretta Heuer, The Homeschooler's Guide to Portfolios and Transcripts

The unconventionality of homeschooling and other alternative programs may make it more difficult to gain admission to the college of your choice. How can you get around this problem? While eligibility most certainly depends on the education laws and rules in your home state, in many places you can produce a portfolio, instead of report cards and transcripts, to prove your qualifications.

Portfolio Assessment

An increasing number of colleges and universities will accept a portfolio representing your education if you do not have report cards and transcripts. Portfolios tend to more accurately portray your level of knowledge, skills, and experiences.

A portfolio is a collection of your best work as well as a compilation of your educational experiences. Did you act in any plays? Volunteer for any organizations? Take any adult education or community college courses? Do Red Cross training? All of these experiences go into your portfolio. In preparation for creating a portfolio, here are some items you should hang on to:

1. Lists of books read, especially separated into grade levels or genres. If you complete book reports or essays, keep those too.

2. Tickets or playbills from theatrical productions you've attended. If you completed essays about the plays you've seen, those should be kept as well.

3. Photocopies of both First Aid and CPR cards.

4. Essays written. File away all of your essays.

5. Evaluation letters from auxiliary teachers (those that are not parents, such as music or sign language teachers).

6. Museum programs or receipts.

7. Audiocassettes of you either having a conversation with someone in the foreign language you have studied or reciting portions of text in that language.

8. Community college transcripts and/or report cards.

9. Adult school transcripts and/or report cards.

10. High school transcripts and/or report cards (if any).

11. Programs of music you've performed.

12. Programs of plays you've performed.

13. Poetry you've written.

14. Certificates or other papers as proof of sports team or martial arts participation.

And this is just the tip of the iceberg! While it may seem like an excessive list, it's always easier to throw away something you didn't think you'd need than it is to later try to find proof that you did something. Based on this list, you should be able to tell the importance of starting early and keeping good records.

Transcripts

Transcripts provide a written account of a student's academic accomplishments. It may be possible to produce your own report cards. Either you or your parent could do this. One thing to clarify with your state department of education is whether you can legally create your own transcripts. If you already established your homeschooling as a private school, then there should be no problem.

Both to preserve the integrity of the grading system and to make sure that your grades accurately reflect your level of knowledge, it's best to create documents as you progress through high school.

The typical transcript includes course names, grades, and the amount of credit earned. Many states use the Carnegie system that assigns one unit for each yearlong course and one-half unit for each semester course. A notable exception to this rule is California, which assigns ten units for yearlong courses and five units for semester courses. Regardless of what was actually taught, it is best to choose standard names for courses. In other words, call Algebra 1 exactly that. Remember that the goal is to put the information into a format that an admissions clerk can readily follow.

The closer your transcripts look to public school transcripts, the better. Below you will find the graduation requirements for the three largest states. Though the requirements are similar, they have differences as well. While you should certainly check with your state of residence, using the information below can help you get started.

It should be noted that these are the minimum requirements for graduation. Anyone actively considering college should strengthen the number of courses taken in English, math, and science. Most alternative education students will be surprised at the lack of academic rigor required by these minimal standards and will readily qualify.

California

1. Three courses in English.

2. Two courses in mathematics (one of which must be algebra).

3. Two courses in science (including biological and physical sciences).

4. Three courses in social studies, including U.S. history and geography (which must include the Declaration of Independence, the U.S. Constitution, including the Bill of Rights, the Federalist Papers, the Emancipation Proclamation, the Gettysburg Address, and George Washington's Farewell Address); world history, culture, and geography; and one semester course in American government and civics and a one semester course in economics.

5. One course in visual or performing arts or a foreign language.

6. Two courses in physical education (unless exempted).

Texas

1. Four years of English.

2. Three years of math (to include Algebra 1).

3. Two years of science: biology, chemistry, or physics.

4. Two and one-half years of social studies, inluding world history or world geography (one year); U.S. history since Reconstruction (one year); and U.S. government (one semester).

5. One semester of economics (emphasis on the free enterprise system and its benefits).

6. Science/social studies elective or other academic elective such as world history studies, world geography studies, and any science course approved by state board of education.

7. One and a half years of physical education.

8. One semester of health education or health science technology.

9. One semester of speech.

New York

1. Four courses in English (equals four years).

2. Four years of social studies (to include one year of U.S. history and government, two years of global history, one semester of participation in government, and one semester of economics).

3. Three years of math.

4. Three years of science.

5. One semester of health.

6. One year of the arts (dance, music, theater, or visual arts).

7. One year of a foreign language.

8. Seven semester courses of electives (or the equivalent of three and a half years).

Sources

This is clearly a general introduction to a rather important topic. When it comes time to submit portfolios and transcripts, I encourage you to find additional information. The two best sources for information on portfolios, transcripts, and making it all legal are:

And What About College? Cafi Cohen wrote this book for Holt/GWS in 2000. Not only does it tell you everything that you need to know about portfolios and transcripts for homeschooling, but it provides a great deal of general information about how to get into the college of your choice.

The Homeschooler's Guide to Portfolios and Transcripts. Loretta Heuer wrote this book for IDG Books Worldwide in 2000. It is the only book, to my knowledge, that focuses strictly on how to create portfolios and transcripts.

With the information available in both of these books, you can't go wrong. However, remember to check your state's rules regarding transcripts and portfolios. Every state has slightly different criteria.

State Departments of Education

Deciding which is the best choice for earning a high school diploma may come down to what is legal in your state. If you have any doubts, please contact your state's department of education. It will be able to provide answers to most of your questions concerning legality.

Alabama Department of Education

50 North Ripley Street
PO Box 302101
Montgomery, AL 36104

PHONE: (334) 242-9700
FAX: (334) 242-9708
WEBSITE: www.alsde.edu

Alaska Department of Education and Early Development

801 West Tenth Street, Suite 200
Juneau, AK 99801

PHONE: (907) 465-2800
FAX: (907) 465-3452
WEBSITE: www.educ.state.ak.us
EMAIL: webmaster@eed.state.ak.us

Arizona Department of Education

1535 West Jefferson Avenue
Phoenix, AZ 85007

PHONE: (602) 542-5460
FAX: (602) 542-5440
WEBSITE: www.ade.state.az

Arkansas Department of Education

General Education Division, Room 304A
4 State Capitol Mall
Little Rock, AR 72201

PHONE: (501) 682-4202
FAX: (501) 682-1079
WEBSITE: http://arkedu.state.ar.us

California Department of Education

721 Capitol Mall, Second Floor
Sacramento, CA 95814

PHONE: (916) 657-2577
FAX: (916) 657-2577
WEBSITE: www.cde.ca.gov

Colorado Department of Education

201 East Colfax Avenue
Denver, CO 80203

PHONE: (303) 866-6600
FAX: (303) 830-0793
WEBSITE: www.cde.state.co.us

Connecticut Department of Education

State Office Building, Room 305
165 Capitol Avenue
Hartford, CT 06106

PHONE: (860) 713-6548
FAX: (860) 566-8964
WEBSITE: www.state.ct.us/sde

Delaware Department of Education

John G. Townsend Building
PO Box 1402
Federal and Lockerman Streets
Dover, DE 19903

PHONE: (302) 739-4601
FAX: (302) 739-4654
WEBSITE: www.doe.state.de.us

District of Columbia Public Schools

The Presidential Building
835 North Capitol Street NE
Washington, DC 20002

PHONE: (202) 724-4222
FAX: (202) 442-5026
WEBSITE: www.k12.dc.us

Florida Department of Education

325 West Gaines Street, Suite 1514
Tallahassee, FL 32399

PHONE: (850) 201-7400
FAX: (850) 201-7405
WEBSITE: www.fldoe.org
EMAIL: commissioner@fldoe.org

Georgia Department of Education

2054 Twin Towers East
205 Butler Street
Atlanta, GA 30334

PHONE: (404) 656-2800
FAX: (404) 651-6867
WEBSITE: www.doe.k12.ga.us
EMAIL: state.superintendent@doe.k12.ga.us

Hawaii Department of Education

1390 Miller Street
Honolulu, HI 96813

PHONE: (808) 586-3310
FAX: (808) 586-3320
WEBSITE: http://doe.k12.hi.us
EMAIL: supt_doe@notes.k12.hi.us

Idaho Department of Education

Len B. Jordan Office Building
650 West State Street
PO Box 83720
Boise, ID 83720

PHONE: (208) 332-6800
FAX: (208) 334-2228
WEBSITE: www.sde.state.id.us/dept

Illinois State Board of Education

100 North First Street
The Alzina Building
Springfield, IL 62777

PHONE: (217) 782-4321
FAX: (217) 524-4928
WEBSITE: www.isbe.state.il.us

Indiana Department of Education

State House, Room 229
Indianapolis, IN 46204

PHONE: (317) 232-6610
FAX: (317) 232-8004
WEBSITE: www.doe.state.in.us
EMAIL: webmaster@doe.state.in.us

Iowa Department of Education

Grimes State Office Building
East 14th and Grand Streets
Des Moines, IA 50319

PHONE: (515) 281-3436
FAX: (515) 281-4122
WEBSITE: www.state.ia.us

Kansas Department of Education

120 South East Tenth Avenue
Topeka, KS 66612

PHONE: (785) 296-3201
FAX: (785) 296-7933
WEBSITE: www.ksbe.state.ka.us

Kentucky Department of Education

500 Mero Street
Capital Plaza Tower
Frankfort, KY 40601

PHONE: (502) 564-3421
FAX: (502) 564-6470
WEBSITE: www.kde.state.ky.us

Louisiana Department of Education

626 North Fourth Street
PO Box 94064
Baton Rouge, LA 70704

PHONE: (225) 342-4411
FAX: (225) 342-7316
WEBSITE: www.doe.state.la.us

Maine Department of Education

23 State House Station
Augusta, ME 04333

PHONE: (207) 287-5800
FAX: (207) 287-5802
WEBSITE: www.state.me.us/education

Maryland Department of Education

200 West Baltimore Street
Baltimore, MD 21201

PHONE: (410) 767-0462
FAX: (410) 333-6033
WEBSITE: www.msde.state.md.us

Massachusetts Department of Education

350 Main Street
Malden, MA 02148

PHONE: (781) 388-3300
FAX: (781) 388-3396
WEBSITE: www.doe.mass.edu

Michigan Department of Education

Hannah Building, Fourth Floor
608 West Allegan Street
Lansing, MI 48933

PHONE: (517) 373-3324
FAX: (517) 335-45645
WEBSITE: www.michigan.gov/mde
EMAIL: mdeweb@michigan.gov

Minnesota Department of Children, Families, and Learning

1500 Highway 36 West
Roseville, MN 55113

PHONE: (651) 582-8200
FAX: (651) 582-8724
WEBSITE: www.educ.state.mn.us
EMAIL: children@state.mn.us

Mississippi State Department of Education

359 North West Street, Suite 365
Jackson, MS 39201

PHONE: (601) 359-3513
FAX: (601) 359-3242
WEBSITE: www.mde.k12.ms.us
EMAIL: webhelp@mde.k12.ms.us

Missouri Department of Elementary and Secondary Education

PO Box 480
Jefferson, MO 65102

PHONE: (573) 751-4212
FAX: (573) 751-8613
WEBSITE: www.dese.state.mo.us
EMAIL: pubinfo@mail.dese.state.mo.us

Montana Office of Public Instruction

PO Box 202501
Helena, MT 59620

PHONE: (406) 444-2082
FAX: (406) 444-3924
WEBSITE: www.opi.state.mt.us

Nebraska Department of Education

301 Centennial Mall South
PO Box 94987
Lincoln, NE 68509

PHONE: (402) 471-2295
FAX: (402) 471-0017
WEBSITE: www.nde.state.ne.us
EMAIL: eduneb@nde.state.ne.us

Nevada State Department of Education

700 East Fifth Street
Carson City, NV 89701

PHONE: (775) 687-9141
FAX: (775) 687-9101
WEBSITE: www.nde.state.nv.us

New Hampshire Department of Education

State Office Park South
101 Pleasant Street
Concord, NH 03301

PHONE: (603) 271-3144
FAX: (603) 271-1953
WEBSITE: www.ed.state.nh.us

New Jersey Department of Education

100 Riverview Plaza
PO Box 500
Trenton, NJ 08625

PHONE: (609) 292-4469
FAX: (609) 777-4099
WEBSITE: www.state.nj.us/education

New Mexico Department of Education

300 Don Gaspar
Santa Fe, NM 87501

PHONE: (505) 827-6582
FAX: (505) 827-6696
WEBSITE: www.sde.state.nm.us

New York State Education Department

Office for Nonpublic School Services
Room 481 EBA
Albany, NY 12234

PHONE: (518) 474-3879
FAX: (518) 473-4909
WEBSITE: www.nysed.gov

North Carolina Department of Public Instruction

301 North Wilmington Street
Raleigh, NC 27601

PHONE: (919) 807-3300
FAX: (919) 715-1278
WEBSITE: www.ncdnpe.org (for homeschool information)
and www.ncpublicschools.org/about_dpi/ (for public
schools information)

North Dakota Department of Public Instruction

600 East Boulevard
Bismarck, ND 58505

PHONE: (701) 328-4572
FAX: (701) 328-2461
WEBSITE: www.dpi.state.nd.us

Ohio Department of Education

65 Front Street
Columbus, OH 43215

PHONE: (614) 466-2937
FAX: (614) 644-5960
WEBSITE: www.ode.state.oh.us
EMAIL: ims_help@ode.state.oh.us

Oklahoma State Department of Education

2500 North Lincoln Boulevard
Oklahoma City, OK 73105

PHONE: (405) 521-3301
FAX: (405) 521-6205
WEBSITE: www.sde.state.ok.us

Oregon Department of Education

255 Capitol Street NE
Salem, OR 97310

PHONE: (503) 378-3569
FAX: (503) 373-7968
WEBSITE: www.ode.state.or.us

Pennsylvania Department of Education

333 Market Street, Fifth Floor
Harrisburg, PA 17126

PHONE: (717) 787-4860
FAX: (717) 787-7222
WEBSITE: www.pde.state.pa.us

Rhode Island Department of Education

225 Westminster Street, Fourth Floor
Providence, RI 02903

PHONE: (401) 222-4600, ext. 2503
FAX: (401) 222-4600
WEBSITE: www.ridoe.net
EMAIL: ride0015@ride.ri.net

South Carolina Department of Education

1429 Senate Street
Columbia, SC 29201

PHONE: (803) 734-8493
FAX: (803) 734-8492
WEBSITE: www.myscschools.com

South Dakota Department of Education

700 Governor's Drive
Pierre, SD 57501

PHONE: (605) 773-6934
FAX: (605) 773-3134
WEBSITE: www.state.sd.us/deca

Tennessee State Department of Education

2730 Island Home Boulevard
Knoxville, TN 37920

PHONE: (865) 579-3749
FAX: (865) 532-4791
WEBSITE: www.state.tn.us/education

Texas Education Agency

1701 Congress Avenue
Austin, TX 78701

PHONE: (512) 463-9630
FAX: (512) 463-9008
WEBSITE: www.tea.state.tx.us

Utah State Office of Education

250 East 500 South
Salt Lake City, UT 84111

PHONE: (801) 538-7801
FAX: (801) 538-7521
WEBSITE: www.usoe.k12.ut.us

Vermont Department of Education

120 State Street
Montpelier, VT 05620

PHONE: (802) 828-5406
FAX: (802) 828-3140
WEBSITE: www.state.vt.us/educ
EMAIL: edinfo@doe.state.vt.us

Virginia Department of Education

PO Box 2120
Richmond, VA 23218

PHONE: (804) 786-9421
WEBSITE: www.pen.k12.va.us

Washington Office of Superintendent of Public Instruction

Old Capitol Building
PO Box 47200
Olympia, WA 98504

PHONE: (360) 664-3574
FAX: (360) 753-6712
WEBSITE: www.k12.wa.us
EMAIL: webmaster@ospi.wednet.edu

West Virginia Department of Education

1900 Kanawha Boulevard East
Building 6, Room 262
Charleston, WV 25305

PHONE: (304) 558-2118
FAX: (304) 558-0304
WEBSITE: http://wvde.state.wv.us
EMAIL: wvde@access.k12.wv.us

Wisconsin Department of Public Instruction

125 South Webster Street
PO Box 7841
Madison, WI 53707

PHONE: (608) 266-3390 or (800) 441-4563
FAX: (608) 267-1052
WEBSITE: www.dpi.state.wi.us
EMAIL: webadmin@dpi.state.wi.us

Wyoming Department of Education

Hathaway Building, Second Floor
2300 Capitol Avenue
Cheyenne, WY 82002

PHONE: (307) 777-7670
FAX: (307) 777-6234
WEBSITE: www.k12.wy.us

Accreditation

Six regional and one national association provide accreditation for high school programs within the United States. The Council for Higher Education Accreditation oversees this nongovernmental process.

Regional Accreditation

Regional accreditation is voluntary, nongovernmental, and self-regulatory. Despite being voluntary, there are few reputable colleges and universities that don't go through this process. It is somewhat different at the high school level, where many private schools elect not to go through what can be a quite expensive process. However, if your primary concern is for transferability of credits and acceptability to college admissions officers, going to an accredited school is certainly your safest bet.

Middle States Association of Colleges and Schools

Commission on Secondary Schools
3624 Market Street
Philadelphia, PA 19104

PHONE: (215) 662-5603
FAX: (215) 662-0957
WEBSITE: www.css-msa.org
EMAIL: info@css-msa.org

Provides accreditation for secondary schools in Delaware, the District of Columbia, Maryland, New Jersey, New York, Pennsylvania, Puerto Rico, the U.S. Virgin Islands, and other locations overseas.

New England Association of Schools and Colleges

Commission on Public Secondary Schools
209 Burlington Road
Bedford, MA 01730

PHONE: (781) 271-0022
FAX: (781) 271-0950
WEBSITE: www.neasc.org/cpss/cpss.htm

Provides accreditation for public secondary schools in Connecticut, Maine, Massachusetts, New Hampshire, Rhode Island, and Vermont and ninety-two American/international schools around the world.

North Central Association of Colleges and Schools

Commission on Accreditation and School Improvement
Arizona State University
PO Box 873011
Tempe, AZ 85287

PHONE: (480) 965-8700 or (800) 525-9517
WEBSITE: www.ncacasi.org
EMAIL: nca@nca.asu.edu

Provides accreditation for nineteen states—Arizona, Arkansas, Colorado, Illinois, Indiana, Iowa, Kansas, Michigan, Minnesota, Missouri, Nebraska, New Mexico, North Dakota, Ohio, Oklahoma, South Dakota, West Virginia, Wisconsin, Wyoming—as well as the Department of Defense Dependents Schools and the Navajo Nation.

Northwest Association of Schools and Colleges

Commission on Schools
Boise State University
1910 University Drive
Boise, ID 83725

PHONE: (208) 426-5727
FAX: (208) 334-3228
WEBSITE: www2.boisestate.edu/nasc

Provides accreditation for schools in Alaska, Idaho, Montana, Nevada, Oregon, Utah, and Washington, as well as Canada, China, Egypt, Jamaica, Macedonia, Mexico, Panama, Poland, Russia, Saudi Arabia, and Western Samoa.

Southern Association of Colleges and Schools

Commission on Secondary and Middle Schools
1866 Southern Lane
Decatur, GA 30033

PHONE: (404) 679-4500 or (800) 248-7701
FAX: (404) 679-4541
WEBSITE: www.sacs.org/pub/sec/index.htm
EMAIL: csms@sacs.org

Accredits schools in Alabama, Florida, Georgia, Kentucky, Louisiana, Mississippi, North Carolina, South Carolina, Tennessee, Texas, and Virginia, as well as Latin America.

Western Association of Schools and Colleges

Accrediting Commission for Schools
533 Airport Boulevard, Suite 200
Burlingame, CA 94010

PHONE: (650) 696-1060
FAX: (650) 696-1867
WEBSITE: www.acswasc.org
EMAIL: mail@acswasc.org

Accredits all schools below the college level in California, Hawaii, East Asia, and the Pacific Basin.

National Accreditation

The Distance Education and Training Council is the only national accreditation body for high school programs. Some of the distance-learning high schools accredited by DETC have been in existence for more than one hundred years.

In conducting completely unscientific research on acceptability, fifteen colleges and universities throughout the United States were contacted and asked one question: is DETC accreditation of a high school program acceptable for admission to your school? Out of the fifteen, only one gave a definite no. The overwhelming majority found DETC accreditation acceptable, provided the other pieces (test scores, grades, and so on) were in place.

Distance Education and Training Council

1601 18th Street NW
Washington, DC 20009

PHONE: (202) 234-5100
FAX: (202) 332-1386
WEBSITE: www.detc.org
EMAIL: detc@detc.org

Accreditation Oversight

The Council for Higher Education Accreditation is the final arbiter of all things accredited. Although it is technically nongovernmental, it is the body that recognizes accreditors. Even more important, it is the body that the government looks to in matters of accreditation. If you have a complaint about your regional accreditor, you can contact the council at

Council for Higher Education Accreditation

One Dupont Circle NW, Suite 510
Washington, DC 20036

PHONE: (202) 955-6126
FAX: (202) 955-6129
WEBSITE: www.chea.org
EMAIL: chea@chea.org

Colleges That Accept Nontraditional Students

The following colleges and universities have accepted nontraditional students. Students have gone to these schools after passing the GED, homeschooling, or attending an alternative high school, in addition to other methods of earning a high school diploma. While a school's inclusion on this list in no way guarantees that you will be accepted there, it is at least confirmation that the school will consider your circumstances.

This information has been compiled from numerous sources and is an incomplete list. Not included on the list are the thousands of community and junior colleges throughout the country. Most of them will also accept nontraditional learners and will have policies in place that reflect that admissions goal.

There are a number of sources both in print and online where lists such as this are available. Hopefully, as more and more schools admit nontraditional learners, all of these lists will become obsolete.

* Denotes a school that is either highly selective or highly prestigious or both.

A
Adrian College, MI
Agnes Scott College, GA
Alaska Bible College, AK
Albion College, MI
Allegheny College, PA
Allentown College of St. Francis de Sales, PA
American College, AR
American Institute of Business, IA
*American University, DC
*Amherst College, MA
Anderson University, IN
Antioch College, OH
Appalachian Bible College, WV
Arizona College of the Bible, AZ
Arkansas Bible College, AR
Arkansas Christian College, AR
Arkansas State University, AR
Asbury College, KY
Ashland University, OH
Assumption College, MA
Auburn University, AL
Austin College, TX
Azusa Pacific University, CA

B
Ball State University, IN
Baptist Bible College of Pennsylvania, PA
Barat College, IL
Bartlesville Wesleyan College, OK
*Bates College, ME
Baylor University, TX

Belhaven College, MS
Bell and Howell Institute, AZ
Bethany Theological Seminary and College, AL
Bethel College, IN
Bethel College, MN
Binghamton University (State University of New York), NY
Biola University, CA
Blackburn College, IL
Boise State University, ID
*Boston College, MA
*Boston University, MA
Bridgewater State College, MA
Brigham Young University, UT
*Brown University, RI
Butler University, IN

C
California Baptist University, CA
*California Institute of Technology, CA
California State Polytechnic University-Pomona, CA
California State Polytechnic University-San Luis Obispo, CA
California State University-Dominguez Hills, CA
California State University-Fresno, CA
California State University-Monterrey Bay, CA
California State University-Sacramento, CA
California State University-Stanislaus, CA
Calvin College, MI
*Carleton College, MN
*Carnegie Mellon University, PA
Case Western Reserve University, OH

Central Missouri State University, MO
Chapman University, CA
Christian Brothers University, TN
*The Citadel, SC
Clearwater Christian College, FL
College of the Ozarks, AR
College of Saint Benedict/St. John's University, MN
*College of William and Mary, VA
Colorado College, CO
Concordia College, MN

D

Dallas Christian College, TX
*Dartmouth College, NH
Davidson College, NC
Dekalb College, GA
Delaware State College, DE
Delaware Valley College, PA
Denver Baptist Bible College, CO
DePaul University, IL
Drake University, IA
*Duke University, NC
Duquesne University, PA

E

East Texas Baptist University, TX
Eastern Connecticut State University, CT
Eastern Michigan University, MI
Eastern Nazarene College, MA
Eastern New Mexico University, NM
Edinboro University of Pennsylvania, PA
Elizabethtown College, PA
Embry Riddle Aeronautical University, AL
Emmanuel College, GA
Emmaus Bible College, IA
Emory University, GA
Evergreen State College, WA

F

Fitchburg State College, MA
Florida Atlantic University, FL
Florida College, FL
Florida Institute of Technology, FL
Florida Southern College, FL
Florida State University, FL
Fort Hays State University, KS
Framingham State College, MA
Franciscan University of Steubenville, OH
Friends University, KS
Fresno Pacific University, CA

G

George Fox College, OR
George Mason University, VA
George Washington University, DC
Georgia Institute of Technology, GA
Georgia State University, GA
Gonzaga University, WA
Gordon College, MA
Grand Canyon University, AZ

H

Hampshire College, MA
*Harvard University, MA
*Harvey Mudd College, CA
Hastings College, NE
Hawaii Pacific University, HI
Henderson State University, AR
Hendrix College, AR
Hobart and William Smith College, NY
Hood College, MD
Houghton College, NY
Houston Baptist University, TX
Humboldt State University, CA
Huntington College, AL
Huntington College, IN

I

Idaho State University, ID
Illinois Institute of Technology, IL
Indiana University, IN
Indiana University of Pennsylvania, PA
Indiana Wesleyan University, IN
Iowa State University, IA
Ithaca College, NY

J

Jacksonville State University, AL
John Brown University, AR
*Johns Hopkins University, MD
Johnson and Wales University, RI
Judson College, AL
Judson College, IL
Juniata College, PA

K

Kalamazoo College, MI
Kansas State University, KS
Kent State University, OH
Kentucky Mountain Bible College, KY
Kenyon College, OH
Knox College, IL
Kutztown University of Pennsylvania, PA

L

Lafayette College, PA
Lake Forest College, IL
Lawrence Technological University, MI
Lawrence University, WI
Lesley College, MA
Lewis and Clark College, OR
Liberty University, VA
Linfield College, OR
Loma Linda University, CA
Longwood College, VA
Louisiana Baptist University, LA
Loyola College, MD
Loyola University, IL
Lubbock Christian University, TX
Lyon College, AR

M

*Macalaster College, MN
Manchester College, IN
Mansfield University of Pennsylvania, PA
Maranatha Baptist Bible College, WI
Marlboro College, VT
Marquette University, WI
Mary Baldwin College, VA
Maryland Institute College of Art, MD
*Massachusetts Institute of Technology, MA
Mesa State College, CO
Michigan State University, MI
Michigan Technological University, MI
Middle Tennessee State University, TN
Middlebury College, VT
Midwestern State University, TX
Mills College, CA
Minneapolis College of Art and Design, MN
Mississippi College, MS
Mississippi State University, MS
Mississippi University for Women, MS
Monmouth University, NJ
Montana State University-Billings, MT
Montana State University-Bozeman, MT
Moody Bible Institute, IL
*Mount Holyoke College, MA
Murray State University, KY

N

Nebraska College of Technical Agriculture, NE
New College of Florida, FL
New Mexico Institute of Mining and Technology, NM
New Mexico State University, NM
*New York University, NY
Niagara University, NY
North Carolina State University, NC
North Central Texas College, TX

Northern Michigan University, MI
Northwest Nazarene College, ID
Northwestern College, IA
Northwestern College, MN
*Northwestern University, IL
Notre Dame College of Ohio, OH
Nyack College, NY

O

Oakland University, MI
Oberlin College, OH
*Occidental College, CA
Oglethorpe University, GA
Ohio State University-Columbus, OH
Ohio Wesleyan University, OH
Oklahoma City University, OK
Oklahoma State University, OK
Old Dominion University, VA
Oral Roberts University, OK
Oregon Institute of Technology, OR
Oregon State University, OR

P

Pacific Lutheran University, WA
Pacific Union College, CA
Pennsylvania College of Technology, PA
Pepperdine University, CA
Point Loma College, CA
Point Loma Nazarene College, CA
*Pomona College, CA
Portland State University, OR
Prescott College, AZ
*Princeton University, NJ
Purdue University, IN

R

Radford University, VA
Randolph-Macon Woman's College, VA
Reed College, OR
Regis University, CO
*Rensselaer Polytechnic Institute, NY
Rhode Island School of Design, RI
*Rice University, TX
Ripon College, WI
Roger Williams University, RI
Rose Hill College, SC
Rutgers University, NJ

S

Salem-Teikyo University, WV
Salve Regina College, RI
Sam Houston State University, TX
Samford University, AL
*Sarah Lawrence College, NY

Seattle Pacific University, WA
Seattle University, WA
Shippensburg University of Pennsylvania, PA
Simpson College, CA
Southern Illinois University, IL
Southern Methodist University, TX
Spring Arbor College, MI
Spring Hill College, AL
Springfield College, MA
Southeastern Bible College, AL
Southwest State Technical Institute, AL
Southwestern College, AZ
St. Edward's University, TX
St. John's College, MD
St. Joseph's University, PA
St. Louis University, MO
St. Mary's University, TX
St. Mary's University of Minnesota, MN
St. Olaf College, MN
*Stanford University, CA
Stephen F. Austin State University, TX
Stephens College, MO
Stetson University, FL
Sul Ross State University, TX
*Swarthmore College, PA
*Syracuse University, NY

T
Temple College, TX
Temple University, PA
Texas A & M (all campuses), TX
Texas Christian University, TX
Texas Tech University, TX
Texas Woman's University, TX
Thomas Aquinas College, CA
Thomas More College of Liberal Arts, NH
*Trinity College, CT
Trinity University, TX
Troy State University, AL
Truman State University, MO

U
Union College, NE
*Union College, NY
Union University, TN
*United States Air Force Academy, CO
*United States Coast Guard Academy, CT
*United States Military Academy (West Point), NY
*United States Naval Academy (Annapolis), MD
University of Akron, OH
University of Alabama-Birmingham, AL
University of Alabama-Huntsville, AL
University of Alabama-Tuscaloosa, AL
University of Alaska-Fairbanks, AK

University of Alaska-Southeast, AK
University of Arizona, AZ
*University of California-Berkeley, CA
*University of California-Davis, CA
*University of California-Los Angeles, CA
*University of California-Riverside, CA
*University of California-Santa Barbara, CA
*University of California-Santa Cruz, CA
University of Charleston, WV
*University of Chicago, IL
University of Colorado-Boulder, CO
*University of Connecticut, CT
University of Delaware, DE
University of Florida, FL
University of Georgia, GA
University of Hawaii-Hilo, HI
University of Hawaii-Manoa, HI
University of Houston, TX
University of Idaho, ID
*University of Illinois-Urbana-Champaign, IL
*University of Iowa, IA
University of Judaism, CA
University of Kansas, KS
University of Kentucky, KY
University of La Verne, CA
University of Maine, ME
University of Maryland-Baltimore, MD
University of Maryland-College Park, MD
University of Maryland-University College, MD
*University of Massachusetts-Amherst, MA
*University of Michigan, MI
University of Minnesota-Crookston, MN
University of Minnesota-Duluth, MN
University of Minnesota, Twin Cities, MN
University of Mississippi, MS
University of Missouri-Columbia, MO
University of Montana, MT
University of Nebraska-Lincoln, NE
University of Nevada-Las Vegas, NV
University of Nevada-Reno, NV
University of New England, ME
University of North Carolina-Chapel Hill, NC
University of North Carolina-Greensboro, NC
University of North Dakota, ND
University of North Texas, TX
*University of Oregon, OR
*University of Pennsylvania, PA
University of Portland, OR
University of Puget Sound, WA
University of Redlands, CA
University of Rhode Island, RI
University of San Francisco, CA
University of South Carolina, SC
University of South Dakota, SD

*University of Southern California, CA
University of Tennessee, TN
University of Texas-Arlington, TX
*University of Texas-Austin, TX
University of Texas-El Paso, TX
University of Texas-San Antonio, TX
University of the Pacific, CA
*University of the South (Sewanee), TN
University of Toledo, OH
University of Utah, UT
University of Vermont, VT
*University of Virginia, VA
University of Washington, WA
University of West Alabama, AL
University of Wisconsin-Eau Claire, WI
*University of Wisconsin-Madison, WI
University of Wisconsin-Superior, WI

V

Valdosta State University, GA
Valparaiso University, IN
*Vanderbilt University, TN
*Vassar College, NY
Villanova University, PA
*Virginia Military Institute, VA
Virginia Polytechnic Institute and State University, VA
Virginia Wesleyan College, VA

W

*Washington and Lee University, VA
Washington State University, WA
Wayne State College, NE
*Wellesley College, MA
Wells College, NY
Wesleyan University, CT
Western Baptist College, OR
Western Michigan University, MI
Westmont College, CA
Wheaton College, IL
Whittier College, CA
Whitworth College, WA
Willamette University, OR
Wisconsin Lutheran College, WI
Wittenburg University, OH
Worcester State University, MA
Wright State University, OH

X, Y

Xavier University, OH
*Yale University, CT
York College, NE
York College of Pennsylvania, PA

For specific information on which schools have accepted homeschoolers (as opposed to other nontraditional students), check out the following websites. They list many, many more schools than I have been able to compile.

College and University Reviews—Homeschool Admission Policies

http://eho.org/collrev.htm

College Internet Connection—Private and Homeschool Friendly Colleges and Universities

http://rsts.net/colleges

Learn In Freedom

www.learninfreedom.org

Do you work at a college or university not listed here? Do you readily admit home-schoolers? Or do you think that your school should be designated as prestigious or highly selective? Please send a note to hsd@degree.net and I will evaluate and possibly update my database for any future editions.

Recommended Reading

If it's here, you should buy it. Many books were read and consulted in the making of this book. These were the best to be found.

Distance Learning

Bears' Guide to Earning Degrees by Distance Learning (Ten Speed Press; [800] 841-2665). In print more than twenty-five years, this is the "mother" publication of the Bears' Guide series and profiles over 2,500 schools that offer nontraditional programs in virtually all fields, from accounting to Zulu. It goes into more depth on issues such as alternative means of earning credit, accreditation and state licensure, honorary doctorates, non-U.S. schools, and research doctorates. 432 pages, $29.95.

Baker's Guide to Christian Distance Education: Online Learning for All Ages (Baker Books; www.bakerbooks.com). Now the single best book on Christian distance learning. Jason Baker has provided a solid reference tool for this most interesting topic. 224 pages, $13.99

Charter Schools

National Charter School Directory: 2001 (Center for Education Reform; [202] 822-9000). Melanie L. Looney and the Center for Education Reform have produced a spectacular reference for folks interested in all of the many charter schools out there. 381 pages, $39.95

The GED

See recommended reading in chapter 8.

Homeschooling

And What About College: How Homeschooling Leads to Admissions to the Best Colleges and Universities (Holt/GWS; available from Amazon.com). Cafi Cohen has become the source on college admissions for homeschoolers. If that is your focus, this is the book you must buy. 224 pages, $18.95.

Homeschooling Almanac, 2002–2003 (Prima Publishing; [800] 632-8676; www.primalifestyles.com). This book by Mary and Michael Leppert is a must-buy for homeschoolers. Includes everything there is to know about homeschooling. 688 pages, $24.95.

The Homeschooler's Guide to Portfolios and Transcripts (IDG Books Worldwide; available from Amazon.com). Loretta Heuer, to my knowledge, provides the only book specifically on this topic. 365 pages, $14.95.

Homeschooling the Teen Years (Prima Publishing, [800] 632-8676; www.primalifestyles.com). Cafi Cohen has produced this book that greatly complements her other writings. It provides all of the information that anyone would need on how to homeschool a teenager. 368 pages, $16.95.

Nontraditional Education

Dumbing Us Down: The Hidden Curriculum of Compulsory Schooling (New Society Publishers; [800] 567-6772; www.newsociety.com). John Taylor Gatto, a former New York State Teacher of the Year, tells us why the current public school system doesn't succeed, and how it must either be changed or gotten rid of completely. 104 pages, $11.95.

The Teenagers' Guide to School Outside the Box (Free Spirit Publishing; [612] 338-2068; www.freespirit.com). This book, written for teenagers, provides complete information on internships, mentorships, study abroad, apprenticeships, and volunteering. Rebecca Greene has provided a valuable reference for the nontraditional learner. 248 pages, $15.95.

For those interested in homeschooling, unschooling, and the larger field of nontraditional learning, these two books by Grace Llewellyn are a great place to begin your search. *Guerrilla Learning: How to Give Your Kids a Real Education with or without School* (John Wiley and Sons; available from Amazon.com). 224 pages, $14.95. *The Teenage Liberation Handbook: How to Quit School and Get a Real Life and Education* (Lowry House Publishers; [541] 686-2315; lowryhousepub@aol.com). 448 pages, $20.

For More Information

There are several reasons why someone would want to contact me concerning this book:

- You own or operate a school or program, and the information on your school or program is incorrect.

- You own or operate a school or program, and you wish to be included in any future editions (should they come to pass).

- You are a student and wish to share information about a particular program.

- You are a student and wish further information on a program.

- You wish to share an additional way to earn a high school diploma.

- You are a magazine publisher desperately in search of someone to write your next article on nontraditional high school education.

I am quite happy to correspond with anyone who has shown the intelligence to purchase my book. However, before you send me information on your program, you should check out www.degree.net/updates/hsd to see if it's been added as an update. Schools can and do change addresses, telephone numbers, and the programs offered. Then write to me at

High School Diplomas

c/o Thomas Nixon
PO Box 19021
Fresno, CA 93790

Or email me at hsd@degree.net. Please bear with me as I do receive many emails. However, I always eventually respond to all mail, electronic or otherwise.

For information on book sales, please contact the fine folks at Ten Speed Press at

Degree.net

A division of Ten Speed Press
PO Box 7123
Berkeley, California 94707
www.degree.net

PHONE: (510) 559-1600 or (800) 841-BOOK
FAX: (510) 559-1629

Finally, I am on the Internet at www.tomnixon.net. This website provides information on this book as well as my other writings. It also offers updated information on this book.

Schools and Programs Index

Index

A

Accreditation
    importance of, ix
    independent study high schools and, 22, 23, 26
    national, 185
    online high schools and, 2–3, 5–6, 7, 14
    oversight, 185
    regional, 184–85
Alternative high schools
    definition of, 70
    example experience at, 73–75
    listings of, 70–72, 75–77
American Council on Education, 148, 160
American Homeschool Association, 32

B

Bear, Mariah, 73–75
Bowman, Leslie, 5–6

C

California Proficiency Testing, 162, 163–64
Center for Education Reform, 79, 138, 139
Charter Friends National Network, 138
CharterSchooLaw.com, 138
Charter schools
    ages of, 81–82
    choosing, 79–80
    cost of, 81
    directory of, 82, 191
    frequently asked questions about, 80–81
    Internet resources for, 138–39
    listings of, 82–137
    rankings of, 79–80, 139
    sizes of, 81
    types of, 81
CHSPE, 162, 163–64
Cohen, Cafi, 63, 177
Colleges
    accepting nontraditional students, 186–90
    community, 166–67
Council for Higher Education Accreditation, 185

D

Departments of education
    state, 179–83
    U.S., 138–39
Distance Education and Training Council (DETC),
    2, 185
Douglas, Rich, 163–64

E

Education Week, 139
Examinations
    GED, 148–60
    high school proficiency, 161–64
Exchange programs, 167–68

G

GED, 148–60
    books, 158–59
    contacts in U.S., 151–55
    disability accommodations, 149
    international testing sites, 156–58
    Internet resources, 160
    minimum age requirements, 150
    passing score, 149
    test structure, 148

H

Head, Tom, 60–61
Heritage Foundation, 138
Hernandez, Beverly, 62
High school exchange programs, 167–68
High school proficiency examinations, 161–64
High schools
    alternative, 70–77
    charter, 79–139
    independent study, 21–28
    online, 2–19
    skipping, 166–69
    university-based, 141–46
Homeschooling
    advantages of, 29, 30
    arguments against, 30
    books about, 191, 192
    example experiences of, 33–34, 60–61
    frequently asked questions about, 29–32
    Internet resources for, 62–63
    magazines and periodicals for, 59, 61–62
    organizations for, 32
    state laws and, 30, 32, 34–35, 63
    state listings for, 35–59
    types of, 29
    unschooling vs., 29
Home School Legal Defense Association, 30, 32, 63

More books on distance learning and alternative education from Degree.net and Ten Speed Press

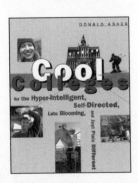